Scripting the Son

Studies in Early Christology

SERIES EDITORS:
Michael Bird, David Capes, and Scott Harrower

The purpose of the Studies in Early Christology (SEC) series is to foster public research in a range of disputed questions relating to early Christology with a view to clarifying the issues, furthering the debate, and—most of all—offering compelling accounts of the emergence of early Christology/Jesus devotion by Christian groups in the Greco-Roman world. The ambition of the series is to attract leading researchers in the fields of Second Temple Judaism, Hellenistic Religion, New Testament, Christian Origins, and patristic studies, with a view to exploring how various Christologies and patterns of devotion to Jesus emerged and why they took on the shape that they did. The series will include monographs by emerging scholars, contributions from senior researchers, and conference proceedings on salient topics related to early Christology. The editors of the series invite submissions for consideration that contribute to discussions on early Christology, demonstrate a sophisticated knowledge of primary sources, interact thoroughly with secondary literature, and use appropriate methodologies.

"Kyle Hughes continues his groundbreaking work on prosopological exegesis and the early church in this newest venture, *Scripting the Son*. Weaving together rich biblical exegesis with careful historical theology, he shows that Christology flowered in part through early Christians' ability to 'hear' the Son's voice in the pages of the Old Testament. The result is a valuable resource that illuminates both historical and theological considerations about early Christology in the New Testament and pre-Nicene Christianity–areas in continual need of deep study."

—**Brandon D. Smith**, chair of the Hobbs School of Theology & Ministry, and associate professor of theology & early Christianity, Oklahoma Baptist University

"A chorus of scholarly voices in recent years has (re)called our attention to the unabashedly christological reading of the Old Testament by early Christian theologians. In this excellent exploration of second- and third-century exegetes, Kyle Hughes tells us both how they came to read Scripture this way, and why. Highly recommended!"

—**Joel Scandrett**, associate professor of historical theology, Trinity Anglican Seminary

"When reading the Old Testament, early Christians identified moments when the Father, Son, and Spirit conversed about salvation history. In *Scripting the Son*, Kyle Hughes offers a rich and comprehensive theological exploration of these divine dialogues alongside the rule of faith, showing how they contributed to developments in Christology and the doctrine of the Trinity. Highly recommended."

—**Matthew W. Bates**, professor of New Testament, Northern Seminary

"*Scripting the Son* expands our understanding of the forces that shaped early Christology. By weaving together various threads, Hughes provides a compelling account of key early Christian doctrines. After gleaning lines from the major sources of early Christianity, he reconstructs a comprehensive 'script' of the inter-trinitarian theodrama, a tool which will be of help to scholars, clergy, and interested laity."

—**David E. Wilhite**, professor of historical theology, George W. Truett Theological Seminary, Baylor University

"In his new book, Kyle Hughes pulls back the ancient exegetical curtain so we can watch the performance of Scripture and Christology in the early church. This was no routine drama, but a lively dialogue between the Old Testament and the apostolic testimony, with the person of Christ playing the leading role. Anyone interested in patristic exegesis, biblical interpretation, or Christology should pick up a copy and follow along with the script."

—**Stephen Presley**, senior fellow for religion and public life, the Center for Religion, Culture & Democracy, and associate professor of church history, The Southern Baptist Theological Seminary

Scripting the Son

Scriptural Exegesis and the Making of
Early Christology

Kyle R. Hughes

FOREWORD BY
Shawn J. Wilhite

CASCADE *Books* • Eugene, Oregon

SCRIPTING THE SON
Scriptural Exegesis and the Making of Early Christology

Studies in Early Christology

Copyright © 2024 Kyle R. Hughes. All rights reserved. Except for brief quotations in critical publications or reviews, no part of this book may be reproduced in any manner without prior written permission from the publisher. Write: Permissions, Wipf and Stock Publishers, 199 W. 8th Ave., Suite 3, Eugene, OR 97401.

Cascade Books
An Imprint of Wipf and Stock Publishers
199 W. 8th Ave., Suite 3
Eugene, OR 97401

www.wipfandstock.com

PAPERBACK ISBN: 978-1-6667-4213-8
HARDCOVER ISBN: 978-1-6667-4214-5
EBOOK ISBN: 978-1-6667-4215-2

Cataloguing-in-Publication data:

Names: Hughes, Kyle R. [author]. | Wilhite, Shawn J. [foreword writer].

Title: Scripting the Son : scriptural exegesis and the making of early Christology / by Kyle R. Hughes ; foreword by Shawn J. Wilhite.

Description: Eugene, OR: Cascade Books, 2024 | Series: Studies in Early Christology | Includes bibliographical references and index.

Identifiers: ISBN 978-1-6667-4213-8 (paperback) | ISBN 978-1-6667-4214-5 (hardcover) | ISBN 978-1-6667-4215-2 (ebook)

Subjects: LCSH: Jesus Christ—History of doctrines—Early church, approximately 30–600. | Bible—Old Testament—Criticism, interpretation, etc.—History—Early church, approximately 30–600. | God (Christianity). | Theology, Doctrinal. | Hermeneutics—Religious aspects—Christianity—History.

Classification: BT198 H84 2024 (paperback) | BT198 (ebook)

VERSION NUMBER 11/01/24

Unless otherwise indicated, all Scripture quotations are from The Holy Bible, English Standard Version, published by Crossway Bibles, a division of Good News Publishers © 2001, 2006, 2011, 2016. Used by permission. All rights reserved. Septuagint quotations, unless otherwise indicated, are from The Lexham English Septuagint © 2019 by Lexham Press. Used by permission.

For my parents,
Bob and Stephanie Hughes

Contents

Foreword by Shawn J. Wilhite | ix
Acknowledgments | xiii
List of Abbreviations | xiv

1. Introduction: The Trinity and the Old Testament | 1
2. The New Testament and Other Early Christian Literature | 22
3. Justin Martyr | 43
4. Irenaeus of Lyons | 72
5. Tertullian of Carthage | 100
6. Later Developments in the West | 144
7. Origen of Alexandria | 156
8. Conclusion: Scripting the Son | 187

Appendix: Tables of Instances of Prosopological Exegesis | 201
Bibliography | 207
Author Index | 215
Ancient Document Index | 217

Foreword

AT THE HEART OF fourth-century trinitarian controversies stood the concern for scriptural exegesis and philosophical arguments about scriptural texts.[1] Articulating the Trinity required a Christian imaginary and skills for reading Christian material. How early Christians argued depended a great deal on what they could see, the patterns of reading and arguing about Christian textual material, and an attempt at speaking metaphysically—all to contemplate the mystery of God's life.

As scholars of early Christianity seek to explore the complex matrix of theological models, we continue to uncover *modes* of scriptural reading strategies that either uphold or are produced by theological ideas. Early Christian theology and reading strategies reside in symbiosis. Several scholars have shown that early Christian theologians utilized, modified, and resourced reading strategies within Greek culture.[2] Reading strategies are not masters but servants for a theologian's contemplation of God. Some reading strategies developed alongside the church's

1. Mark Edwards, *Aristotle and Early Christian Thought*, Studies in Philosophy and Theology in Late Antiquity (London: Routledge, 2019), 78: "When Christians of the fourth century undertook to defend the Nicene Creed by philosophical reasoning, the terms of greatest moment to them were *ousia* and *dunamis* ('being' and 'power' or 'potentiality').... To Christians, they were scriptural, but the meanings grafted upon them by all parties to theological controversy in this epoch are derived, by way of Plotinus and Porphyry, from the Aristotelian lexicon."

2. Kathy Eden, *Hermeneutics and the Rhetorical Tradition: Chapters in the Ancient Legacy and Its Humanist Reception*, Yale Studies in Hermeneutics (New Haven, CT: Yale University Press, 1997); Martin Irvine, *The Making of Textual Culture: "Grammatica" and Literary Theory, 350–1100*, Cambridge Studies in Medieval Literature 19 (Cambridge: Cambridge University Press, 1994).

theological maturation; as the debates of theology matured, so too did Christian reading patterns. However, we see the writers of Scripture practicing several strategies from ancient Greek rhetoric. We can observe some of this practice in their appropriation of older textual material (namely, in how a New Testament writer uses the Greek Bible).

One such reading strategy used by writers of Scripture and the earliest Christians is *prosopology*—the very topic of this book. It is not necessarily my responsibility to prove that early Christians used this practice (although I am convinced that they did) or show its viability for modern theological discourse; instead, I want to situate the following book in a stream of scholarship that has focused more predominantly upon *prosopological exegesis*. Michael Slusser was among the first to bring this discussion into English-speaking scholarship because, up to that point, prosopology had been primarily discussed in German and French scholarship.[3] In the past fifteen years, Matthew Bates, David Downs, Kyle Hughes, and Madison Pierce (ordering their work by date) have been the more prominent scholars raising awareness about this exegetical strategy.[4] Downs and Hughes have predominantly looked at this practice in early Christian literature. Bates and Pierce, on the other hand, have concerned themselves with Christian Scripture.

The writer of Hebrews reads several older passages prosopologically. An easier and more obvious example to see is found in Hebrews 1:5:

> For to which of the angels did God ever say,
> "You are my Son;
> today I have begotten you" [Ps 2:7]?

---

3. Michael Slusser, "The Exegetical Roots of Trinitarian Theology," *Theological Studies* 49 (1988) 461–76.

4. Matthew W. Bates, *The Hermeneutics of the Apostolic Proclamation: The Center of Paul's Method of Scriptural Interpretation* (Waco, TX: Baylor University Press, 2012); David J. Downs, "Prosopological Exegesis in Cyprian's *De Opere et Eleemosynis*," *Journal of Theological Interpretation* 6.2 (2012) 279–93; Matthew W. Bates, *The Birth of the Trinity: Jesus, God, and Spirit in New Testament and Early Christian Interpretations of the Old Testament* (Oxford: Oxford University Press, 2015); Kyle R. Hughes, "The Spirit Speaks: Pneumatological Innovation in the Scriptural Exegesis of Justin and Tertullian," *Vigiliae Christianae* 69 (2015) 463–83; Kyle R. Hughes, *The Trinitarian Testimony of the Spirit: Prosopological Exegesis and the Development of Pre-Nicene Pneumatology*, Supplements to Vigiliae Christianae 147 (Leiden: Brill, 2018); Kyle R. Hughes, "The Spirit and the Scriptures: Revisiting Cyprian's Use of Prosopological Exegesis," *Journal of Early Christian History* 8.2 (2018) 35–48; Madison N. Pierce, *Divine Discourse in the Epistle to the Hebrews: The Recontextualization of Spoken Quotations in Scripture*, Society for New Testament Studies Monograph Series 178 (Cambridge: Cambridge University Press, 2020).

Or again,
> "I will be his Father,
> and he will be my Son" [2 Sam 7:14; 1 Chr 17:13]?

God the Father is speaking to God the Son; to discern the meaning in the scriptural texts, one may assign divine persons to each of the pronouns. I am particularly drawn to (1) *who* the persons in dialogue are, (2) *where* the dialogue occurs, and (3) *when* the dialogue transpires. Prosopology is different to *prosopopoeia* (or performative exegesis), whereby the author *performs* the character of the spoken person; instead, prosopology invites us to "listen in" on two divine persons in dialogue with one another!

In my own research, I have found this practice appearing in Cyril of Alexandria (*d.* 444). He believed that he followed the scriptural pattern in his prosopological reading of Hebrews 1.[5] If the practice is done by scriptural authors (as argued by Bates and Pierce), by those in earliest Christian communities (as argued by Downs and Hughes), and by pro-Nicene theologians (as seen in Cyril), then it may be helpful to begin asking *how can modern theologians incorporate prosopological reading strategies in their own theological discourse?*[6]

Hughes has provided us with yet another resource on the topic in *Scripting the Son*. He is a careful reader of both biblical and patristic texts. This book is added to his research profile on early Christian scriptural exegesis and theology before the Nicene and pro-Nicene traditions:

> "The Spirit Speaks: Pneumatological Innovation in the Scriptural Exegesis of Justin and Tertullian." *Vigiliae Christianae* 69 (2015) 463–83.
>
> *The Trinitarian Testimony of the Spirit: Prosopological Exegesis and the Development of Pre-Nicene Pneumatology*. Supplements to Vigiliae Christianae 147. Leiden: Brill, 2018.
>
> "The Spirit and the Scriptures: Revisiting Cyprian's Use of Prosopological Exegesis." *Journal of Early Christian History* 8.2 (2018) 35–48.
>
> *How the Spirit Became God: The Mosaic of Early Christian Pneumatology*. Eugene, OR: Cascade, 2020.

---

5. Shawn J. Wilhite, "'Was It Not the Only Begotten That Was Speaking Long Ago': Cyril of Alexandria's Christological Exegesis in His Commentary on Hebrews (Heb. 1:1–2)," *Studia Patristica* 129 (2021) 39–50.

6. See Fred Sanders, *The Triune God*, New Studies in Dogmatics (Grand Rapids: Zondervan, 2016).

Hughes has displayed that before the creedal formulation of the Nicene faith, early Christians were trinitarian and creative in their scriptural exegesis. May we learn alongside Hughes and discern from these earliest Christians *how* to read Scripture for trinitarian theology. *Scripting the Son* directly contributes to the growing trends of trinitarian theology among Christian theologians and, more specifically, to the relationship of early Christian scriptural exegesis and trinitarian theology. Many may be drawn to the Nicene and pro-Nicene traditions, but Hughes displays how much more there is to learn about these pre-Nicene traditions. *Tolle lege*!

Shawn J. Wilhite

Associate professor of Christian studies, California Baptist University; fellow and director of the Center for Ancient Christian Studies (https://www.ancientchristianstudies.com)

Acknowledgments

As with every book I have written, my wife Karisa was my north star along the journey, encouraging me onwards and sacrificially giving her time to allow me to bring this project to completion. Karisa, you are a crown unto your grateful husband (Prov 12:4). My children, Aliya, Asher, and Judah, were likewise gracious to me over this long process of researching, writing, and editing; I owe them several bonus games of Everdell (and probably another expansion as well).

Additional thanks are due to a variety of friends and colleagues who supported me over the course of this project: Blake Adams, R. J. Barthelmes, Brett Edwards, Jesse Farris, Fr. Tony Melton, and Trevor Moore. Over the past ten years that I have spent working on prosopological exegesis, Matthew Bates has been generous with his time, encouragement, and friendship. Special words of gratitude are also due to David Capes, who saw the early potential in this project and kindly invited me to submit the proposal for what would become this book, and to Shawn Wilhite for his interest in my scholarship and generous foreword for this volume.

At Cascade, I am again grateful for Michael Thomson, George Callihan, Robin Parry, Calvin Jaffarian, James Stock, and Matthew Wimer.

This book is dedicated to my parents, Bob and Stephanie Hughes. Thank you for your decades of love and investment in me. May the love of Christ shine brightly upon you for all your days.

Kyle Hughes

Feast of Pope St. Gregory the Great 2024

Abbreviations

Ancient

1 Apol.	Justin, *1 Apology*
1 Clem.	Clement of Rome, 1 Clement
2 Clem.	Clement of Rome, 2 Clement
Adv. Jud.	Tertullian, *Against the Jews*
An.	Tertullian, *The Soul*
Antichr.	Hippolytus, *Christ and Antichrist*
Barn.	Epistle of Barnabas
Carn. Chr.	Tertullian, *The Flesh of Christ*
Cels.	Origen, *Against Celsus*
Comm. Cant.	Origen, *Commentary on the Song of Songs*
Comm. John	Origen, *Commentary on John*
Comm. Matt.	Origen, *Commentary on Matthew*
Comm. Rom.	Origen, *Commentary on Romans*
Demetr.	Cyprian, *To Demetrian*
Dial.	Justin, *Dialogue with Trypho*
Dial. Herac.	Origen, *Dialogue with Heraclides*
Dom. or.	Cyprian, *The Lord's Prayer*
Eccl. Hist.	Eusebius, *Ecclesiastical History*

Eleem.	Cyprian, *Works and Almsgiving*
Ep.	Cyprian, *Epistles*
Epid.	Irenaeus, *Demonstration of the Apostolic Preaching*
Fort.	Cyprian, *To Fortunatus: Exhortation to Martyrdom*
Hab. virg.	Cyprian, *The Dress of Virgins*
Haer.	Irenaeus, *Against Heresies*
Herm.	Tertullian, *Against Hermogenes*
Hist. eccl.	Eusebius, *Ecclesiastical History*
Hom. Cant.	Origen, *Homilies on the Song of Songs*
Hom. Ezech.	Origen, *Homilies on Ezekiel*
Hom. Gen.	Origen, *Homilies on Genesis*
Hom. Isa.	Origen, *Homilies on Isaiah*
Hom. Jer.	Origen, *Homilies on Jeremiah*
Hom. Lev.	Origen, *Homilies on Leviticus*
Hom. Luc.	Origen, *Homilies on Luke*
Hom. Num.	Origen, *Homilies on Numbers*
Hom. Ps.	Origen, *Homilies on the Psalms*
Laps.	Cyprian, *The Lapsed*
LXX	Septuagint
Marc.	Tertullian, *Against Marcion*
Mort.	Cyprian, *Mortality*
MT	Masoretic Text
Noet.	Hippolytus, *Against Noetus*
Or.	Origen, *Prayer*
Paed.	Clement of Alexandria, *Christ the Educator*
Pat.	Cyprian, *The Advantage of Patience*
Praesc.	Tertullian, *Prescription against Heretics*
Prax.	Tertullian, *Against Praxeas*
Princ.	Origen, *First Principles*
Protr.	Clement of Alexandria, *Exhortation to the Greeks*
Res.	Tertullian, *The Resurrection of the Flesh*

Strom.	Clement of Alexandria, *Miscellanies*
Symp.	Methodius, *Symposium*
Test.	Cyprian, *To Quirinius: Testimonies against the Jews*
Trin.	Novatian, *The Trinity*
Unit. eccl.	Cyprian, *The Unity of the Catholic Church*
Virg.	Tertullian, *The Veiling of Virgins*
Zel. liv.	Cyprian, *Jealousy and Envy*

Modern

ACW	*Ancient Christian Writers*
ANF	*Ante-Nicene Fathers*
BAC	The Bible in Ancient Christianity
BGBH	Beiträge zur Geschichte der biblischen Hermeneutik
BHT	Beiträge zur historischen Theologie
BTCB	Brazos Theological Commentary on the Bible
CEECW	*The Cambridge Edition of Early Christian Writings*
CTC	Christian Theology in Context
CUASEC	Catholic University of America Studies in Early Christianity
CUASST	Catholic University of America Studies in Sacred Theology
CWS	The Classics of Western Spirituality
ECF	The Early Church Fathers
FOTC	The Fathers of the Church: A New Translation
GSECP	Gorgias Studies in Early Christianity and Patristics
HDR	Harvard Dissertations in Religion
JECH	*Journal of Early Christian History*
JSOTSup	Journal for the Study of the Old Testament Supplement Series
JTI	*Journal of Theological Interpretation*
LCL	The Loeb Classical Library
LNTS	Library of New Testament Studies

LW	*Luther's Works*
NICNT	New International Commentary on the New Testament
NovTSup	Supplements to Novum Testamentum
NSD	New Studies in Dogmatics
OECS	Oxford Early Christian Studies
OECT	Oxford Early Christian Texts
PPS	Popular Patristics Series
ProEccl	*Pro Ecclesia*
PTMS	Princeton Theological Monograph Series
RSECW	Routledge Studies in the Early Christian World
SBLMS	Society of Biblical Literature Monograph Series
SBLSBS	Society of Biblical Literature Sources for Biblical Study
SBLSS	Society of Biblical Literature Symposium Series
SBR	Studies of the Bible and Its Reception
SecCent	*Second Century*
SFC	Selections from the Fathers of the Church
SJLA	Studies in Judaism in Late Antiquity
SNTSMS	Society for New Testament Studies Monograph Series
StPatr	Studia Patristica
ThH	Théologie historique
TJ	*Trinity Journal*
TS	*Theological Studies*
VC	*Vigiliae Christianae*
VCSup	Supplements to Vigiliae Christianae
WUNT	Wissenschaftliche Untersuchungen zum Neuen Testament
ZNW	*Zeitschrift für die neutestamentliche Wissenschaft und die Kunde der älteren Kirche*

1

Introduction

The Trinity and the Old Testament

THE HISTORY OF THEOLOGICAL development in early Christianity could largely be written as the story of early Christian interpretation of what would come to be called the Old Testament. According to the Gospels, the process of reflecting on the life, death, and resurrection of Jesus began on that very first Easter Sunday. In an intriguing pericope found at the end of Luke's Gospel, the Evangelist recounts how Jesus, even before he had appeared to the Eleven, met two of his followers on the road to Emmaus (Luke 24:13–35). Not recognizing Jesus, the two men recounted their great disappointment regarding recent events that had taken place in Jerusalem, earning them a rebuke from Jesus, who claimed that the prophets had in fact taught that it was necessary for the Messiah to suffer and die. To this Luke appends the following note: "And beginning with Moses and all the Prophets, he interpreted to them in all the Scriptures the things concerning himself" (Luke 24:27). Likewise, the apostle Paul tells the Corinthians, "For I delivered to you as of first importance what I also received: that Christ died for our sins in accordance with the Scriptures, that he was buried, that he was raised on the third day according to the Scriptures, and that he appeared to Cephas, then to the twelve" (1 Cor 15:3–5). By "the Scriptures," Paul of course meant the Law, the Psalms, and the Prophets—again, what Christians would come to call the Old Testament. As John Behr points out, Paul's primary concern in this passage is not "the historicity of the events behind their reports, but that the reports are continuous with, in accordance with, Scripture."[1] From the beginning, then, the gospel of Jesus Christ was inextricably tied into a re-reading of the Old Testament in light of the death and resurrection of Christ; "because God has acted in Christ in a definitive, and unexpected, manner, making everything new, Scripture itself must be read anew."[2]

Over the course of the following decades and centuries, the interpretation of the Old Testament, and in particular the early Christians' claim that Jesus Christ was himself the center of all the Scriptures, would serve as a major flashpoint in the struggle for Christian self-definition with respect to non-believing Jews on the one hand and assorted groups that would come to be labeled "heretics" on the other. Surely one of the most remarkable claims advanced by the early Christians was the suggestion that the one God described in these Scriptures could—and, in fact, must—be understood as Father, Son, and Holy Spirit. For example, by the middle of the second century, Justin Martyr was making the audacious claim, in his debate with his Jewish interlocutor Trypho, that "Scripture declares that the Son was begotten of the Father before all creatures, and everybody will admit that the Son is numerically distinct from the Father!"[3] While Justin's account, whatever its historical basis, reflects the reality that many Jews rejected Justin's interpretation of their Scriptures that identified Jesus as a "second God," the Christians of Rome were hardly united behind Justin's approach. Justin's time in Rome overlapped with that of another teacher, Marcion, who like Justin sought to make sense of the Christian faith with respect to the Old Testament. As Judith Lieu explains, Marcion advocated for a very different interpretation of the Scriptures in which the Creator is shown to be "morally distinct and inferior" to the true, transcendent, absolutely good God revealed by Jesus.[4] This, of course, has important implications for how Marcion understood the purpose and authority of the Old Testament; as Lieu argues, "Given that the weaknesses of the Creator was pre-eminently displayed within it, and was crucial for his own narrative of God's revelation in Jesus Christ, the 'Old Testament' must, at least initially, have retained some necessary status," while

---

1. Behr, *Way to Nicaea*, 16.

2. Behr, *Way to Nicaea*, 27. As Young writes, "There can be little doubt that in the earliest Christianity a massive rereading of scripture took place" (*Scripture*, 42).

3. *Dial.* 129.3 (trans. Falls).

4. Lieu, *Marcion*, 366. On Marcion and Marcionism, see further Behr, *Way to Nicaea*, 17–19; Ehrman, *Lost Christianities*, 103–9.

INTRODUCTION: THE TRINITY AND THE OLD TESTAMENT   3

nevertheless "the sole record of the revelation of God" was to be found in the writings of Jesus' apostles.[5] The fact that anti-Marcionite polemics were written well into the fourth century demonstrates that the issues raised by Marcion concerning the Old Testament and the nature of the deity revealed therein continued to occupy Christian thinkers long after the death of Marcion.[6]

Aptly, therefore, does Brevard Childs write, "The church's struggle with the Trinity was not a battle *against* the Old Testament, but rather a battle *for* the Old Testament."[7] To the extent that early Christians wished to affirm the status of the Old Testament as *Christian* Scripture that revealed the workings of one God across both Old and New Testaments, the foundational elements of Christology would need to pass through the forge of the Old Testament. It is the purpose of this book, then, to contribute to our understanding of the role the Old Testament played in the formation of early trinitarian theology by examining how Christians of the first, second, and third centuries appealed to dialogical passages of the Old Testament for support in constructing their understanding of the person and work of Jesus Christ, the incarnate Son of God who co-existed with the Father before all worlds, was born of the Virgin Mary, suffered and was crucified under Pontius Pilate, was dead and buried, and ascended into heaven to be seated at the right hand of God, from whence he shall return to judge the world. In these passages, I contend, we find something of a "script" by which we can trace the emergence of the narrative logic of early Christology along these very lines.

In the broadest sense, then, this book examines the relationship between biblical exegesis and the development of trinitarian theology. More narrowly, I seek to analyze the fashioning of christological doctrine in the pre-Nicene period through the lens of early Christian reflection on the Old Testament. To be still more specific, the primary thesis of this work is that the early Christian reading strategy of prosopological exegesis (which will be defined in more detail below) made an important and often under-appreciated contribution to the development of Christology in the pre-Nicene period. Such a conclusion fits within a broadly recognized perspective among scholars that "scriptural exegesis

---

5. Lieu, *Marcion*, 431–32.

6. On Marcion in the Christian heresiological tradition, see Lieu, *Marcion*, 86–125.

7. Childs, *Biblical Theology*, 376 (italics original). I was introduced to this quotation in Rowe, "Biblical Pressure," 295.

[was] shaped by contemporary exegetical procedures and assumptions."[8] This volume, therefore, is both a historical and a theological investigation that seeks to understand the process by which early Christian exegetes looked to Scripture for refining their view of the person and work of Christ. In so doing, I make both historical and theological claims, and while I contend that theological and historical investigations can be mutually illuminating, I recognize that various readers may find one set of claims more compelling than the other and welcome engagement with the argument set forth in this book from scholars approaching this subject from a variety of persuasions and perspectives.

On the one hand, this work is a historical investigation that seeks to understand the process by which Christian writers used Scripture to develop their understanding of the person and work of Christ. To the extent that recent scholarship has seen what Christopher Beeley and Mark Weedman have called an "unprecedented" amount of attention to early Christian interpretation of the Bible,[9] this book participates in this larger conversation that seeks to unite the study of early Christian biblical interpretation with the study of early Christian theology. Following Beeley and Weedman, I take it as a "fundamental presupposition" that "biblical exegesis played a decisive role in the development of early trinitarian theology."[10] Within this stream of scholarship, one current of particular relevance for this text is that which has emphasized how early Christian exegetes were indebted to the interpretive methods and tools of the broader Greco-Roman culture of their time.[11] Studies such as this present volume can therefore rightly be described as historical inquiries into the fundamental logic by which the early Christians developed their theology with respect to their reading of the Scriptures.[12]

Still, on the other hand, this book is deeply and unapologetically theological in nature. While traditional historical-critical scholarship of the Bible has generally sought to free the interpretation of Scripture from Christian doctrine, one recent strand of scholarship has instead sought to restore the connection between the two. Following David

8. Young, *Scripture*, 45.
9. Beeley and Weedman, "Introduction," 1.
10. Beeley and Weedman, "Introduction," 8.
11. The classic work here is Young, *Biblical Exegesis*.
12. As Skarsaune observes, "In many respects, Christian literature of the period 30–250 CE may be said to be one single large commentary on the Scriptures, the Hebrew Bible" ("Scriptural Interpretation," 375).

Yeago's call for a return to "theological exegesis" that would take seriously the fact that the crafters of doctrine in the first Christian centuries believed that they were doing so in accordance with the teaching of Scripture,[13] a recent wave of scholarship has, in the words of C. Clifton Black, attempted a reading of Scripture that involves a "forthright reclamation of the church's canonical resources, especially its doctrine of the Triune God and its appeal to the *regula fidei*."[14] Accordingly, there has been renewed attention to the means by which early Christian exegetes read the Scriptures through the eyes of faith. One particularly promising avenue of inquiry has involved exploring the proposition that the Scriptures themselves exert some kind of "pressure" that leads interpreters to understand God, across both Old and New Testaments, as Trinity.[15] For C. Kavin Rowe, the doctrine of the Trinity emerged not in opposition to the witness of the Old Testament but rather "precisely because the writers of the New Testament presupposed the authority of the Old Testament and made explicit use of the theological grammar that undergirds the Old Testament's language about the one God."[16] Extending this a step forward, Matthew Bates's work on prosopological exegesis has analyzed how dialogical texts in the Old Testament presented early Christian exegetes with riddles that were best solved through a person-centered reading strategy that identified multiple divine speakers, again demonstrating how the very words of Scripture exerted a pressure for a trinitarian understanding of God that was deeply rooted in the Old Testament.[17] It is in line with this trajectory of scholarship, then, that this present book identifies the intersection of scriptural interpretation and

---

13. Yeago, "New Testament," 159–64. For example, according to Yeago, the doctrine of the Trinity is best understood as the attempt by the early church to make sense of the primitive Christian identification of Jesus as Yahweh ("New Testament," 153–58); cf. Phil 2:9–11 and its invocation of Isa 45:21–24.

14. Black, "Trinity and Exegesis," 151. See further, e.g., Wilken, *Spirit*; O'Keefe and Reno, *Sanctified Vision*; Treier, *Introducing Theological Interpretation*; Black, *Reading Scripture*. For a concise summary of early Christian writers' appeals to Scripture in their development of trinitarian thought, see Edwards, "Exegesis," 80–89. A helpful overview of approaches to trinitarian exegesis is found in Sanders, *Triune God*, 155–237.

15. Rowe, "Biblical Pressure," 295–312. See further Seitz, *Elder Testament*, 21–34.

16. Rowe, "Biblical Pressure," 299. Rowe points to New Testament texts that posit an ontological identity between Yahweh and Jesus Christ, such as Rom 10:13 and John 20:28 ("Biblical Pressure," 301–3).

17. Bates, *Birth*. As a classic example, early Christian exegetes interpreted Ps 110:1 as the words of the Father to the Son, as at Mark 12:35–37 and Acts 2:33–35; cf. Bates, *Birth*, 44–62.

the early development of Trinitarianism as fertile ground for theological investigation. With Frances Young, then, I maintain that "doctrine was generated by the need to make sense of scripture."[18] Still, whatever its implications for the work of theology today, this book's central task is rooted in the careful work of historical investigation through the close reading of literary texts in their historical contexts.

Threading the Labyrinth of Early Christology

This text aims to pull together three scholarly strands that, together, become the golden thread by which we will explore the labyrinth of early Christology: prosopological exegesis, the *testimonia* hypothesis, and the *regula fidei*. This section aims to briefly describe each of these key areas of focus, placing each in its current scholarly setting and identifying its function in the argument of this volume, before beginning the argument proper.

Prosopological Exegesis

First, this work explores as its primary focus the subject of how early Christian interpreters used a person-centered reading strategy called prosopological exegesis to find the voice of Christ speaking through the dialogues of the Old Testament. Indeed, most of the pages of this book are devoted to analyzing specific examples of prosopological exegesis in Christian writings from the first three centuries. From the method's roots in the pages of the New Testament through its careful application in the hands of church fathers such as Justin, Irenaeus, Tertullian, and Origen, I trace how prosopological exegesis contributed to the development of Christology in the pre-Nicene period. This book is, to my knowledge, the first comprehensive account of prosopological exegesis in the pre-Nicene period, the result of a careful examination of all the many thousands of pages of extant writings from this period.[19] Given

---

18. Young, *Scripture*, 13.

19. Because of the book's focus on prosopological exegesis to, from, or concerning the Son, some instances of prosopological exegesis, such as when "the church" or "the angels" are identified as the speakers of Old Testament passages in which they are not in view and the Son is not referenced, are not included in this book's analysis. That sub-category of prosopological exegesis, however, is very small, and thus this volume includes the vast majority of early Christian instances of prosopological exegesis.

INTRODUCTION: THE TRINITY AND THE OLD TESTAMENT   7

its foundational role in this volume, prosopological exegesis must now be introduced in more detail.

The term "prosopological exegesis" has been used by modern scholars to describe the early Christian exegetical practice of identifying various "characters" or "persons" (Greek *prosōpa*; Latin *personae*) participating in dialogical passages of the Old Testament.[20] Though the roots of this ancient reading method lie in the exegetical practices of the Greco-Roman rhetorical schools and the language was initially drawn from the world of the theater (*prosōpon* meaning "mask"), early Christian interpreters of Scripture used prosopological exegesis to identify Father, Son, and Spirit as the true or ultimate speakers of texts in which the speaker or addressee was otherwise ambiguous.[21] To set up the arguments to come in this book, there are two specific points concerning prosopological exegesis that warrant our further attention.

First, scholars have demonstrated that early Christian writers utilized prosopological exegesis to provide a scriptural warrant for the use of "person" language that would eventually be identified as the predominant metaphor for speaking of diversity within the Godhead. It is this contribution of prosopological exegesis to the development of Trinitarianism that was first identified by Carl Andresen in a landmark 1961 article. For Andresen, the trinitarian notion of person was not a later patristic innovation but instead grounded in a form of scriptural exegesis; for instance, the early christological interpretation of Ps 110:1 has been well documented from the origins of the Christian movement.[22] Andresen suggested that when the early Christians began to draw upon the literary language of *prosōpon*, this created theological pressures insofar as such readings could suggest that, perhaps, the speaker was merely a fictional character and not a real divine person. In response, Christian exegetes crafted increasingly careful introductory formulas and refined the possible applications of prosopological exegesis.[23] For Andresen, it was Tertullian who first recognized that prosopological exegesis could be used to

20. Key works include Andresen, "Zur Entstehung," 1–39; Rondeau, *Les commentaires patristiques*; Slusser, "Exegetical Roots," 461–76; Bates, *Hermeneutics*; *Birth*; Hughes, "Spirit Speaks," 463–83; "Spirit and the Scriptures," 35–48; *Trinitarian Testimony*; *How the Spirit Became God*. For recent summaries of the history of scholarship on prosopological exegesis, see Bates, *Hermeneutics*, 183–87; Hughes, *Trinitarian Testimony*, 12–21.

21. For a formal definition, see Bates, *Hermeneutics*, 218.

22. Andresen, "Zur Entstehung," 18; cf. Hay, *Glory*.

23. Andresen, "Zur Entstehung," 21.

include not just the Father and the Son but also the Holy Spirit in what could now truly be spoken of as a trinitarian conversation, though my recent work has demonstrated that evidence for the Holy Spirit speaking prosopologically as his own distinct divine person may be found as early as Justin Martyr.[24] Building on this foundation, Michael Slusser went so far as to identify prosopological exegesis as the "exegetical roots" of trinitarian theology, suggesting that "when early Christian prosopological exegesis accords places to the trinitarian persons which are congruent with both Christian piety and Christian worship, it raises the real possibility that the trinitarian distinctions were arrived at in a methodical way."[25] Matthew Bates's *The Birth of the Trinity* developed this argument further, arguing that "prosopological exegesis contributed decisively to the development of the concept of the Trinity, since it was this way of reading that especially led to the consolidation of 'person' language to express the three-in-one mystery."[26] According to Bates, the use of prosopological exegesis was far more common and more significant for later Christian interpreters of Scripture than even Andresen recognized; as such, Bates explores what he terms "Trinitarianism by continuity in prosopological exegesis," insofar as the use of "person" language in prosopological readings of the Old Testament provided "a divinely authorized metaphor that could suitably parse God's oneness."[27] Likewise, Madison Pierce's *Divine Discourse in the Epistle to the Hebrews* demonstrated how an understanding of prosopological exegesis can illuminate the author's use of intradivine dialogue in that epistle.[28] In the wake of these studies, there can now be little doubt that prosopological exegesis played a significant role in the development of trinitarian theology.[29]

---

24. Andresen, "Zur Entstehung," 23; Hughes, *Trinitarian Testimony*, 54–63.

25. Slusser, "Exegetical Roots," 475.

26. Bates, *Birth*, 7.

27. Bates, *Birth*, 26–27, 36–40 (here 37). Or put another way, as Bates writes, this metaphor became "the premier divinely authorized way to parse and differentiate identities and relationships with respect to the one God" (*Birth*, 203). Despite its title, *The Birth of the Trinity* was almost exclusively devoted to analyzing how prosopological exegesis was used to illustrate the relationship between the Father and the Son, and as a result my books *The Trinitarian Testimony of the Spirit* and *How the Spirit Became God* aimed to extend Bates's work to show that prosopological exegesis likewise contributed to pneumatological development by providing scriptural warrant for the use of "person" language that would eventually be applied to the Spirit as the third divine person of the Trinity.

28. For her summary of prosopological exegesis, see Pierce, *Divine Discourse*, 3–22.

29. The importance of prosopological exegesis for the development of trinitarian

Second, the scholarly study of prosopological exegesis has the potential to illuminate not just the emergence of trinitarian theology but also Christology more specifically. Older works on prosopological exegesis, such as those of Rondeau and Slusser, largely focused on how Christian exegetes of the third and fourth centuries used prosopological exegesis to distinguish between the human and divine natures of Christ.[30] The aforementioned newer wave of research into prosopological exegesis, however, has moved the goalposts into the first and second centuries of the Christian era, probing at the christological implications of prosopological exegesis during this earlier time period. In order to explore how prosopological exegesis contributed to christological claims, it is worth further exploring Bates's notion of the "theodrama," which he describes as "the dramatic world invoked by an ancient reader of Scripture as that reader construed a prophet to be speaking from or observing the person (*prosōpon*) of a divine or human character."[31] It is within these theodramatic scriptural interpretations, Bates demonstrates, that we find "snapshots of the relationship between divine persons as envisioned by the earliest Christian readers of Scripture, and when stitched together, these individual pictures form a panorama of the interior divine life."[32] Most significantly for this book is the fact that this panorama is not "a static portrait" but "an unfolding story" of God's engagement with his creation through the ages.[33] It is, therefore, a *narrative* account of the actions of the economic Trinity, and as such Bates's book traces how, for early Christian writers, "intra-divine dialogue covers the full spectrum of the life of the Godhead as economically revealed in the Old Testament," focusing on conversations between the Father and the Son concerning the Son's pre-existence, mission, suffering and death, resurrection, and enthronement.[34] In other words, careful attention to early Christian writers' use of prosopological exegesis, and the theodramatic

---

theology is starting to break through into more popular-level literature, such as in Sanders, *Triune God*, 226–35, where it is given the idiosyncratic name of "prosoponic exegesis."

30. Rondeau, *Les commentaires patristiques*; Slusser, "Exegetical Roots," 470–75.

31. Bates, *Birth*, 5n38; for more on Bates's conception of the theodrama, see *Birth*, 34–36.

32. Bates, *Birth*, 41.

33. Bates, *Birth*, 40.

34. Bates, *Birth*, 8.

settings envisioned by such interpretations of Scripture, provides an outline for the basic narrative of the Son's economic mission.

Towards the conclusion of his book, Bates gestures at the notion that valid prosopological exegesis, from the position of Christian orthodoxy, is that which coheres with the claims of the apostolic proclamation.[35] Seeing as Bates's interests are primarily at the theological level, it is not surprising that he concludes with the following observation:

> Does the apostolic proclamation undergird prosopological exegesis or is prosopological exegesis part of the "in accordance with the scriptures" portion of the apostolic proclamation that certifies the truthfulness of the early Christian testimony? For this present author, a choice between the two cannot be made, for they are mutually reinforcing when, beginning from either direction, a spiraling process of formulating theses and seeking verifications is undertaken.[36]

While there is undoubtedly much truth in the notion of a "spiraling process" between prosopological exegesis and the apostolic proclamation, Bates's thematic approach in his book does little to explore the details of this process itself. After all, the apostolic proclamation, at least as reflected in the *regula fidei*, could take flexible forms, as noted below. Likewise, different early Christian authors used prosopological exegesis in different ways and with different emphases. Indeed, as will be explored over the course of this book, Bates's proposal, for all its emphasis on the early Christian portrayal of the *divine* narrative, lacks sufficient attention to the *historical* narrative by which these early Christian writers engaged with scriptural exegesis as a means of reflecting upon and developing their theological ideas, particularly with reference to the christological content of the apostolic proclamation or what would come to be termed the rule of faith.

In order to better understand the context within which prosopological exegesis was employed by early Christian writers, it will be necessary at times to turn our attention to the following two secondary concerns that serve as the other two significant threads traced in this book.

---

35. Bates, *Birth*, 198–200.
36. Bates, *Birth*, 200.

The *Testimonia* Hypothesis

A second major thread in this volume concerns the *testimonia* hypothesis, which posits the existence of written collections of quotations pulled from the Old Testament that could function as proof-texts to reinforce significant points of theology. Broadly speaking, the *testimonia* hypothesis refers to the notion that the first generations of Christians gathered together and edited groups of quotations from the Septuagint, to which they attached certain authoritative interpretations, to function as proof-texts in defense of important early Christian beliefs.[37] The basic evidence for this hypothesis is found in the fact that certain scriptural passages (e.g., Psalm 22 and Psalm 110) were far more extensively quoted in early Christian writings than other Old Testament texts (e.g., Leviticus); moreover, the fact that these same passages are consistently incorrectly attributed, mixed, or linked with other quotations, and are different from extant scriptural text-types (MT or LXX), suggests the existence of some kind of scriptural extract collections from which Christian writers could draw.[38] Indeed, we have numerous undisputed examples of such *testimonia* collections among patristic writers as early as the third century,[39] but in light of the fact that we possess no such extract collection from the first or second centuries, the existence of *testimonia* collections in the first and second centuries remains speculative.

The first major study of Christian *testimonia* collections was made by Edwin Hatch, who argued in the late nineteenth century that the early Christians took over what was originally a Jewish practice of making written collections of Old Testament quotations for various purposes, though Hatch provided no relevant evidence from Jewish sources for his thesis.[40] J. Rendel Harris took this a step further by hypothesizing the existence of a single *Testimony Book* of Old Testament passages organized under the headings of "against the Jews" and "concerning the Christ," which he then related to Papias's statement about Matthew composing the *logia*.[41] Criticism of these views as overly simplistic led to the development of alternative understandings of the form and function of

---

37. Albl, *Scripture*, xv.
38. See further Fitzmyer, "4QTestimonia," 61–68, on each of these features.
39. For examples, see Albl, *Scripture*, 97–157.
40. This practice would continue within Judaism as the midrashic practice of "pearl-stringing"; see further Boyarin, *Intertextuality*.
41. On Hatch and Harris, see Albl, *Scripture*, 10–25; Fitzmyer, "4QTestimonia," 67–70; Barnard, "Use of Testimonies," 109–11.

these *testimonia* collections. For instance, according to C. H. Dodd, the early Christian *testimonia* were located not in a single written volume but within the realm of oral tradition. Early Christian writers, such as Paul, John, and the author of Hebrews, drew on these key collections of Old Testament passages, as well as their broader contexts, in formulating their theology, thus making the oral *testimonia* the "substructure of all Christian theology."[42]

The publication of the Qumran document 4QTestimonia in 1956, however, greatly strengthened the case for the existence of *written* extract collections around the turn of the era. In particular, 4QTestimonia demonstrated that Jews strung together Old Testament quotations in this manner from before the advent of Christianity.[43] Building on this example of a written *testimonia* collection, Harry Gamble further challenged Dodd by demonstrating how otherwise unexplainable similarities in the wording and combination of these quotations are clear evidence of written, and not merely oral, *testimonia* collections, which likely had a wide variety of uses in the lives of early Christians.[44] Similarly, in his comprehensive study of extract collections in the ancient world, Martin C. Albl has further demonstrated the existence of Greco-Roman and Jewish extract collections that can be dated to before the time of the New Testament, providing additional literary background for the claim that there existed early written Christian *testimonia* collections in Justin's day and earlier.[45] Thus, Albl concludes, against Dodd and others who have claimed a primarily oral mode of development for Christian *testimonia* collections, in all probability there must have been written scriptural extract collections prior to the writing of the New Testament documents. Though no such Christian *testimonia* collections are extant from the first century, it is nevertheless highly likely that such collections preceded the writing of many, if not all, of the New Testament documents.[46] Albl goes on to propose that it was in fact these *testimonia* collections that gave rise to the codex in early Christianity, positing that the compact codex form would have been particularly convenient for missionaries to carry

---

42. Dodd, *According to the Scriptures*, 127. On Dodd, see Albl, *Scripture*, 27–32; Fitzmyer, "4QTestimonia," 73–74.
43. Fitzmyer, "4QTestimonia," 86.
44. Gamble, *Books and Readers*, 26–27.
45. See the evidence summarized in Albl, *Scripture*, 70–96.
46. Albl, *Scripture*, 6.

and would have allowed for easy marking of passages of special interest.⁴⁷ Certainly by the time of Justin Martyr we have clear evidence of the existence and use of Christian *testimonia* collections.⁴⁸

Engagement with the *testimonia* hypothesis will be necessary to determine the source of the major innovations traced through this book. In particular, we will want to determine how the early Christian writers studied in this work made use of such collections in formulating this important trajectory of biblical interpretation. I will propose that it was primarily the early Christian exegetes themselves who were responsible for the prosopological interpretations that contributed to the development of Christology, though the existence of *testimonia* collections that featured passages organized according to the presumed prosopological speaker could have come into existence sometime around the time of Tertullian.

The *Regula Fidei*

A third and final important strand of analysis in this volume concerns the rule of faith (often known by its Latin name, the *regula fidei*). The term "rule of faith" and its synonyms were used in early Christian literature to refer to a basic summary of the apostolic kerygma.⁴⁹ Whereas earlier scholarship was inclined to see the rule of faith as identical with the primitive baptismal confession, the majority of modern scholars instead see the rule of faith as developing in parallel with the baptismal confession in order to guide the teaching that preceded baptism.⁵⁰ Whatever the

---

47. Albl, *Scripture*, 99, contra Gamble (*Books and Readers*, 54–66), who argues that a codex collection of Paul's letters is what influenced the physical form of other Christian writings. But we need not choose just one explanation for the Christian adoption of the codex.

48. As demonstrated in the magisterial work of Skarsaune, *Proof from Prophecy*; cf. the summary in Young, *Scripture*, 49n10.

49. This parallels, e.g., the definitions offered by Kelly ("an outline summary of Christian teaching used for catechetical instruction and other purposes"; *Early Christian Creeds*, 2); Ferguson ("a summary of apostolic preaching and teaching"; *Rule of Faith*, xi); Hartog ("a concise statement of early Christian public preaching and communal belief, a normative compendium of the *kerygma*"; "Rule of Faith," 65–66); Grech ("[a] compendium of Christian kerygma"; "Regula Fidei," 590); Young ("summaries of the faith"; *Making of the Creeds*, 9).

50. On the history of scholarship concerning the rule of faith and its relation to the baptismal confession, see Armstrong, "Rule of Faith," 32–43; Ferguson, *Rule of Faith*, 48–65; Laing, *Irenaeus*, 115–17. On the rule of faith as developing in parallel to the

precise *Sitz im Leben* of the rule of faith, the following three points are of particular importance for this work.

First, I assume a dynamic interplay, from the earliest decades of the Christian movement, between the rule of faith and the Scriptures, each of which had a distinct function within early Christian communities even as much of their content overlapped.[51] Specifically, I assume that the rule of faith was not only derived from the Scriptures but also that it shaped the interpretation, canonization, and perhaps even the writing of the Scriptures themselves.[52] Much recent scholarship has demonstrated the significance of the rule of faith as an important hermeneutical principle for interpreting Scripture; if a proposed interpretation was not in line with the rule of faith, it was to be rejected.[53] Paul Hartog has cautioned us against seeing this functioning as an impersonal mechanism for interpretation; rather, its use "stressed a disposition or orientation more than a method," and as such it is to be taken for granted that exegetes came to the text with what one might term a "hermeneutics of faith."[54] Likewise, it appears that the rule of faith played an important role in the formation of the biblical canon, insofar as one of the criteria by which early Christian writings came to be accepted as canonical was their conformity to the rule of faith—a rule that was, of course, largely developed from these very writings.[55] Indeed, we may plausibly suspect that the rule of faith, the early development of which almost certainly preceded the writing of any of the books of the New Testament,[56] influenced the writing of the Christian Scriptures themselves.

Second, the rule of faith could take flexible forms as it developed in the pre-Nicene period even as it preserved a central fixed narrative.

---

baptismal confession, with some minor differences on the precise function of the rule of faith, see Behr, *Way to Nicaea*, 33–37; Kelly, *Early Christian Creeds*, 49–52; Countryman, "Tertullian and the Regula Fidei," 218–21; Blowers, "*Regula Fidei*," 225; Ferguson, *Rule of Faith*, 70; Young, *Making of the Creeds*, 6–12.

51. See further Bokedal, "Rule of Faith," 233–55; Ferguson, *Rule of Faith*, 67–68; Johnson, *Jesus Christ*, 22–23.

52. This point has been developed by, e.g., Williams, *Evangelicals and Tradition*, 52–57.

53. See further Donovan, *One Right Reading?*, 11–14; Hartog calls the rule of faith a "road map" for the correct interpretation of Scripture ("Rule of Faith," 66).

54. Hartog, "Rule of Faith," 68–69.

55. As Armstrong writes, "The development of a definitive body of Christian literature came to define the orthodoxy by which the final form of the canon was adjudicated" ("Rule of Faith," 44). See further Armstrong, *Role of the Rule of Faith*.

56. Cf. proto-creedal statements in the New Testament such as 1 Cor 15:3–7; Rom 1:3–5; 8:34; 1 Pet 3:18–22; see further Young, *Making of the Creeds*, 8.

Writers such as Irenaeus and Tertullian felt liberty to present various forms of the rule of faith even as a basic structure remained consistent across each particular usage.[57] This combination of stability and variety is characteristic of oral transmission of tradition, a view developed with respect to the rule of faith by L. W. Countryman, who proposed an "oral-social" theory of understanding the rule of faith.[58] Paul Blowers, in contesting and developing some of the finer points of Countryman's argument, draws parallels between the rule of faith and the sermons in Acts in order to suggest that the early church "committed itself not to a universally invariable statement of faith but to variable local tellings of a *particular* story that aspired to universal significance."[59] Indeed, for Blowers, the realities of divine accommodation and evolving doctrinal challenges meant that, in the words of Irenaeus, the process of "bringing out more fully" the meaning of the Scriptures lent itself to what we might call different "performances" of the rule of faith.[60] As such, the rule of faith locates Christian identity as participation within a sweeping, cosmic narrative; as Blowers has argued, the rule of faith "served the primitive Christian hope of articulating and authenticating a world-encompassing story or metanarrative of creation, incarnation, redemption, and consummation," and as such it "set forth the basic 'dramatic' structure of a Christian vision of the world" for the purposes of exegeting both Scripture and experience.[61] This emphasis on narrative, and on early Christians telling and inhabiting a shared story concerning God's revelation in Christ and its implications for the world, has been set forth expansively by N. T. Wright.[62] Blowers builds on this approach in arguing that diversity among the early apostolic churches could be bridged and unified in a distinctive Christian identity through an appeal to a larger, authoritative narrative.[63] The rule of faith, then, is "Scripture's own intrin-

---

57. For Irenaeus, see Ferguson, *Rule of Faith*, 35–39; on Tertullian's varying usages of the rule of faith, Countryman concludes that the rule of faith was "an authority which [Tertullian's readers] were prepared to recognize and accept in a variety of versions, long and short, allowing considerable latitude in wording, but expecting a consistent and traditional pattern to emerge" ("Tertullian and the Regula Fidei," 214). See also Johnson, *Jesus Christ*, 24–30.

58. Countryman, "Tertullian and the Regula Fidei," 217–18.

59. Blowers, "*Regula Fidei*," 208 (italics original); Blowers's critique of Countryman is found in "*Regula Fidei*," 206–9.

60. Blowers, "*Regula Fidei*," 215–20 (referencing *Haer.* 1.10.3). For a constructive synthesis of Countryman and Blowers, see Johnson, *Jesus Christ*, 30n52.

61. Blowers, "*Regula Fidei*," 202.

62. Wright, *New Testament and the People of God*, 65–80.

63. Blowers, "*Regula Fidei*," 203–5.

sic story-line," helping locate the church within the true plot of Scripture and providing a way of life for those seeking to inhabit this narrative for themselves.[64] Thus, there is a close relationship between the rule of faith and the *hypothesis*, or plot, of Scripture. The center of this narrative is of course Christology, insofar as Christ is not only the literal central and most expansive article of the trinitarian *regula fidei* but the very hermeneutical key for unlocking the meaning of the Scriptures.[65]

Third, the roots of the Christology found in the *regula fidei* are located within the original apostolic proclamation or *kerygma*. As J. N. D. Kelly summarizes, not only the content of the *regula fidei* but even its very "characteristic lineaments and outline found their prototypes in the confessions and credal summaries contained in the New Testament documents."[66] For instance, Paul's gospel emphasized that Christ's death and resurrection took place "in accordance with the Scriptures" (1 Cor 15:3), suggesting that the central christological claims of the *kerygma* took place in the context of reflection on Scripture.[67] C. H. Dodd, in his classic study of the apostolic preaching, identified seven elements as making up the outline of the primitive *kerygma*,[68] which Matthew Bates has recently modified to encompass the following eight points:

> Jesus the king
> 1. preexisted with the Father,
> 2. took on human flesh, fulfilling God's promises to David,
> 3. died for sins in accordance with the Scriptures,
> 4. was buried,
> 5. was raised on the third day in accordance with the Scriptures,
> 6. appeared to many,
> 7. is seated at the right hand of God as Lord, and
> 8. will come again as judge.[69]

---

64. Blowers, "*Regula Fidei*," 212–15. See also Hartog, "Rule of Faith," 70–76.

65. Hartog, "Rule of Faith," 74–76. See also O'Keefe and Reno, *Sanctified Vision*, 24–44.

66. Kelly, *Early Christian Creeds*, 29.

67. Osborn, "Reason and the Rule of Faith," 46–47; as Osborn explains, "For Paul there is no distinction between the gospel, the kerygma, and the rule; it is concerned with the recital or proclamation of an event: Christ and him crucified" ("Reason and the Rule of Faith," 47). Cf. Kelly, *Early Christian Creeds*, 16–17; Hartog, "Rule of Faith," 72.

68. Dodd, *Apostolic Preaching*, 17.

69. Bates, *Salvation*, 52. Bates's primary adjustment to Dodd's outline is the addition of the first point; for Bates's defense of pre-existence in the Synoptics, see *Salvation*,

INTRODUCTION: THE TRINITY AND THE OLD TESTAMENT   17

It is precisely these details that are most frequently emphasized in the christological section of later statements of the *regula fidei*, and thus the link between *kerygma* and *regula* is evident, with these elements being found or assumed across the Gospels, Acts, Pauline epistles, and Johannine writings.[70]

Still, one significant question stands out: why were these particular details (and not others) selected as the core of the primitive *kerygma*, therefore establishing these points as the basis for the future development of the *regula fidei* and the creeds? Indeed, as Frances Young has explained, the *regula fidei* is "clearly an important precursor" to the later creeds of orthodox Christianity; specifically, she argues, "the overall selection" found in the *regula fidei* and its "use of traditional phrases" meant that it "profoundly affected the expansion of the second baptismal question," which concerns the nature of belief in God the Son.[71] Thus, a complete understanding of the development of the christological content of the creeds will take into account the development of the christological content of the *regula fidei*, and it is precisely this task that will be taken up in this book. I will propose that a prosopological reading of the Old Testament could have provided justification for every christological point emphasized in the *regula fidei* of the early church, suggesting a more dynamic interplay between biblical interpretation and doctrinal formulation than is sometimes assumed. My attempts to expand my thesis to try and get at the underlying forces and sources that shaped early Christian use of prosopological exegesis will, I hope, be recognized by the reader as a quest for what seems on balance to be likely or probable given the impossibility of having certainty on such matters.

Overview

Having introduced the topic and scope of this book, we can now proceed to briefly overview the contents of the coming chapters. Chapter 2 rounds out the introductory portion of the book and sets the stage for subsequent analysis of the selected pre-Nicene church fathers by exploring the origins of prosopological exegesis in the New Testament and the Apostolic Fathers. As we will see, the first decades after Christ also saw

---

54–58. See also Bates, *Birth*, 50–59.

70. See further Dodd, *Apostolic Preaching*, 17–89.

71. Young, *Making of the Creeds*, 9; see also Blowers, "Regula Fidei," 220–22.

the emergence of Christians prosopologically interpreting the Old Testament. The Gospels reflect early interest in person-centered reading strategies, while Hebrews and 1–2 Clement have the first substantive instances of prosopological exegesis in which Christ is the speaker or addressee of Old Testament dialogue. While the total amount of relevant material in these writings is far less than that found in later Christian works, these instances nevertheless formed a precedent that would be expanded upon in subsequent decades and centuries.

In chapter 3, we commence our first in-depth analysis of an early Christian writer who made a significant contribution to Christology through his use of prosopological exegesis. In this chapter, we will find that Justin Martyr expanded upon and repurposed existing *testimonia* collections to generate novel instances of prosopological exegesis, which he interpreted as conversations among Father, Son, and Spirit. When his use of prosopological exegesis is brought into parallel with his proto-creedal formulations, we can better understand how and why Justin advanced a high Christology over and against the views of his opponents. In particular, Justin stands out as the first Christian writer to explicitly articulate his approach to prosopological exegesis, an approach he would apply with increased sophistication in his *Dialogue with Trypho* to defend Christ's role in salvation history from his pre-existence through his present reign.

In chapter 4, our focus turns to Irenaeus of Lyons, who makes more extensive use of prosopological exegesis from the person of the Son than Justin had. Like Justin, Irenaeus uses prosopological exegesis to advance a high Christology, tracing the Son of God's pre-existence with the Father through his present reign. Irenaeus demonstrates the flexibility of prosopological exegesis by adapting, expanding, and repurposing Justin's approach for his own polemical ends. Indeed, such were the needs of his anti-gnostic arguments that Irenaeus was particularly keen to provide prosopological readings of the Old Testament that would support his understanding of the rule of faith. Still, the gnostics' own use of person-centered reading strategies prevented Irenaeus from the more enthusiastic embrace of the method seen in later writers such as Tertullian and Origen.

In chapter 5, we examine the writings of Tertullian of Carthage, who greatly expands both the scope and the depth of prosopological exegesis in advancing a high Christology in light of his own polemical needs. Besides being the first to use prosopological exegesis to support

INTRODUCTION: THE TRINITY AND THE OLD TESTAMENT   19

claims concerning Christ's virgin birth and return to judge the world, Tertullian's use of the Latin word *persona* shifts the focus of prosopological exegesis away from its origins in a theatrical context towards a more concrete definition of the Son as a distinct divine person. Tertullian also demonstrates a much higher degree of convergence between prosopological exegesis, the *regula fidei*, and even the development of early Christian *testimonia* collections, suggesting the consolidation of early Christology around a common set of themes. As will be noted, however, Tertullian's approach to prosopological exegesis contains some potential shortcomings such that it would be up to later Christian writers to refine and better articulate how this method was best used.

In chapter 6, we briefly assess the diminished emphasis on prosopological exegesis in Latin writers of the third century who wrote after Tertullian. The writings of Hippolytus, Novatian, and Cyprian all demonstrate that prosopological exegesis was increasingly sidelined, with Tertullian's Montanist persuasions and the rise of new scriptural battles calling for new methods being among the reasons for this decline. Even so, we discover with Cyprian a newfound emphasis on Christ as the ultimate speaker of the words of the Old Testament to an audience of Christians in Cyprian's own day.

In chapter 7, we explore how Origen's use of prosopological exegesis served to advance his christological claims. While demonstrating the continued utility and flexibility of this form of interpretation, as well as the continued alignment between the rule of faith and prosopological exegesis with respect to the Son, Origen provides a more nuanced approach to its use through his appeal to the multiple senses of Scripture. Likewise, Origen advances a homiletical and pastoral interest in using prosopological exegesis to show how the words of the Old Testament could be re-presented as the words of the Son to Origen's own congregation, to believers who he exhorted to themselves take on the very *persona* of Christ. Additional elements of Origen's use of prosopological exegesis, including its relevance for so-called partitive exegesis and his particular interest in reading the Song of Songs as a dialogue between Christ and the church, would have long-term implications for Christian theology.

In chapter 8, having demonstrated the extent to which prosopological exegesis served as a highly significant and creative element in the construction of christological doctrine, the book concludes with some theological, homiletical, and pastoral applications before setting out a "script" of Old Testament passages placed on the lips of the Son by early Christian writers, organized into "acts" and "scenes" to demonstrate the method's comprehensive application to every aspect of early Christology.

Two final notes are in order before we proceed to the book proper. First, many of the ideas developed in this book were initially explored in my monograph *The Trinitarian Testimony of the Spirit: Prosopological Exegesis and the Development of Pre-Nicene Pneumatology* (Brill, 2018), which was a revision of my doctoral dissertation at Radboud University, Nijmegen. While that book focused on how early Christian use of prosopological exegesis contributed to the development of emerging beliefs about the distinct divine personhood of the Holy Spirit, I was able to make some passing observations about the nature of prosopological exegesis as it was applied to the Father and the Son that served as foundations for the further analysis supplied in this present volume. Readers less inclined to wade through scholarly minutiae will be comforted to know that all of the most relevant points of that earlier work have been distilled and extended here in service of this volume's distinct argument. Likewise, readers interested in the topic of prosopological exegesis from the person of the Holy Spirit, which receives relatively minor attention in this volume, should consult my book *How the Spirit Became God: The Mosaic of Early Christian Pneumatology* (Cascade, 2020) for a further exploration of the role that prosopological exegesis had in the development of early Christian views of the distinct personhood of the Holy Spirit. Additionally, I proposed some initial thoughts regarding the relationship between prosopological exegesis and the *regula fidei* to the Development of Early Christian Theology section at the 2018 Society of Biblical Literature Annual Meeting with a paper entitled, "The Prosopological Speech of the Son and the Development of Pre-Nicene Christology." The encouragement I received from that presentation played a significant role in my desire to continue working on this project.

Second, regarding primary sources, I have often supplied my own translations in cases where the author's appeal to prosopological exegesis needs to be more carefully clarified with respect to the original Greek or Latin text. My own translations are marked with "(AT)" after the reference. Published translations may be modernized to change archaic language (indicated in the footnotes) or slightly modified to provide a unified format throughout much of the book; for instance, for all quotations of the Old Testament outside of the New Testament, the Old Testament quotations are placed in italics with the scriptural reference following the quotation in brackets. The ESV is used for direct biblical quotations;

however, when various early Christian writers cite Scripture, their form of the quotation is provided. References are given to the Hebrew (MT) numbering of the Psalms, as that is what most English readers are familiar with, though it is of course worth noting that early Christians used the Greek (LXX) version of the Old Testament, which often differed in small but significant ways from the wording of the MT. While interesting, these textual differences between the MT and LXX are beyond the scope of this book, though readers confused by why New Testament or early Christian citations of the Old Testament often do not match what they find in the English (MT-based) Old Testament would do well to consult an edition of the LXX, even if only in English translation.

With these preliminaries out of the way, we can now proceed to consider the significance of prosopological exegesis within the New Testament and other first-century Christian writings for the development of early Christology.

2

The New Testament and Other Early Christian Literature

JOHN BEHR HAS SUGGESTED, with reference to Jesus' question, "But who do you say that I am?" (Matt 16:15), that "the reflection provoked by this question in the formative years of the history of the Christian Church" is in fact at the heart of Christian theology.[1] As the account of Jesus' appearance on the road to Emmaus (Luke 24:13–35) indicated, the early Christians looked to the Old Testament to deepen their answer to this question, a phenomenon attested to on nearly every page of the New Testament writings themselves as well as across much of early Christian literature more generally.[2] Given their belief that God was the ultimate author of Scripture, the early Christians saw the disparate books of the Old Testament as telling a single story, a story centered on Jesus Christ, whose presence was found not just in prophecies regarding his coming but through typological and allegorical readings of the biblical text as well. Perhaps one of the most intriguing and under-appreciated ways in which the first believers in Jesus searched the Scriptures was their identification of the voice of Christ himself speaking in the Old Testament. This chapter briefly traces initial moves towards person-centered reading as an interpretive method in the Gospels and Acts before examining the beginnings of a more formal approach to prosopological exegesis in the Epistle to the Hebrews and the second-generation writings known to us as 1–2 Clement.

1. Behr, *Way to Nicaea*, 1.
2. Cf. Behr, *Way to Nicaea*, 49–70. See also Juel, *Messianic Exegesis*, 5–29.

Prosopological Exegesis in the New Testament

At the broadest level, the New Testament writings consistently make the point that the Old Testament, when understood in light of what God had done in Christ, was prophesying or typologically speaking about Christ, who was himself the fulfillment of the Law and the Prophets. For instance, Matthew's Gospel, following an opening genealogy placing Jesus in the line of David, identifies Jesus' virgin birth as a fulfillment of Isa 7:14 (Matt 1:22–23). The Gospel accounts often portray Jesus as quoting the words of the prophets and applying them to himself.[3] The opening of John's Gospel famously retells Gen 1:1 to emphasize the pre-existence of the Word and the role of the Word in creation (John 1:1–4). The book of Acts recounts Philip teaching the Ethiopian eunuch that the prophecy of Isa 53:7–8 was fulfilled in Christ's sacrificial, willing death (Acts 8:32–33). Paul identifies Jesus as the fulfillment of God's promises concerning the gentiles (Rom 15:8–12). Such examples are so numerous and familiar throughout the New Testament as to require no further comment here.

Our focus, then, is on those relatively infrequent instances in which the words of the Old Testament—as we will see, at this point primarily those from the Psalter—are interpreted as being spoken *to* or *by* Jesus. In turning to this one strand of early Christian biblical interpretation, we need to distinguish this phenomenon from simple statements of prophetic fulfillment; there are, in fact, two streams of christological interpretation that are similar and yet different in some crucial ways.[4] On the one hand, the voice of Christ may connect back to the voice of a prophet only insofar as the prophet's words are used to prove that Jesus is the Christ and that he is the final referent of Old Testament prophecy. This emphasis on Jesus fulfilling the Old Testament prophecies is a common one in the New Testament, with the Gospel of Matthew making particular use of this approach. To take just one example, in Matt 13:34–35, the Evangelist reports that Jesus' habit of teaching in parables "was to fulfill what was spoken by the prophet," which is then followed by a quotation from Ps 78:2 in Matt 13:35: "I will open my mouth in parables; I will utter what has been hidden since the foundation of the world." The words of the psalmist find a further, final fulfillment in Christ, but the words are truly the words of the

---

3. E.g., Ps 118:22–23 at Matt 21:42 pars.

4. The identification of these two distinct streams of interpretation is indebted especially to the analysis of Andresen ("Zur Entstehung," 20), who applied it to the way Psalm 110 was interpreted in the early church.

psalmist and are not invoked for any purpose beyond proving that Jesus was the Christ predicted by the prophets.[5]

There is, however, an alternative way of reading that displaced this mediating role for the prophet and instead presented the words of certain psalms *as the words of Christ himself*.[6] Perhaps the clearest example in the Gospel narratives is Jesus' invocation of Psalm 22 from the cross: "My God, my God, why have you forsaken me?" (Mark 15:34, quoting Ps 22:1).[7] Here the voice of David has become the voice of Christ. This would seem to open up a whole new vista on the psalms in question: perhaps, then, "the words of the psalms are the words of Jesus; Jesus becomes David and David Jesus."[8] Perhaps, in other words, the words of these psalms were not merely reflective of the psalmist talking *about* Christ but were, in some mysterious sense, the words of Christ himself. Paul, likewise, at times seems to think that we should understand Christ to be the speaker of words from the Psalter without explicitly indicating this (e.g., Rom 15:3); as Richard Hays notes, "Paul does not seek to explain or justify his identification of the psalmist's first-person singular pronoun with the figure of Christ," suggesting that "the christological interpretation of this psalm must have been an established tradition in early Christianity before Paul's writing of Romans."[9]

What, though, could possibly justify such a reading of the Psalms? An understanding of the phenomenon of *prosopological exegesis* in the ancient world can help clarify how this move came about. Prosopological exegesis, as we understand it from ancient rhetorical handbooks and early Christian writers who made explicit use of person-centered reading strategies,[10] sought to identify the various "characters" or "persons" (Greek *prosōpa*; Latin *personae*) participating in scenes of dialogue in which the speaker or audience was perceived to be unclear. Particularly in the Psalms and the writings of the prophets, where dialogical passages often contain abrupt shifts in speaking characters, early Christian interpreters attempted to show how Father, Son, and Holy Spirit could be

---

5. For further examples, see, e.g., Matt 13:14–15; 15:8–9; Luke 4:18–19; John 19:24.

6. Attridge, "Giving Voice," 107.

7. On the role of Psalm 22 in shaping the Gospel accounts of Jesus' passion, see Juel, *Messianic Exegesis*, 99–103, 110–16.

8. Attridge, "Giving Voice," 107.

9. Hays, *Conversion*, 102.

10. See further the more thorough introduction to prosopological exegesis in chapter 1 above; see also Bates, *Hermeneutics*, 187–215.

identified as conversation partners in these texts. In these instances, the human prophet takes on the identity of one of these divine persons; the prophet's own person slips fully into the background as he takes on the role of an actor in the divine theodrama.[11]

Specifically, then, prosopological exegesis refers to those instances in which the human prophet actually takes on the role of a divine person and, within the theodramatic setting, speaks to or is spoken to as that character. Over time, this understanding of personhood would evolve out of its theatrical or literary context to contribute to the early church's articulation of the Trinity as three distinct persons who share one divine essence.[12] The exact extent to which prosopological exegesis was used by the New Testament authors is open for debate. While Matthew Bates often uses contextual inference to reclassify many examples of what others have identified as instances of typological interpretations as examples of prosopological exegesis, here and throughout this study my focus is on those instances in which the prosopological interpretation is deliberate, "marked" by the writer's explicit introduction of a speaker and/or audience not in view in the original text.[13] The New Testament, then, gives us a window of insight into how early Christian interpreters used a christological hermeneutic to discover the speech of the Son in the pages of the Old Testament, paving the way for a more formal, systematic approach to prosopological exegesis in the following generations of Christian exegetes.

Person-Centered Reading in the Gospels and Acts

Within the Gospel accounts, we see explicit evidence of a person-centered reading strategy being used to interpret a dialogical passage

11. See again Bates, *Birth*, 35.

12. See further Bates, *Birth*, 25–27, 36–40; Hughes, *How the Spirit Became God*, 71–75.

13. For a more thorough treatment of prosopological exegesis in the New Testament, see Bates, *Hermeneutics*; Bates, *Birth*. Indeed, this chapter's analysis is very much indebted to Bates's work, as will become evident in the pages that follow, though as noted here I am not as sanguine as Bates about seeing prosopological rather than typological interpretation as the operative method in many of the passages that he analyzes. To use his terminology, I would prefer to focus on instances of "explicitly introduced prosopological exegesis or marked prosopological exegesis," whereas Bates's survey also encompasses what Bates calls "unmarked prosopological exegesis" in which the prosopological interpretation is inferred from "context and additional indicators" (*Hermeneutics*, 220).

from the Psalms from no less an authority than Jesus himself. In Mark 12:35–37 and parallels, the Gospel writers present Jesus debating the scribes in the temple concerning the right interpretation of David's words in Ps 110:1:

> And as Jesus taught in the temple, he said, "How can the scribes say that the Christ is the son of David? David himself, in the Holy Spirit, declared, 'The Lord said to my Lord, "Sit at my right hand, until I put your enemies under your feet."' David himself calls him Lord. So how is he his son?"

The implication is that the person to whom the dialogue of Ps 110:1 is spoken, to whom David refers as "my Lord," is greater than merely being the son of David. This point is underscored by the context of this verse in the rest of Psalm 110.[14] Indeed, many scholars have made a compelling case that early Christian interpreters' reference to one part of a biblical passage could evoke the broader context of the passage.[15] Regardless of whether Jesus himself expected his opponents to read the entirety of Psalm 110 in reference to his own person and ministry,[16] Jesus' interpretation of Ps 110:1 opens the door for reading at least this portion of the psalm as the words of the Father to the Son, as seems to be the plain conclusion we are to draw from Jesus' question. As Bates points out, "Jesus, as he is portrayed, has seemingly noticed a puzzle in the text of the psalm that he seeks to tease out."[17] In particular, the ambiguity around the person called "my Lord" in Ps 110:1 opens up the text to a reading that draws in Christ as the true addressee of the speech that David gives in the character of God. If one teases out the implications of such a reading along the lines that prosopological exegesis will follow, then Ps 110:1 is to be understood as David reporting the words of the Father to the Son; the theodramatic setting or time value of the speech would appear to be at the time of Christ's enthronement following his ascension.[18] To the extent that this reference to Ps 110:1 activates a read-

---

14. Bates, *Birth*, 53–54. For a more traditional reading of Jesus' interpretation of Ps 110:1 as simply an example of a pesher interpretation of Scripture, see Longenecker, *Biblical Exegesis*, 73–74.

15. See, e.g., Hays, *Echoes*, 20–21.

16. As suggested by Bates, *Salvation*, 57.

17. Bates, *Birth*, 44.

18. Bates, *Birth*, 47–52. Later Christian writers would come to identify the Holy Spirit, as a theodramatic person in his own right, as the ultimate "speaker" of Ps 110:1; see further Hughes, *How the Spirit Became God*, 54–76.

ing of the rest of the psalm as the words of the Father to the Son, Jesus could even be making a claim about his own pre-existence and divine begottenness.[19] While the extent to which Jesus or the Gospel writers intend us to draw these implications is, in my mind, unclear, the fact that the Gospel tradition records Jesus interpreting certain psalms according to a person-centered reading strategy testifies to the early and privileged place that such readings of the Psalms had in early Christianity. Jesus, in other words, appears to intend that we read this psalm along the lines of later Christian prosopological exegesis, although it is worth noting that the method is not explicitly marked as such, and David is still in view as the speaker of the psalm.

The book of Acts provides us with further examples of how person-centered reading strategies may have emerged among early Christians. Perhaps the most instructive case study is Peter's Pentecost sermon (Acts 2:14–36). In the middle of this sermon, Peter says,

> For David says concerning him, "I saw the Lord always before me, for he is at my right hand that I may not be shaken; therefore my heart was glad, and my tongue rejoiced; my flesh also will dwell in hope. For you will not abandon my soul to Hades, or let your Holy One see corruption. You have made known to me the paths of life; you will make me full of gladness with your presence." (Acts 2:25–28, quoting Ps 16:8–11)

In the broader context, in which Peter notes that David "foresaw and spoke about the resurrection of the Christ" (Acts 2:31), it seems clear that Peter would have us understand the words of Ps 16:8–11 as the words of Christ. The introductory formula, however, identifies David as the speaker, who "says" these words "concerning [Christ]" (Acts 2:25). The awkward juxtaposition of these two elements makes it difficult to determine if this should be understood as an example of typological or prosopological exegesis. Harold Attridge takes the former view, arguing, "The 'I' of the psalm remains David, who reports a vision of God that presages what God will do to his 'Holy One.' In the hands of other early Christians the psalm could have been construed differently," with Jesus identified as the true, ultimate speaker of this psalm.[20] Indeed, later Christians would make just such a move, but here "the voice of the psalm

---

19. So Bates, *Birth*, 52–56.
20. Attridge, "Giving Voice," 104.

is that of Jesus only by inference, not by dramatic presentation."[21] The reader, therefore, is invited to read these quotations as the words of the prophet that nevertheless find a further fulfillment in Christ.

Matthew Bates, on the other hand, has argued that prosopological exegesis is the best way to account for this passage. While conceding the difficulty of the introductory formula, Bates nevertheless points to the significant differences between the lives of David and Jesus, which he sees as diminishing the evidence for a typological reading.[22] Ultimately, the issue comes down to how seriously one takes the category of "unmarked" prosopological exegesis. Bates is correct to observe that there is something going on here that transcends a mere typological reading, and yet this kind of interpretation still seems significantly different from what we will find in the Epistle to the Hebrews and, even more so, from the writings of Justin, Irenaeus, or Tertullian. I suggest, therefore, that this example, like the case of Ps 110:1 in Mark 12:35–37, reflects a period in which Christians were still trying to make sense of how exactly the words of Christ related to the words of David in the Psalms.[23] While I hesitate to see these instances as full-fledged examples of what will emerge as a clear method of prosopological exegesis, they are very much the forerunners of such a method and would have contributed to the exegetical "pressure" that would force further layers of reflection on early Christian interpreters such that the rise of a more formal, systematic approach to prosopological exegesis was a logical next step for interpreters to take.

Thus, the early Christian search for the *vox Christi* in the Old Testament started, perhaps, in such humble fashion: the example of Jesus speaking the words of Ps 22:1 from the cross, a question from Jesus about the true referent of Ps 110:1, and a sermon that seems to suggest that the words of Ps 16:8–11 were somehow Christ's description of his own suffering. And yet it would be precisely psalms such as these that, over the course of subsequent decades and centuries, would be the

---

21. Attridge, "Giving Voice," 104.
22. Bates, *Birth*, 153–54.
23. As Hays argues, "The interpretation of the lament psalms as *prayers of the Messiah* is already a presupposition of the earliest stratum of New Testament tradition" (*Conversion*, 117; italics original). As he goes on to claim, "the proclamation of a crucified Messiah entails a fundamental revisioning of the messianic hope; however, once one grants the hermeneutical premise that the Messiah is the praying voice of the Psalms, then the homology between the lament psalms and the passion story helps make sense out of the oxymoronic confession that the crucified Jesus is God's anointed" (118).

primary occasion for further reflection on Christ and the presence of his voice in the Old Testament.

Prosopological Exegesis in Hebrews

We observe a step forward in methodological clarity for person-centered reading strategies in the Epistle to the Hebrews, the New Testament book that is most interested in interpreting Old Testament dialogical passages as conversations between the Father and the Son (and perhaps, also, the Holy Spirit).[24] As Madison Pierce observes, "The God who speaks in Hebrews is a God identified as three distinct speakers: Father, Son, and Spirit."[25] Building on what we have already observed in the Gospels, Hebrews furthers the process of early Christian reflection on the presence of Christ in various psalms as either the speaker or the addressee of the words found therein.

The Father Speaks to the Son

Hebrews begins with a striking contrast: while in the past God spoke "by the prophets" (Heb 1:1), God now "has spoken to us by his Son" (Heb 1:2). This preface sets the stage for the following catena of Old Testament quotations (Heb 1:5–14) that establish Christ as superior to the angels. What is particularly intriguing about these quotations is that, as Christopher Seitz observes, God's speaking to us by his Son "can also arguably include God's speaking to the Son," which is in fact what we see in Heb 1:5–14.[26] The fact that the author's examples of God speaking to us by his Son are drawn exclusively from the Old Testament, rather than from the life of the incarnate Jesus, establishes the precedent for seeing "by-the-son [sic] speaking emerging directly from the scriptures of Israel, as the speech of God, of Son, and of Holy Spirit."[27] While the author of Hebrews does not break from the sense of the original quotations in the catena

---

24. On the Holy Spirit speaking as his own theodramatic person, see Bates, *Birth*, 163–65, but note my hesitation in Hughes, *How the Spirit Became God*, 32n71. Pierce (*Divine Discourse*, 135–74) emphasizes the role of the Holy Spirit as a speaker to the community rather than within the Godhead. On the use of Scripture in Hebrews more generally, see Longenecker, *Biblical Exegesis*, 158–85.

25. Pierce, *Divine Discourse*, 1.
26. Seitz, *Elder Testament*, 249.
27. Seitz, *Elder Testament*, 251.

when he identifies their speaker as "God" (Heb 1:5), he does explicitly introduce a new addressee, "the Son" (Heb 1:8).[28]

Starting in Heb 1:5, the author argues that a series of Old Testament quotations could not have been addressed to the angels and therefore must have been addressed to the Son. He begins with Ps 2:7: "You are my Son, today I have begotten you." Though the author of Hebrews does not formally describe his interpretive method, the introductory question in Heb 1:5, as reinforced by the explicit invocation of Christ at Heb 1:8, identifies the audience of Ps 2:7 as the Son, perhaps picking up on the Gospel accounts of Jesus' baptism. Because Christ was not in view in the original text, which was presumably a royal psalm centered on the Davidic king, this is a clearer instance of prosopological exegesis than anything we find in the Gospels. Here the theodramatic reading of Ps 2:7 is fully in focus; the psalmist as the human speaker of these words has fallen entirely out of view. Indeed, the temporal setting of the quotation has been shifted from a particular moment of human history to be set "in the context of the exalted Son's eternal relationship to God—temporally unmarked, as it were."[29]

The citation of Ps 2:7 in this particular context is striking given that, as Bates points out, Ps 2:7 would come to be interpreted as "*a speech within a speech that was originally spoken by the Son*, who was reporting the words the *Father had spoken to him at an earlier time*, all of which has critical implications for how Christology and trinitarian dogma developed."[30] Again, as Bates reminds us, this piece of dialogue is taken from a broader context in the full verse of Ps 2:7: "I will tell of the decree: The LORD said to me, 'You are my Son; today I have begotten you.'" The central part of the verse, quoted in Heb 1:5 as well as alluded to in the Gospel accounts of Jesus' baptism, is thus construed as a record of the Father's speech at an earlier theodramatic time. And given that early Christian interpreters were clear that the Father spoke these words to Jesus, the logical consequence is that the Son must have had the actual conversation with the Father being recounted in Ps 2:7 at some point prior to the time when the Son was recounting it. While the

---

28. Pierce notes the emerging pattern in Hebrews concerning the Father's prosopological speech: "Rather than altering the speaker of these texts, the author of Hebrews changes the addressee or the subject. The Father speaks to and about the Son in almost every instance" (*Divine Discourse*, 35).

29. Seitz, *Elder Testament*, 251.

30. Bates, *Birth*, 64 (italics original); see also *Birth*, 67–68.

author of Hebrews does not comment on this broader context, the following verse, with its reference to "when [God] brings the firstborn into the world," makes clear his understanding of when this divine dialogue took place (Heb 1:6; cf. Deut 32:43). The implication is that the Father originally spoke the words of Ps 2:7 to the pre-existent Son at the time of the Son's incarnation.[31]

The case of Heb 1:5, therefore, demonstrates a prosopological reading of Ps 2:7 that not only presents this portion of dialogue as the Father's words to the Son but also supports the emerging Christian understanding of the Son's pre-existence. Thus, prosopological exegesis, particularly as it activated broader contexts of meaning in a quoted text's original setting, thereby created theological pressure by which Christology could further develop. Nevertheless, it is important to stress that the author of Hebrews does not *explicitly* bring out the full context of Ps 2:7 as later Christian interpreters would, even if its location within the catena of quotations concerning the Son's supremacy and pre-existence is highly suggestive.

The author of Hebrews then quotes 2 Sam 7:14 as the words of the Father concerning (but not spoken to) the Son (Heb 1:5b)[32] and presents the words of Deut 32:43 and Ps 104:4 as the Father's speech concerning the angels (Heb 1:6–7) before returning to three linked quotations interpreted as the words of the Father to the Son (Heb 1:8–13), each of which will be discussed in turn.[33]

First, another psalm originally addressed to the Davidic king is reinterpreted as the words of the Father to the Son: "Your throne, O God, is forever and ever, the scepter of uprightness is the scepter of your kingdom. You have loved righteousness and hated wickedness; therefore God, your God, has anointed you with the oil of gladness beyond your companions" (Heb 1:8–9, quoting Ps 45:6–7). This verse is another good example of

31. Bates, *Birth*, 69–70. Further commentary on interpretive options is offered by Attridge (*Hebrews*, 51) and Pierce (*Divine Discourse*, 41–52).

32. As will be explored in subsequent chapters of this book, later Christian writers included instances of the Father speaking concerning the Son within the approach that we have termed prosopological exegesis; the simplest explanation for including such instances, I think, is that the differentiation of the persons of the Godhead was not in view in the source texts.

33. Bates (*Birth*, 163–65) seeks to show that we should understand the Holy Spirit to be the prosopological speaker of these verses given that Heb 1:9b appears to describe the actions of the Father concerning the Son. While this is in fact the move that later Christian interpreters will make, the author of Hebrews nevertheless seems to want us to read this quotation as the words of the Father to the Son; see further Hughes, *How the Spirit Became God*, 32n71; Pierce, *Divine Discourse*, 56n68.

theological pressure emerging from the text itself; the apparent reference to two gods in the passage serves to ascribe divinity to Christ.[34] The presumed theodramatic setting is the time of Christ's enthronement at the beginning of his present reign.[35]

Second, the author summons still another psalm as an example of the Father speaking to the Son:

> You, Lord, laid the foundation of the earth in the beginning, and the heavens are the work of your hands; they will perish, but you remain; they will all wear out like a garment, like a robe you will roll them up, like a garment they will be changed. But you are the same, and your years will have no end. (Heb 1:10–12, quoting Ps 102:25–27)

Following the Greek text of the psalm, the author of Hebrews understands these verses as direct dialogue, which he interprets as the words of the Father to the Son for the purpose of identifying the Son as not only "God" but also "Lord."[36] The christological implications are profound; as Bates summarizes, the Son is here addressed "as the one who has authored creation and who will consummate it, transcending its fickle mutability."[37] The theodramatic setting of the speech itself is undetermined, but locating it at the time of Christ's enthronement along with the Father's other words in this catena makes sense.[38]

Third, the author of Hebrews cites a crucial text already discussed above in the case of the Gospels: "Sit at my right hand until I make your enemies a footstool for your feet" (Heb 1:13, quoting Ps 110:1). This text was perhaps linked with Ps 102:25–27 because of its introductory formula, which as noted above appears to speak of two Lords and "underlies the logic of [the author's] reading," which is to identify these words as spoken by the Father to the Son concerning the Son's exaltation.[39] The most logical

---

34. See further Pierce, *Divine Discourse*, 54–56.

35. See further Bates, *Birth*, 163–65.

36. Pierce, *Divine Discourse*, 56–59. Following his interpretation of Heb 1:8–9, Bates (*Birth*, 170–71) posits uncertainty on who is addressing the Son in these verses, but as with the previous instance the Father is still the most likely speaker at this point.

37. Bates, *Birth*, 171.

38. On account of his uncertainty regarding the text's speaker, Bates (*Birth*, 171) simply identifies the theodramatic setting with the prophetic setting, although my proposal has the advantage of maintaining a consistent theodramatic setting across all of Heb 1:8–13.

39. Pierce, *Divine Discourse*, 60.

theodramatic setting is, again, at the Son's enthronement.⁴⁰ Together, this chain of prosopological interpretations advances a high Christology that locates pivotal speech from the Father to the Son in the Psalms.

The catena's citation of both Ps 2:7 and Ps 110:1 is interesting in light of a later passage in the epistle. As the author argues,

> So also Christ did not exalt himself to be made a high priest, but was appointed by him who said to him, "You are my Son, today I have begotten you"; as he says also in another place, "You are a priest forever, after the order of Melchizedek." (Heb 5:5–6, quoting Pss 2:7; 110:4)

Here the author gives a prosopological interpretation of Ps 2:7 and Ps 110:4, interpreting both as the words of the Father to the Son. Assuming that Ps 110:1 was part of the very earliest layer of christological reflection that emerged from a Christian reading of the Old Testament, as the historical record seems to indicate, it is surely noteworthy that a subsequent verse from that same psalm is "activated" or brought into consideration by the author of Hebrews. In other words, the appeal to the broader context of Psalm 110, which was at most only implicit in the Gospel accounts of Jesus' controversy with the scribes, is now being invoked in the same christological framework that Ps 110:1 had been. Indeed, the issue of pre-existence seems to be central in a prosopological reading of Ps 110:4 as well.⁴¹ Thus the entirety of Psalm 110, as with Psalm 2,⁴² was very quickly caught up into the emerging christological reflection of the early church.⁴³

Before moving on from the Father's speech to the Son in Hebrews, one final observation is relevant for the later argument of this book. The catena of texts strung together in Heb 1:5–14 is strongly suggestive of the idea that the author of Hebrews is here making use of a previous *testimonia* collection.⁴⁴ The stringing together of related texts with only vague

40. See further Bates, *Birth*, 170.

41. See Bates, *Birth*, 55.

42. See, for instance, the christological interpretation of Ps 2:1–2 in Acts 4:25–26. Outside of the Gospels and Hebrews, Ps 110:1 is also cited in Acts 2:34–35, and Ps 2:7 is also cited in Acts 13:33 (where it is linked with Isa 55:3 and Ps 16:10 as pertaining to Christ's exaltation).

43. Ps 110:4 is also cited in Heb 7:17 and 7:21, suggesting its central importance for the author of Hebrews. Attridge notes that Psalm 110 "runs like a red thread throughout the work" (*Hebrews*, 23). On prosopological exegesis in Heb 5:5–6 and 7:1–21, see further Pierce, *Divine Discourse*, 63–78.

44. Albl, *Scripture*, 201–7; cf. Attridge, *Hebrews*, 50.

citation formulas, especially when similar combinations of quotations are found in other independent sources,[45] points to the likelihood of the existence of a written *testimonia* collection.[46] The catena, Martin Albl comments, "is a reflection of the intense scriptural activity centered on Jesus Christ," with the collection of scriptural texts having been brought together some time before the writing of Hebrews for the purpose of establishing the supremacy of the Son over the angels.[47] Likewise, Attridge comments that "the traditional catena on which the author may have drawn gave expression to the early church's belief in Christ as its exalted Lord," here repurposed to demonstrate "the christological movement of the exordium, from pre-existence through humiliation to exaltation."[48] This shows both the close connection between prosopological exegesis and the use of *testimonia* collections in the early church as well as the connection between these things and the establishment of a basic christological narrative, a topic to which we will return throughout this book as we examine the early *regula fidei*.

The Son Speaks Back to the Father

Hebrews is also noteworthy for the relative clarity with which it posits the Son as the ultimate speaker of some Old Testament quotations. Having presented the words of the Father to the Son in Hebrews 1, the author of Hebrews now provides evidence of the Son speaking back to the Father in Hebrews 2. As the author argues,

> For he who sanctifies and those who are sanctified all have one source. That is why he [that is, Christ] is not ashamed to call them brothers, saying, "I will tell of your name to my brothers; in the midst of the congregation I will sing your praise." And again, "I will put my trust in him." And again, "Behold, I and the children God has given me." (Heb 2:11–13)

This catena includes three quotations, all of which the author invites us to read prosopologically, not as the words of the psalmist or the

---

45. In this case, e.g., 1 Clem. 36.2–6.
46. Albl, *Scripture*, 202.
47. Albl, *Scripture*, 207.
48. Attridge, *Hebrews*, 50. Attridge even suggests the process by which this reading of Ps 2:7 could have been generated: the text was stripped from its original context, the pronoun became ambiguous, and Christ was supplied as the referent (*Hebrews*, 57).

prophet but as the words of Christ to or concerning the Father. The first quotation, Ps 22:22, activates a reading of one of the most important psalms for early Christology: Psalm 22. In this psalm, the psalmist's cry of dereliction expresses agony over his perceived abandonment by God (22:1–18), begs God for rescue (22:19–21), and vows to praise God for his impending deliverance (22:22–31). Given that Jesus spoke the words of Ps 22:1 ("My God, my God, why have you forsaken me?") from the cross (Mark 15:34 pars.), this psalm became a natural source of early Christian typological and prosopological exegesis.[49] Here the author of Hebrews assigns the words of Ps 22:22 to the Son, though the precise theodramatic setting of this speech is unclear. While Pierce favors a time prior to the Son's rescue, Bates understands the words to have been spoken after Christ's resurrection; as Bates contends, while both the original and theodramatic settings emphasize the still-future time in which the words of praise will be offered, "*this future is now present* for the author of Hebrews, as the exalted Son through the Spirit is expressing praise to the Father in the gathered assembly, the church."[50] While both options are plausible, the reference to sanctified believers favors Bates's view. Still, for the author of Hebrews the most important element of the quotation is that it provides evidence of Christ speaking of his followers as his "brothers," justifying the author's claims about Jesus' humanity and the resulting implications for soteriology.[51]

The following quotations, from Isa 8:17–18, are likewise interpreted prosopologically as the words of the Son, presumably spoken before God to the "congregation" of God's people referenced in Heb 2:12, underscoring his similarities with his brothers and sisters as he leads them in singing praise to the Father.[52] While the source text is not an obvious place for drawing upon speech from the Son (the identity of the speaker is, admittedly, very unclear), this verse would nevertheless come to be an important point of reflection for later writers such as Origen.

---

49. On Psalm 22 and early Christology, see further Bates, *Birth*, 136–37; Pierce, *Divine Discourse*, 99–101.

50. Bates, *Birth*, 138 (italics original); see further Pierce, *Divine Discourse*, 111–13.

51. Pierce, *Divine Discourse*, 100.

52. On Isa 8:17 as the likely source of the second quotation in the catena, see Bates, *Birth*, 141–46; Pierce, *Divine Discourse*, 103–10. The theodramatic setting is again unclear, but following the logic of the previous quotation Christ's present reign would again make the most sense.

A second example of the Son's speech to the Father is found in the author's discussion of Christ's once-for-all sacrifice in Hebrews 10. As the author writes,

> Consequently, when Christ came into the world, he said, "Sacrifices and offerings you have not desired, but a body have you prepared for me; in burnt offerings and sin offerings you have taken no pleasure. Then I said, 'Behold, I have come to do your will, O God, as it is written of me in the scroll of the book.'" (Heb 10:5–7, quoting Ps 40:6–8)

This citation recontextualizes the psalmist's words to God as speech from Christ to his Father, perhaps providing a response to the Father's words about his eternal priesthood (Heb 5:5–6; 7:17; 7:21) in line with what Hebrews has already established about the Son's obedience.[53] As a still further instance of prosopological exegesis in this epistle, this text is given the theodramatic setting of the time "when Christ came into the world" (Heb 10:5), presumably referring to the time of the incarnation.[54] The theological implications are profound, particularly insofar as the text identifies the Father as having prepared a body for the Son in advance of the incarnation. As Bates argues,

> The Father *initiates* the gracious gift-giving with the presentation of the incarnational body to the Son, yet the Son *consummates* the gift-giving by offering this very same body back to the Father as an act of willing obedience to him, recognizing that this is what the Father ultimately desires.[55]

The incarnation is thus a symmetrical mission, carried out jointly between the Father and the Son for the redemption of humankind.

Hebrews, therefore, mines the Psalter for evidence of divine dialogues between Father and Son. While the author of this epistle does not announce his use of prosopological exegesis as later Christian writers will do, his reliance on the method is clear enough, as the above analysis has shown. Indeed, the author's method of pulling together distinct quotations from various psalms to be spoken by either the Father or the Son on

---

53. See Pierce, *Divine Discourse*, 113–16. For more on the textual variations between the Hebrews quotation and the "standard" LXX, see *Divine Discourse*, 116–21.

54. On the possible significance of the author marking this speech as taking place at the time of the incarnation, as opposed to other instances of divine dialogue that lack a set temporal framework, see Seitz, *Elder Testament*, 249–59. See also Pierce, *Divine Discourse*, 122–23.

55. Bates, *Birth*, 87 (italics original).

a distinct topic or theme in many ways anticipates the more prosopological interpretations of writers such as Justin, Irenaeus, Tertullian, and Origen. Thus, this brief examination of the New Testament writings both connects the pre-Nicene fathers to the first generation of Christian writers as well as introduces some of the key biblical texts that will recur over the subsequent chapters of this book. We have, in other words, some of the first lines of a "script" of Old Testament texts placed on the lips of the Son (or spoken by the Father to the Son), establishing a precedent that would continue to develop across the following centuries.

Prosopological Exegesis in the Apostolic Fathers

The only other clear examples of the use of prosopological exegesis from before the middle of the second century are found in the writings attributed to Clement of Rome, works that have been traditionally included in the set of texts known as the Apostolic Fathers. Like the New Testament Epistle to the Hebrews, these writings employ a less formal or systematic approach to this interpretive strategy than Justin or his successors will employ.

Prosopological Exegesis in 1 Clement

As has been recognized as far back as Eusebius, Hebrews and 1 Clement share a number of intriguing similarities, even leading some to speculate that Clement was the author of Hebrews, though this view is largely rejected by scholars today.[56] One of these similarities is how both texts use the reading strategy of prosopological exegesis to find evidence of conversations between the Father and the Son in the Psalter.

In response to a schism in the church at Corinth,[57] Clement appeals to Christ's example of humility (1 Clem. 16.1–2). As support, Clement quotes the prophecy of Isa 53:1–14 (1 Clem. 16.3–14), which "the Holy Spirit spoke" concerning Christ (1 Clem. 16.2). Here we have the very common early Christian use of the Old Testament as a source of inspired prophecies concerning the suffering of the Messiah, with the Holy Spirit simply inspiring the words of the prophet rather than speaking as his own

---

56. See further Lindemann, "First Clement," 59; cf. Eusebius, *Hist. eccl.* 3.38; 6.25.

57. Cf. 1 Clem. 44. For a proposal on the nature of the schism through the lens of generational conflict, see Welborn, *Young against the Old*, 21–38.

38 SCRIPTING THE SON

person. Clement's more novel interpretive move, however, is how he pairs this text, a third-person description of Christ, with a text spoken in the first-person which he attributes to Christ himself:

> And again he himself says: *But I am a worm and not a man, a reproach among humans and an object of contempt to the people. All those who saw me mocked me; they spoke with their lips; they shook their heads, saying, He hoped in the Lord; let him deliver him, let him save him, because he takes pleasure in him* [Ps 22:6–8].[58]

The transition between the two texts is awkward, reflecting the shift from third-person description to first-person dialogue as well as the use of a pronoun rather than Christ's name in the introductory formula; nevertheless, the dialogue makes clear that the "he" of the introductory formula is Christ himself, identified here as the true speaker of Ps 22:6–8. Thus we have a further example of prosopological exegesis from the person of the Son. As was the case with Hebrews, Clement identifies Psalm 22 as the words of the Son; again, the fact that Jesus himself had spoken the words of Ps 22:1 from the cross seems to have made it easy for early Christian interpreters to read the rest of the psalm as the *vox Christi*, as Hebrews had done with Ps 22:22 at Heb 2:12. Still, Clement does not pause to comment on his interpretive method at this point, nor does he attempt to propose a theodramatic context for the passage he has quoted, though Christ is here clearly reflecting on his crucifixion. We may still wonder, however, why Christ shifts from the present tense to the past tense in the source text; should we understand this as Christ speaking from the cross (as with Ps 22:1 in the Gospels) or at some later time?[59] But Clement is not, unfortunately, interested in pursuing this line of inquiry further, instead shifting back to his moral exhortation to the Corinthians to emulate Christ's humility (1 Clem. 16.17). It is also interesting that Clement does not take advantage of what would seem to be other obvious opportunities to employ the same reading strategy in other instances. For example, Clement introduces quotations of Ps 28:7, Ps 3:5, and Job 19:26 as proof-texts for the bodily resurrection rather than as the words of Christ.[60] Despite

---

58. 1 Clem. 16.15–16 (trans. Holmes).

59. Bates notes that Christ "is clearly deemed to be speaking sometime *after* the moment of mockery," speaking these words to God the Father, presumably on the basis that Psalm 22 more generally is read as directed to the Father (*Birth*, 131; italics original).

60. 1 Clem. 26.1–3.

the tantalizing example of 1 Clem. 16.15–16, the prosopological voice of Christ is otherwise absent from this letter.

Indeed, the only other clear use of prosopological exegesis in 1 Clement is an instance of the Father speaking to the Son. Echoing Hebrews by drawing a contrast between Christ and the angels, Clement writes,

> But of his Son the Master spoke thus: *You are my Son; today I have begotten you. Ask of me, and I will give you the Gentiles for your inheritance, and the ends of the earth for your possession* [Ps 2:7–8]. And again he says to him: *Sit at my right hand, until I make your enemies a footstool for your feet* [Ps 110:1].[61]

Here Clement interprets the words of Ps 2:7–8 and Ps 110:1 as the words of the Father to the Son. These verses should be familiar, insofar as both Ps 2:7 and Ps 110:1 were quoted in Hebrews 1. Clement has, however, expanded the appeal to Psalm 2 with an additional verse beyond what was quoted in Hebrews, perhaps to reinforce how Christ will triumph over his enemies all the way to the ends of the earth. The theodramatic context is therefore underdetermined, though based on the texts themselves the most plausible reading is at Christ's enthronement at the start of his present reign.

First Clement, therefore, follows Hebrews in mining Psalms 2, 22, and 110 for evidence of dialogue between the Father and the Son, and yet appears to be less interested than Hebrews in drawing attention to these conversations or their significance. This could perhaps be construed as further evidence that 1 Clement is not literarily dependent on Hebrews but rather simply making use of a shared *testimonia* collection.[62]

Prosopological Exegesis in 2 Clement

Scholarly opinion today largely rejects Clementine authorship of the so-called Second Letter of Clement,[63] and yet it is interesting that besides 1 Clement the only other place in the Apostolic Fathers that we find evidence of prosopological exegesis is in the one other text attributed to Clement of Rome.

Second Clement uses prosopological exegesis twice, in both instances placing Old Testament speeches onto the lips of the Son. In the

---

61. 1 Clem. 36.4–5 (trans. Holmes).
62. Cf. Albl, *Scripture*, 204.
63. See, e.g., the discussions in Jefford, *Apostolic Fathers*, 125–28; Pratscher, "Second Clement," 87–88.

first instance, Christ says, "in Isaiah," that "*this people honors me with their lips, but their heart is far from me* [Isa 29:13]."[64] In the Gospels, Jesus quotes Isa 29:13 at Mark 7:6 pars., and yet the author of 2 Clement seems to go out of his way to note that Jesus spoke these words, not as recorded in the Gospels in the course of his earthly ministry but rather "in Isaiah." A prosopological interpretation therefore appears to be in view. The theodramatic setting of the speech is undefined, but in context the Son's words appear to be describing those Christians whose moral deficiencies occasioned 2 Clement in the first place. Thus, the words of God to the Israelites have, in 2 Clement, been re-cast as the words of the Son to the church in the present age.

Likewise, in the second instance, "the Lord" (how 2 Clement prefers to refer to Christ) says, "*My name is continually blasphemed among all the nations* [Isa 52:5]," and then continues, "Woe to him on whose account my name is blasphemed."[65] The source for the latter quotation is not clear, but in any event the citation of the Isaiah passage, which does not appear on the lips of Jesus in the New Testament, further underscores our analysis of how the author is interpreting Isa 29:13. As with the previous instance, the theodramatic setting of the speech is undefined but appears to be the present day, as the author of 2 Clement re-presents the Isaianic text as the words of the Son to his own audience, whose hypocrisy is causing the pagans to blaspheme God.[66]

The fact that 2 Clement pulls both its examples of prosopological exegesis from Isaiah is striking. The only prior example of the *vox Christi* being found in Isaiah was the citation of Isa 8:17–18 at Heb 2:12–13. As with the earlier instance from Isaiah, neither Isa 29:13 nor Isa 52:5 would appear to be a natural fit for a prosopological reading. Isa 29:13 was quoted by Jesus at Mark 7:6 pars. as a prophecy of Isaiah, perhaps lending inspiration for a prosopological reading; moreover, the introduction of Isa 29:13 as the words of "the Lord" (LXX *kyrios*) naturally links up with the next verse in 2 Clement, which is that we should not merely call Jesus "Lord" (*kyrios*) but obey him as such.[67] Isa 52:5 is even more unusual; the speaker in its original context is "the Lord God," who goes on to prophesy concerning a servant who will redeem God's people (Isa 52:13—53:12); the speech in Isaiah, then, would appear to be best understood as the words of God the Father concerning God the Son.

---

64. 2 Clem. 3.5 (trans. Holmes).
65. 2 Clem. 13.2 (trans. Holmes).
66. 2 Clem. 13.3.
67. 2 Clem. 4.1.

This seeming discrepancy between the nature of the source text and its interpretation in 2 Clement suggests that in 2 Clem. 13.2 the author was drawing upon a *testimonia* collection that included both quotations, a theory that is helped by the fact that the source of the second quotation remains unknown. In any event, it is clear in both instances that the author of 2 Clement is simply interested in using these quotations, spoken by "the Lord," as scriptural proofs for his argument rather than as an occasion for reflection on biblical hermeneutics.

Conclusion: Scripting the Son in the New Testament and the Apostolic Fathers

The first century of the Christian movement saw the emergence of a Christian prosopological reading of the Old Testament. While the Jesus tradition recorded in the Gospels reflects an awareness of person-centered reading strategies, it is not until Hebrews that we find more sustained reflection on the presence of Christ in the Psalms, as either the speaker or the addressee of the dialogue between Father and Son. While the authors of Hebrews and 1–2 Clement do not explicitly introduce their prosopological method, their use of person-centered reading provides a clear precedent for later, more intentional applications of this approach to scriptural exegesis. In concluding this chapter, we can pull together our observations in a table that sets out all the instances in which writers of the New Testament and Apostolic Fathers prosopologically interpret Old Testament dialogical passages that involve speech to, from, or about the Son. In this and subsequent tables, the rows represent christological themes while the columns indicate the prosopological speaker; verses in bold are instances in which the passage is dialogue addressed by one divine person to another (intra-divine dialogue):

	From the Father	From the Son	From the Spirit
Divine Pre-Existence	2 Sam 7:14 Ps 2:7b–8	Ps 40:6–8	—
Crucifixion	—	Ps 22:6–8	—
Ascension, Enthronement, and Reign	Ps 45:6–7 Ps 102:25–27 Ps 110:1b–c Ps 110:4	Ps 22:22 Isa 8:17–18 Isa 29:13 Isa 52:5	—

Considering the length of the writings of the New Testament and Apostolic Fathers, this chart shows a relatively meager number of instances, particularly insofar as they are clustered in just a couple of books. Still, we can see that the Psalms and Isaiah lead the way as the most important sources of prosopological exegesis and that the Son's pre-existence and present reign are the most important categories for which there is evidence of relevant prosopological speech. We can also note that, at this time, the Holy Spirit does not talk to or concerning the Son as his own speaking person.

The exact process by which these authors went about reading the Scriptures prosopologically remains veiled in mystery. At minimum, however, we can note that written *testimonia* collections likely lie behind at least some of the groupings of verses interpreted prosopologically in Hebrews and 1–2 Clement. This fact signals that in the following chapters, as authors' use of prosopological exegesis becomes more clearly defined and we have more data points to review, we will need to pay closer attention to the role of this particular thread in our story of christological development. Likewise, Attridge's observation that at least one catena in Hebrews reflects the sequence of the basic christological narrative pushes us to consider the role of the rule of faith in later Christian writings and its impact on prosopological exegesis.[68] It would fall, then, to a later writer, Justin Martyr, to make further exegetical inroads using prosopological exegesis and these other threads that contributed to the fashioning of early Christology.

---

68. Language regarding the *regula fidei* is absent from the New Testament and Apostolic Fathers, but proto-creedal material can be found in, e.g., Phil 2:5–10; Col 1:15–20; 1 Tim 3:16.

3

Justin Martyr

JUSTIN MARTYR (CA. 100–165), the great early Christian apologist, represents an important milestone in the complex story of early Christian self-definition, as Christians sought to make better sense of their identity with respect to both Judaism and the broader Greco-Roman culture. A gentile convert to Christianity, Justin had received extensive training in the methods of Greco-Roman philosophy and rhetoric; as such, his writings demonstrate more explicit and systematic use of the principles of textual interpretation that would have been commonly understood by any well-educated person of his time.[1] As an heir to the Christian exegetical tradition that preceded him, as well as to the classical rhetorical approach to how to understand, interpret, and apply written texts, Justin's engagement with the reading strategy of prosopological exegesis represents a significant innovation in the early Christian understanding of the Old Testament's *vox Christi*.

This chapter will survey how Justin uses prosopological exegesis first in his *1 Apology* and then in his *Dialogue with Trypho* before considering how Justin's use of *testimonia* collections and his understanding of the *regula fidei* contributed to the search for the voice of Christ in the Old Testament. As will be demonstrated, Justin expanded upon existing *testimonia* collections to produce examples of prosopological exegesis that, he believed, should be interpreted as conversations amongst divine

---

1. On Justin's education and background, see further Barnard, *Justin Martyr*, 4–13; Osborn, *Justin Martyr*, 1–10.

persons.[2] In concert with his proto-creedal formulations, then, Justin was able to advance a high Christology in support of his polemical objectives against his Jewish and Marcionite opponents.

Prosopological Exegesis in 1 *Apology*

Justin's *1 Apology* (ca. 155) is the first extant Christian writing that explicitly describes how the lens of prosopological exegesis can be brought to bear upon the Scriptures.[3] Having set out examples of how Christ fulfilled Old Testament prophecies (*1 Apol.* 30–35), Justin notes a contrast with a second way in which Christ can be found in the Old Testament (*1 Apol.* 36):

> But whenever you hear the sayings of the prophets spoken as from a person, do not suppose that they are spoken from the inspired ones themselves, but from the divine Logos who moves them. For sometimes he speaks as one announcing beforehand things that are about to happen, but sometimes he speaks as from the person of God, the Master and Father of all, still other times as from the person of Christ, and at still other times from the person of the people answering the Lord or his Father. This sort of thing is also seen in your writers, when the writer of the whole is one individual but he puts forward the dialoguing persons.[4]

Justin here claims that the "divine Logos" can take on the identities of different characters as he inspires the writing of Scripture, speaking in various "persons" (*prosōpa*) such as the Father or the Son.[5] As Justin notes, this way of reading would have been easily recognizable to his audience, which would likely have had no objection to prosopological exegesis in principle even if some of the details of its application might be contested. By contrast, Justin claims, the Jews had failed to follow this most basic principle

---

2. This portion of the chapter builds on my initial analysis of some of these passages in Hughes, *Trinitarian Testimony*, 35–68.

3. On the genre, purpose, audience, and rhetorical strategy of *1 Apology*, see Nyström, *Apology*, esp. 29–66; Cline, *Petition and Performance*, esp. 19–64.

4. *1 Apol.* 36.1–2 (AT). For further commentary on this passage, see Bates, *Hermeneutics*, 199–204.

5. By the "divine Logos," Justin likely intends us to understand the Holy Spirit as it participates in the divine Logos; see further Hughes, *Trinitarian Testimony*, 37–38; cf. Nyström, *Apology*, 124–29. On the Logos in Justin more generally, see Osborn, *Justin Martyr*, 28–43.

of textual analysis and therefore were guilty of reading the Scriptures incorrectly.[6] Anticipating his readers' desire for illustrations of this method in action, Justin then spends the next several chapters providing examples of Old Testament texts that he reads prosopologically.

From the Father

Justin first sets out Old Testament passages that he attributes to the "person" of the Father:

> And that this too may become clear to you, these words were spoken as from the person of the Father through Isaiah the aforementioned prophet: *The ox knows its owner, and the ass its master's manger, but Israel does not know me and my people have not understood. Woe, sinful nation, a people full of sins, an evil seed, lawless sons; you have forsaken the Lord* [Isa 1:3–4]. And again elsewhere, when the same prophet says likewise as from [the person of] the Father, *What sort of house will you build for me? says the Lord. The heaven is my throne, and the earth is the footstool of my feet* [Isa 66:1]. And again elsewhere, *Your new moons and sabbaths my soul hates, and I am not content with the great day of the fast and of idleness; nor, if you should come to be seen by me, will I hear you. Your hands are full of blood. And if you offer the finest wheaten flour and incense, it is an abomination to me. The fat of lambs and the blood of bulls I do not desire. For who demanded these things from your hands? But break every bond of injustice, tear asunder the knots of violent dealings, cover the homeless and naked, distribute your bread to the hungry* [Isa 1:11–15; 58:6–7]. Thus you can now perceive what sort of things are taught through the prophets as from [the person of] God.[7]

Based on the examples of prosopological exegesis we identified in the previous chapter of this book, we would expect Justin to cite Ps 2:7 or Ps 110:1, or at least to include a verse that could be interpreted as spoken to or about the Son. Justin, however, does not give any examples of intra-divine discourse. Rather, the three passages selected from Isaiah as examples of Scriptures spoken from the person of God the Father all focus on the theme of how Israelite religion failed to satisfy God's righteous requirements.[8] While this topic makes sense in light of Justin's overall polemic,

---

6. *1 Apol.* 36.3.
7. *1 Apol.* 37.1–9 (AT).
8. Interestingly, the one other time in *1 Apology* that Justin attributes a quotation

it is less clear why Justin offers these texts as examples of prosopological exegesis. Also surprising is that when Justin quotes Ps 110:1–3 and we would expect to have a prosopological interpretation based on how earlier Christian writers had understood this passage, Justin instead merely introduces the quotation as the words of "David the prophet," casting them more as a prophecy of Christ's resurrection and ascension than as direct dialogue theodramatically spoken by the Father to the Son.[9]

We might wonder, furthermore, if we should even consider such passages as genuine instances of prosopological exegesis; after all, the Old Testament portrayed these verses as spoken by God to Israel, and so simply extending the interpretation to specify that it is "God the Father" speaking hardly seems like much of an innovation. It is possible, though, given the Christians' emerging trinitarian doctrine of God, that assigning texts to "God the Father" as opposed to "God the Son" reflects the same impulses that gave rise to the use of person-centered reading strategies elsewhere in Scripture. The differentiation of the persons of the Godhead was not, after all, in view in the source texts, so there is a sense in which we can indeed speak of this as a form of prosopological exegesis.

In sum, Justin's understanding in *1 Apology* of prosopological exegesis from the person of the Father limits the texts placed on the lips of God the Father to a small number of passages from Isaiah that concern the failures of Israel's cultic worship. While Justin gives an explicit statement of his prosopological method, his actual use of that method in *1 Apology* reads as considerably less sophisticated than what we saw in Hebrews.

From the Son

Before examining Justin's examples of prosopological speech from the Son (*1 Apol.* 38), a comparison with the chapters that immediately precede this digression on prosopological exegesis is instructive. In these earlier chapters, Justin considers some of the ways in which Christ is the fulfillment of prophecy (*1 Apol.* 30–35). Justin primarily appeals to Isaiah but also draws on Numbers, the Psalter, Micah, and Zephaniah.[10] In *1 Apol.* 38, Justin

---

directly to God the Father is at *1 Apol.* 44.2–4, in which the Father is identified as the speaker of the words of Isa 1:16–20, which also concerns the Jews' disobedience and the resulting consequences.

9. *1 Apol.* 45.2–4. See also how Ps 2:7 is only cast as a prophecy and not theodramatic dialogue when Justin quotes all of Pss 1–2 in *1 Apol.* 40.

10. Specifically, in order Justin cites Gen 49:10–11; Isa 11:1; 51:5; Num 24:17; Isa

will go on to treat other verses from Deutero-Isaiah and Psalm 22 as the actual words of Christ, but in *1 Apol.* 35 the nuance is slightly different: the "prophet Isaiah, inspired by the prophetic Spirit" is the speaker of Isa 65:2 and Isa 58:2, while an ambiguous subject "says through another prophet" the words of Ps 22:16 and Ps 22:18.[11] Justin comments on the quotations of the Psalter: "And indeed David, the king and prophet, who said this, suffered none of these things," for it was in fact Christ who suffered all these things.[12] The emphasis in these passages seems to be that Isaiah and David were in fact the real speakers of these prophecies, and yet there also seems to be a sense in which, especially in these quotations of first-person dialogues that fit the story of Christ's passion, they seem to have taken on the literary *persona* of Christ even as they function for Justin simply as the Scriptures "announcing beforehand things that are about to happen."[13] This tension, then, appears to motivate Justin's declaration that "whenever you hear the sayings of the prophets spoken as from a person, do not suppose that they are spoken from the inspired ones themselves, but from the divine Logos who moves them."[14]

With this in mind, then, it is interesting that Justin, when he gives his examples of speech from the "person" of the Son following his section devoted to the prosopological speech of the Father, cites some of the exact same passages that he quoted at *1 Apol.* 35 while now completely obscuring the role of the human prophet in favor of a truly prosopological interpretation:

> And when the prophetic Spirit speaks as from the person of Christ, he speaks in this way: *I spread out my hands over a disobedient and disputatious people, over those who walk in a way that is not good* [Isa 65:2]. And again, *I have given my back to scourges and my cheeks to slaps; I did not turn my face away from the shame of spittings. And the Lord became my helper; therefore I was not put to shame, but I set my face as a solid rock and knew that I would not be ashamed, for the one who justifies me is near* [Isa 50:6–8]. And again when it says, *They cast lots for my clothing* [Ps 22:18], *and pierced my feet and hands* [Ps 22:16]. *But I lay down and slept, and rose again, because the Lord helped me*

7:14; Mic 5:2; Isa 9:6; 65:2; 58:2; Pss 22:16; 22:18; Zech 9:9 (which Justin incorrectly attributes to Zephaniah).

11. *1 Apol.* 35.3 (trans. Barnard).
12. *1 Apol.* 35.3 (trans. Barnard).
13. *1 Apol.* 36.2 (AT).
14. *1 Apol.* 36.1 (AT).

> [Ps 3:5]. And again when it says, *They spoke with their lips, they shook the head, saying, Let him deliver himself* [cf. Ps 22:7–8]. That all these things happened to Christ by the Jews, you are able to learn. For when he was crucified they shot out their lips and shook their heads, saying, *Let him who raised the dead save himself* [cf. Matt 27:39–43].[15]

The catena of biblical quotations that Justin provides as examples of speech "from the person of Christ" are all drawn from Isaiah and the Psalter. As with the instances of the Father's speech, a clear theme is evident around which all of the passages cluster—in this case, the rejection, crucifixion, and resurrection of Christ. The first five quotations are recounted in first-person dialogue. The shift, then, to the perspective of the onlookers to Jesus' crucifixion with the quotation of Ps 22:7–8 is thus doubly jarring insofar as in isolation from the rest of the psalm it makes no sense as words spoken from the person of the Son, leading some scholars to claim that Justin's text has likely been corrupted or lost.[16] In identifying portions of Psalm 22 as the words of the Son, Justin follows in the tradition of Hebrews and 1 Clement, and his quotation of Ps 22:16 and Ps 22:18 is straightforward enough. The problematic portion, though, stems from the fact that Justin picks up the quotation at Ps 22:7b, leaving out the preceding content (Ps 22:6–7a) spoken in the first-person. While a lacuna is possible, there is another explanation involving Justin's use of *testimonia* collections, which we will explore further below. Returning, though, to the big picture of what Justin is doing here, we can observe that in contrast to the quotations from the Father, none of which even made reference to the Son, here two quotations at least make reference to the Father (Isa 50:6–8; Ps 3:5), even if none of these texts illustrate the Son speaking directly to the Father. Intra-divine dialogue is still conspicuously absent.

On two other occasions in *1 Apology* Justin identifies Old Testament passages as spoken from the person of the Son. First, Justin presents Isa 65:1–3 as having been spoken "as in the person of Christ Himself."[17] This is simply an expansion of the citation of Isa 65:2, which was attributed to the Son as part of the catena in *1 Apol.* 38, though presented here in support of Justin's argument that the gentiles, and not the Jews, were

---

15. *1 Apol.* 38.1–8 (AT).

16. As Minns and Parvis write, "Either this section is not in its proper place, or if it is in its proper place, some words have fallen out" (*Justin*, 181n9).

17. *1 Apol.* 49.1–4 (trans. Barnard).

the ones who had correctly recognized Christ. Second, Justin identifies Christ as the one who spoke to Moses out of the burning bush (Exod 3:5). The idea that Christ was the subject of the Old Testament theophanies, and was in fact the one who led Israel out of Egypt, is found in the New Testament itself (e.g., 1 Cor 10:4; Jude 5) and is here expanded upon by Justin.[18] Though in a different category from the other examples we have seen thus far, because it is not about Christ's incarnate ministry but rather is interpreted as the ministry of the pre-incarnate Son, it can nevertheless be viewed as an example of prosopological exegesis insofar as it introduces a speaker not in the original source text, which could have been viewed as ambiguous in light of an emerging trinitarian understanding of God that allowed for distinction between the speech of God the Father and God the Son.[19] Contextually, Justin sought to distinguish between the invisible Father and the visible Son as a means of proving, against his interlocutors, that Scripture speaks of two divine persons; the consequences of such a reading of the theophanies will be further unpacked in the next chapters of this book.

In considering Justin's approach in *1 Apol.* 38 (as well as in these later instances) with respect to *1 Apol.* 35, the simplest conclusion is that Justin can deploy the same texts in different ways. On the one hand, a portion of Isaiah or the Psalter that is spoken in the first-person can be described as the words of the inspired human author who is prophetically announcing what will come to pass; on the other hand, these same passages can be understood as the words of the divine Logos himself, who speaks in the character of Christ. How exactly Justin reconciles these two perspectives is unclear.

Perhaps this lack of clarity can partially explain one other puzzling aspect of Justin's method. In none of these instances does Justin analyze the potential theodramatic setting of the quotation or its implications for Christology; not once does Justin encourage us to read any of these passages as being spoken by Christ to the Father. In other words, just as with Justin's examples of prosopological exegesis from the Father, Justin again fails to provide us with an instance of intra-divine discourse. His examples of the Son's prosopological speech do little more than emphasize how Old Testament prophecies had an ultimate reference point in

---

18. *1 Apol.* 62.3. On Justin's christological reading of the Old Testament theophanies, see further Kominiak, *Theophanies*, 23–47; Trakatellis, *Pre-Existence*, 53–92; Lieu, *Marcion*, 23–24.

19. See also Justin's analysis of the burning bush episode at *Dial.* 59–60.

the events surrounding Christ's crucifixion. The intriguing theodramatic implications of the divine dialogue described in Hebrews remain unexplored in Justin's thought in *1 Apology*.

One possible explanation for this gets back to Justin's own rhetorical training and how he would have understood prosopological exegesis. In his own appeal to the commonly accepted principles of textual interpretation,[20] Justin signals that when he is using the Greek term *prosōpon* for "person," we are not supposed to think in ontological terms as much as literary ones, with the theatrical background of masks likely coming into view.[21] The kind of divine dialogue portrayed in Hebrews, with its implied settings such as at some time before the creation of the world, seems to require a different conception of "personhood" in which we are to imagine God the Father and God the Son as distinct divine persons whose conversations have been recorded in the pages of Scripture. Rather, for Justin, the prophet is something like an actor, inspired by the Holy Spirit to put on and take off various masks in order to give prophetic speeches "in-character." The emphasis is on the fulfillment of prophecy, not on anything about Christology proper.

From the Spirit

Indeed, staying on the theme of prophecy, Justin next considers examples of "when the prophetic Spirit speaks as prophesying things that are to come to pass."[22] Interestingly, whereas in the preceding chapters Justin had spoken of quotations "from the person of the Father" and "from the person of the Son," there is no corresponding language of "from the person of the Holy Spirit." Rather, Justin likely intends for us to see the Spirit as the one speaking "as" the Father and the Son in the preceding chapters; in this and the following chapters, then, Justin simply identifies the words of the prophets as having been inspired by the Holy Spirit (*1 Apol.* 39–45). At least in these texts, the Holy Spirit does not seem to speak as his own *prosōpon* in Scripture as do the Father and the Son, for he is himself the architect of Scripture.[23]

20. See again *1 Apol.* 36.2.

21. This is not to deny that Justin had a more robust ontology of divine personhood but simply to recognize that prosopological exegesis does not appear to be the foundation by which he builds this understanding.

22. *1 Apol.* 39.1 (AT).

23. See, e.g., *1 Apol.* 38.1; 44.1; 47.1; 53.6; 61.13.

Summary

Despite his promising overview of his prosopological method, Justin's actual employment of person-centered reading in his *1 Apology* lacks the depth or consistency of earlier texts such as Hebrews. Whereas the latter writing envisioned intra-divine dialogue between the Father and the Son, the former is simply content to offer monologues regarding the failures of Israel's worship or prophecies of Jesus' crucifixion. It is striking, then, that Justin's next work would take considerable steps towards a more mature use of this method along the lines of what was observed in Hebrews.

Prosopological Exegesis in the *Dialogue with Trypho*

Justin's *Dialogue with Trypho* (ca. 160), likely written some five to ten years after his *1 Apology*, is a tour-de-force of early Christian biblical interpretation.[24] Though Justin does not describe his prosopological method in the *Dialogue* as he had in his earlier work, nor does he give set blocks of examples, he nevertheless uses this reading strategy with more frequency and with a broader scope that brings its use more into line with the approach of Hebrews.

From the Father

In *1 Apology*, Justin's examples of speech from the person of the Father centered on the failures of Israel's cultic worship. In the *Dialogue*, however, Justin expands on the Father's speech in several important ways that bring the Father's relationship with the Son more clearly into view. Because Justin does not treat these texts in a systematic fashion, I have organized my analysis by theme, aiming for as "chronological" a presentation as possible of the events in salvation history.

Divine Pre-Existence

As in Hebrews, Justin's *Dialogue* pulls back the curtain on divine dialogues that appear to have taken place before the beginning of time. Unsurprisingly, Psalm 110 is a key text for christological investigation. Throughout the *Dialogue*, Justin insists that Christ is the true referent

---

24. On the genre, purpose, audience, and rhetorical strategy of the *Dialogue*, see Dulk, *Between Jews and Heretics*; Allert, *Revelation*, 37–61.

of this psalm.²⁵ In his first sustained examination of Psalm 110, Justin, having cited the psalm in its entirety,²⁶ then focuses specifically on Ps 110:4, ruling out Hezekiah as the true referent of the psalm.²⁷ Rather, Justin comments,

> God, because of your lack of faith, swore that Jesus is the High Priest *according to the order of Melchizedek* [Ps 110:4]. For, as Melchizedek was the priest of the Most High . . . so has God announced that his eternal priest, called Lord by the Holy Spirit, should be the priest of the uncircumcised.²⁸

While Justin had earlier introduced the entirety of the psalm as the words of David, here Justin specifies that Ps 110:4 should ultimately be read as the words of God concerning Christ; as Justin's interpretation has proceeded, David has faded into the background as the human author while the divine speaker comes into focus. As in this and other instances we will explore below, God is not explicitly referenced as "the Father" in the introductory formula, but we can assume that whenever "God" is speaking to or about the Son, the Father specifically is in view.

What is less clear, however, is precisely when God's announcement of Christ's eternal priesthood took place. Presumably, such an announcement predated creation, as suggested by the preceding verse of Psalm 110, which Justin quotes as, "*In the brightness of the saints, from the womb before the morning star I begot you* [Ps 110:3]." Justin indicates that these words "were addressed to Christ."²⁹ Given what we know of the history of interpretation of Psalm 110, we would expect an interpretation of this verse reflecting a theodramatic setting from before the creation of the world. Conversely, when Justin says elsewhere that "God, through David, announced that he would make him *a priest forever according to the order of Melchizedek* [Ps 110:4],"³⁰ the wording seems to indicate that not until the time of David did God announce this future reality concerning Christ. Thus, while Justin employs a prosopological interpretation of Ps 110:3–4 in service of arguments for Christ's pre-existent divinity, it is the wording of the verses themselves

25. See, e.g., *Dial.* 19.4; 32.3; 33.1–2; 83.1–4; 118.1.
26. *Dial.* 32.6.
27. *Dial.* 33.1.
28. *Dial.* 33.2 (trans. Falls).
29. *Dial.* 83.4 (trans. Falls).
30. *Dial.* 19.4 (trans. Falls).

more than analysis of the possible theodramatic setting of the intra-divine dialogue that Justin draws to our attention.[31]

Of course, the Holy Spirit's identification of the Son as "Lord," not to mention "God,"[32] generated an interpretive problem for Christians who now appeared to worship two gods. In response, Christians such as Justin appealed to biblical texts that appeared to speak of "two powers in heaven." This interpretive tradition had been quite popular in Hellenistic Judaism but was rejected during the rabbinic period even as it was increasingly picked up by Christian exegetes like Justin to be turned against the Jews.[33] For Justin, it was again prosopological exegesis—here from the person of the Father—that provided the most natural way to read such passages. Thus, God's words, "Let us make man in our image, after our likeness" (Gen 1:26), opened themselves to a prosopological interpretation.[34] After dismissing alternative interpretations, Justin identifies this verse as a record of a conversation between God the Father and his pre-existent Son, "who was really begotten of the Father, was with the Father and the Father talked with him before all creation."[35] The conversation even extends into the immediate aftermath of the creation of the world, with Justin casting God's words, "*Behold Adam has become as one of Us, knowing good and evil* [Gen 3:22]" as directed to the Son insofar as these words "clearly show that there were a number of persons together."[36] Here the sense of the words of Scripture actually giving us access to a divine dialogue finally recalls what we observed earlier in Hebrews, with prosopological exegesis providing a window into such intra-divine conversations.

Likewise, other pieces of dialogue in Scripture that speak of two lords or two gods, such as Gen 19:24, Ps 24:7, and Ps 110:1, provide justification for Christian belief in a second pre-existent divine being.[37] As Justin will later remark, "You can see that Scripture declares that the Son was begotten of the Father before all creatures, and everybody will

---

31. See also *Dial.* 63.3–4, where Ps 110:3–4 is linked with Ps 45:6–11. On the use of Psalm 110 in connection with the ascension, see further Daniélou, *Theology of Jewish Christianity*, 257–59.

32. Cf. *Dial.* 33.2; 36.2.

33. See further Segal, *Two Powers in Heaven*, 33–155.

34. See, e.g., *Dial.* 62.1.

35. *Dial.* 62.4 (trans. Falls).

36. *Dial.* 62.3 (trans. Falls).

37. Cf. *Dial.* 127.5; 129.1.

admit that the Son is numerically distinct from the Father!"[38] Given this additional use of prosopological exegesis from the person of the Father to support the Son's pre-existence, it seems to me on balance that Ps 110:3–4 should be interpreted accordingly. In any event, what is clear is that prosopological exegesis played an important role in Justin's defense of the Son's pre-existence.

Ascension

One further potential example of prosopological exegesis from the Father concerning the Son is found in *Dial.* 36, in which Justin reads Psalm 24 as telling of Christ's ascension:

> Now, when these heavenly princes saw that he was in appearance without beauty, honor, or glory, and not recognizing him, they asked, *Who is this King of Glory?* And the Holy Spirit, either in his own name or in the Father's, answered, *The Lord of Hosts. He is the King of Glory* [Ps 24:10].[39]

What is fascinating about this example is that Justin expresses uncertainty regarding how best to prosopologically interpret this passage. Who is the speaker of the dialogue answering the heavenly princes' question? Justin admits the Holy Spirit could be speaking either "in his own name" or "in the Father's." For one thing, this passage appears to suggest that the Holy Spirit is capable of speaking from his own person, a topic to which we will return below. For our present purposes, however, we have another example of explicitly marked prosopological exegesis that records a conversation between the heavenly princes and either God the Father or the Holy Spirit concerning Christ at his ascension. Here Justin does give a specific theodramatic setting, the time of the Son's ascension, a unique observation on his part, which calls further attention to the fact that Justin is otherwise not particularly interested in establishing this setting in other instances.

---

38. *Dial.* 129.3 (trans. Falls).

39. *Dial.* 36.6 (trans. Falls). On the contribution of Psalm 24 to early Christology, see Daniélou, *Theology of Jewish Christianity*, 261.

Present Reign

As in *1 Apology*, Justin in the *Dialogue* quotes Isaiah to criticize the Jews, here emphasizing how God has rejected the Jews on account of their rejection of Christ.[40] In this particular work, however, Justin focuses in on how God, in Christ, has made a new covenant with the gentiles, his new people over whom he now reigns.[41] Indeed, the most extensive cluster of instances of prosopological exegesis marked as spoken by the Father to the Son relates to the gentiles becoming the inheritance of Christ, who now rules over them. Reinforcing Justin's pattern in *1 Apology*, we find that Isaiah is the core text for identifying the prosopological speech of the Father in this regard. Justin sets out his basic interpretive lens in the introduction to his quotation of Isa 42:1–4 towards the end of the *Dialogue*:

> If you have ears to hear it, in Isaiah, God, speaking of Christ in parable, calls him Jacob and Israel. This is what he says: *Jacob is my servant, I will uphold him; Israel is my elect. I will put my spirit upon him and he shall bring forth judgment to the Gentiles* [Isa 42:1] . . .[42]

While this passage does not feature dialogue between Father and Son, it nevertheless establishes that the Son is the true subject matter of these Isaianic passages. When the monologue in Isaiah 42 does shift to speak directly to an unnamed "you" (Isa 42:6–9), Christ is therefore the obvious conversation partner. For example, after citing Isa 42:6–7, Justin comments that these words "have been spoken of Christ and concern the enlightened Gentiles."[43] Indeed, when elsewhere Justin quotes the broader sequence of Isa 42:5–13, he comments that in these verses "God affirms that he will give his glory to him alone whom he has appointed to be the light of the Gentiles."[44] Thus, Justin clearly reads the dialogue in Isaiah 42 as the words of the Father to the Son, though he does not consider the possible theodramatic context or its implications, instead simply focusing on God's covenant in Christ with the gentiles.

---

40. See, e.g., *Dial.* 16.4, quoting Isa 57:1–4.
41. See, e.g., *Dial.* 11.4. While Justin affirms a future, earthly kingdom, he does not deny Christ's present spiritual rule (e.g., *Dial.* 36.5–6). On Justin's millennial teaching, see Hill, *Regnum Caelorum*, 23–27. We also need to remember that "Christ" was itself a royal honorific; see further Bates, *Salvation*, 82–83.
42. *Dial.* 123.8 (trans. Falls; the quotation extends through Isa 42:4).
43. *Dial.* 122.3 (trans. Falls); see also *Dial.* 26.2.
44. *Dial.* 65.7 (trans. Falls).

The same phenomenon is seen with Justin's interpretation of Isaiah 49. As Justin writes,

> We, therefore, were endowed with the special grace of hearing and understanding, of being saved by Christ, and of knowing all truths revealed by the Father. Thus, he says to him, *It is a great thing for you that you should be my servant to raise up the tribes of Jacob and to bring the dispersions of Israel back. I have given you to be the light of the Gentiles, that you may be their salvation even to the farthest part of the earth* [Isa 49:6].⁴⁵

The Father therefore speaks to the Son to commission him as the agent of his salvation to the gentiles. Similarly, when Justin quotes Isa 49:8, he identifies God as the speaker and Christ ("and his proselytes") as the recipient of the speech,⁴⁶ which again focuses on the gentiles as Christ's inheritance. Lest there be any confusion on this point, Justin continues,

> Who, then, is the inheritance of Christ? Is it not the Gentiles? Who is the covenant of God? Is it not Christ? So he states elsewhere in Scripture, *You are my Son, this day have I begotten you. Ask of me, and I will give you the Gentiles for your inheritance and the utmost parts of the earth for your possession* [Ps 2:7–8].⁴⁷

Justin's prosopological interpretation of Ps 2:7 calls to mind to its similar use by Hebrews and 1 Clement, though Justin's introduction of the quotation and his addition of verse 8 mean, in this particular instance, that Justin's focus is on the Son's present rule over the gentiles and not the issue of his divine begottenness.⁴⁸ For Justin, then, the chief place where he finds the Father speaking to the Son in the Old Testament is when the Father commissions the Son to reign over the gentiles, a point particularly resonant in Justin's (literary, if not actually historical) debate with Trypho the Jew.⁴⁹

In sum, therefore, Justin presents the Father as speaking to the Son on the issues of his pre-existence and reign over the gentiles, with

---

45. *Dial.* 121.4 (trans. Falls).
46. *Dial.* 122.5 (trans. Falls).
47. *Dial.* 122.6 (trans. Falls).

48. The other major references to Ps 2:7 in this work, at *Dial.* 88.8 and 103.6, will be discussed below in the section on Justin's use of prosopological exegesis from the person of the Son.

49. For additional examples in which God (that is, the Father) speaks concerning (but not to) the Son on the subject of the gentiles, see, e.g., *Dial.* 11.3; 26.3–4; 91.1; 120.3; 121.1.

a potential further heavenly conversation with the angels at the time of the Son's ascension. The theodramatic setting and possible christological consequences of identifying these passages as the words of the Father to the Son are largely left unexplored. Still, the development from *1 Apology* is clear, with dialogical passages now coming into focus as targets for prosopological exegesis as Justin reads them as intra-divine conversations, something he had not ascribed to the Father in *1 Apology*.

From the Son

Identifying the Son's prosopological speech in the *Dialogue* is not without some degree of challenge. As in *1 Apology*, Justin takes considerable pains to give examples of ways in which Christ is the fulfillment of prophecy.[50] To complicate matters, Justin at times identifies "the Word" as speaking through the prophets.[51] Many of these instances, however, cannot be construed as prosopological exegesis; the emphasis appears simply to be on the Logos' role in inspiring the prophets rather than speech that is in the "person" of the Son.[52] Accordingly, therefore, our analysis will focus on those instances in which Old Testament speech appears to be clearly attributed to the person of the Son. These instances are scattered through the *Dialogue* rather than collected in one place or to support one consistent point; nevertheless, some overall themes emerge that are significant for Justin's Christology.

Divine Pre-Existence

First, Justin attributes Old Testament dialogical passages to the person of the Son that he interprets as the Son commenting on his own divine pre-existence. The key text is one that will increasingly be a focal point for later christological debates: Prov 8:22–36. In the context of Proverbs, this speech is placed on the lips of Lady Wisdom, whose words contrast with those offered by Dame Folly, holding out a choice of two ways of how to live.[53] As we have seen, early Christian belief in the deity of Christ compelled a re-reading of the Old Testament, with texts such as Ps 2:7

---

50. See, e.g., *Dial.* 13.1–9; 14.4–8; 31.1–7; 43.3–8; 53.1–6; 66.1–3; 87.2; 97–106.
51. See, e.g., *Dial.* 49.2; 52.4; 57.2; 58.4; 62.1; 68.5; 86.3; 121.2; 129.1–2.
52. See again *1 Apol.* 36.1.
53. For this reading of Proverbs 8, see Treier, *Proverbs and Ecclesiastes*, 44–49.

produced as evidence of the Son's existence prior to the incarnation (as at Heb 1:5). The specific features of Prov 8:22–36 would prove irresistible to Christians such as Justin seeking to further affirm Christ's pre-existence:

> My statements will now be confirmed by none other than the Word of Wisdom, who is this God begotten from the Father of all, and who is Word and Wisdom and Power and Glory of him who begot him. Here are his words as spoken by Solomon: *If I shall declare to you what happens daily, I shall call to mind events from eternity, and recount them. The Lord begot me in the beginning of his ways for his works. He set me up from eternity, before he made the earth, and before he made the depths, before the fountains of water had sprung out, before the mountains had been established. Before all the hills he begets me* [Prov 8:21–25].[54]

By identifying the Son with God's pre-existent Wisdom, as described in this chapter of Proverbs,[55] Justin has provided an Old Testament precedent for the belief that, in the words of the more famous Johannine formulation, "In the beginning was the Word, and the Word was with God, and the Word was God" (John 1:1). Little did Justin know that this identification of the Word with the Wisdom spoken of in Proverbs 8 would be a major flashpoint for the Arian controversy of the fourth century, with the Septuagint's rendering of Prov 8:22 more precisely speaking of God "creating" Wisdom and thereby appearing to cast the Son as a creature.[56] At this point, however, Justin is not interested in fleshing out a fully-formed doctrine of the eternal generation of the Son, and the quotation suffices for his purposes without him providing any further commentary. That Justin immediately follows this with a quotation from the first chapter of Genesis, "*Let us make man in our image and likeness* [Gen 1:26]," makes clear that he also intends us to read God's words at the time of the creation of the world as spoken by the Father to the Son, again reinforcing the Son's pre-existence.[57]

The importance of Wisdom's speech is highlighted by the fact that Justin quotes from it again near the end of the *Dialogue*, in which Justin

---

54. *Dial.* 61.3 (trans. Falls; the quotation extends through Prov 8:36); cf. *Dial.* 126.1.

55. Note Justin actually starts his quotation at Prov 8:21, but subsequent Christian writers will generally begin with 8:22 as the *crux interpretum*.

56. Athanasius, the great defender of Nicene orthodoxy, therefore had to deal with precisely the problem posed by this verse; see further O'Keefe and Reno, *Sanctified Vision*, 56–63.

57. *Dial.* 62.1–2 (trans. Falls).

is seeking to prove that Scripture speaks of multiple divine persons. Following appeals to Gen 19:24 and Gen 3:22, Justin invokes Prov 8:21–25, from which he draws the conclusion that "Scripture declares that the Son was begotten of the Father before all creatures, and everybody will admit that the Son is numerically distinct from the Father!"[58] Again, Justin is not interested in fleshing out the details of how this generation works, merely employing this Wisdom Christology to make a general point about Christ's pre-existence and role in creation.[59] Still, by pairing this text with Gen 3:22, Justin reinforces his point earlier in the *Dialogue* that the Son was present at the creation of the world.

Finally, also fitting this theme is Justin's interpretation of Christ's baptism in the Jordan. As Justin writes, at the scene of Jesus' baptism, a voice from heaven spoke the same words "uttered by David, when he, in the person of Christ, spoke what was later to be said to Christ by the Father, *You are my Son; this day have I begotten you* [Ps 2:7], meaning that his birth really began for men when they first realized who he was."[60] Here the prosopological interpretation is highlighted by noting that David spoke "in the person of Christ," acknowledging that in its original context, the speaker of Ps 2:7 is actually reporting the words spoken to him by God at an earlier time. The point appears to be that Christ spoke this prior to the Father speaking these words over him at his baptism, again reinforcing Justin's belief in the Son's pre-existence.

Crucifixion

In one of the lengthiest exegetical digressions in the entirety of the *Dialogue*, Justin takes up a christological interpretation of Psalm 22 in *Dial.* 97–106. As is consistent with Justin's inconsistency on such matters, Justin at the outset of this section identifies David as the speaker of this "mystical parable," which was "spoken of Christ,"[61] before he transitions to direct his readers to note how in this psalm, Christ

> reveres his Father and how he refers all things to him, as when he prays to be freed by him from this death; at the same time pointing out in the psalm what sort of men his enemies were,

---

58. *Dial.* 129.3 (trans. Falls).
59. See further Skarsaune, *Proof from Prophecy*, 388–89.
60. *Dial.* 88.8 (trans. Falls).
61. *Dial.* 97.3–4 (trans. Falls).

and proving that he indeed became a man who was capable of suffering.[62]

Indeed, as Justin goes on to exposit each section of the psalm over the subsequent chapters of the *Dialogue*, he intermixes references to the psalm being a prophecy about Christ with interpretive comments that cast the psalm as the words of Christ himself as he looked forward to the time of his crucifixion. Justin, therefore, seems to want to hold together the psalm as both the words of David and the words of Christ. How exactly the text functions in this dual capacity, regrettably, is left unclear.

What is striking for our purposes, though, is that Justin is meditating on almost the entirety of Psalm 22 as the *vox Christi*. The Gospel writers, of course, had recorded Jesus speaking the words of Ps 22:1 from the cross (Mark 15:34 pars.), and other early Christian writers likewise identified other verses of that psalm, such as Ps 22:22 (Heb 2:12) and Ps 22:6–8 (1 Clem. 16.15–16) as the prosopological speech of the Son. Justin himself had quoted pieces of Psalm 22 as examples of the Son's prosopological speech in *1 Apol.* 38. In his *Dialogue*, Justin then takes what would appear to be the next logical step: identifying the great majority of the psalm as the words of Christ. That this psalm sustains a single first-person voice throughout its first twenty-three verses no doubt made such a reading appealing.[63] That the addressee of the Son's speech is the Father is of course clear from the text itself (e.g., Ps 22:1).

The christological implications of Justin reading this psalm through the lens of prosopological exegesis are considerable. That the psalm shows evidence of Jesus being "capable of suffering" counters a docetic Christology;[64] the repetition of this theme suggests that such views may have been common in Justin's time, with Justin insisting that Jesus was aware all along that true suffering would be his fate.[65] Likewise, Jesus' knowledge of his resurrection was known to him from the beginning.[66] In fact, Justin maintains, all the details of Jesus' life and death were part of "the Father's design," and are therefore reflected in this and other

---

62. *Dial.* 98.1 (trans. Falls).

63. The shift in speaker starting at Ps 22:24 likely explains why Justin cuts off his quotation of the psalm after verse 23. Justin does, however, refer to this as the "whole" psalm (*Dial.* 98.1).

64. *Dial.* 98.1; 99.2 (trans. Falls).

65. *Dial.* 99.3.

66. *Dial.* 100.1; 106.1.

portions of the Old Testament.⁶⁷ Justin even uses the psalm to reinforce his belief in Jesus' pre-existence; when Justin reads, *"deliver my soul from the sword, and my only-begotten from the grip of the dog* [Ps 22:20]," it activates Justin's understanding of Jesus as "the Only-begotten of the Father of the universe, having been properly begotten from him as his Word and Power, and afterwards becoming man through the Virgin."⁶⁸ Thus, a text that is primarily interpreted as Jesus speaking about his crucifixion can, secondarily, also touch on his divine pre-existence as well.

Throughout his exposition of the psalm, Justin supplies correspondences from the Gospel accounts of Jesus' passion, highlighting his contention that his Jewish opponents had in fact been "blind" to the true meaning of this psalm, which led them to reject and crucify Jesus.⁶⁹ Justin informs Trypho that Jesus' silence (Ps 22:15) demonstrated that "all your teachers are without wisdom,"⁷⁰ thereby tying the details of his christological interpretation to his own polemical context. The failure of the Jews to accept that Jesus was the true referent of the psalm even with the benefit of hindsight, Justin concludes, contrasts with the example of the apostles (the "brethren" of Ps 22:22), who at least had the wisdom to be "most sorry that they had abandoned him at the crucifixion."⁷¹

Present Reign

A third area in which Justin identifies the Son's prosopological speech concerns Christ's reign over his new people, the gentiles, as consequent upon his rejection by the Jews. As with the Son's divine pre-existence, this reflects a parallel concern that we observed in the Father's prosopological speech. Early in the *Dialogue*, Justin takes up the issue of how Christians should understand the Old Testament's ritual laws. Justin insists that "another covenant, another Law has gone forth from Zion, Jesus Christ."⁷² As Justin then argues,

> The Lord cries out through Isaiah, *I was made manifest to them that seek me not; I was found of them that asked not for me. I*

---

67. *Dial.* 102.2 (trans. Falls).
68. *Dial.* 105.1 (trans. Falls).
69. *Dial.* 97.4 (trans. Falls); cf. *Dial.* 101.2.
70. *Dial.* 103.9 (trans. Falls).
71. *Dial.* 106.1 (trans. Falls).
72. *Dial.* 24.1 (trans. Falls).

> said, *Behold me, to nations that did not call upon my name. I have extended my hands all the day to an unbelieving and contradicting people, who walk in a way that is not good, but after their own sins. It is a people that provokes me to my face* [Isa 65:1–3].[73]

Here "the Lord," that is, Christ, identified as the true speaker of the words of Isaiah, "cries out" concerning the "nations" to which he will extend his gospel and the rejection he faces from his own people. Thus the gentiles who believe in Christ, and not the Jews who do not believe, will inherit God's promises.[74] Though not explicitly indicated, the audience for this address is presumably God the Father. The speech, while describing events in the past tense that presumably referred to Christ's own earthly ministry, is set in the context of the time after the establishment of the new covenant,[75] making the Son's present reign the presumed theodramatic setting for this speech.

In sum, therefore, Justin in his *Dialogue with Trypho* presents the Son speaking from his own person on the themes of his pre-existence, crucifixion, and reign over the gentiles, providing a broader basis of examples of this method than that found in *1 Apology*.

From the Spirit

As noted earlier, Justin appears to open the door to the Holy Spirit speaking not only as a secondary, inspiring agent but as a "person" in his own right in his discussion of Ps 24:10.[76] That Justin believed that the Holy Spirit could in fact speak from his own person according to the principles of prosopological exegesis can be found in a key passage later in the *Dialogue*:

> "Not only because of that quotation [that is, Gen 19:23–25, which had been quoted previously]," I said, "must we certainly admit that, besides the Creator of the universe, another was called Lord by the Holy Spirit. For this was attested to, not only by Moses, but also by David, when he said, *The Lord said to my Lord: Sit at my right hand, until I make your enemies your footstool* [Ps 110:1]. And in other words, *Your throne, O God, is forever and ever; the scepter of your kingdom is a scepter of*

---

73. *Dial.* 24.3 (trans. Falls).
74. Cf. *Dial.* 26.1.
75. See, e.g., *Dial.* 24.1.
76. *Dial.* 36.6.

> *uprightness. You have loved justice, and hated iniquity; therefore God, your God, has anointed you with the oil of gladness above your fellow kings* [Ps 45:6–7]. Tell me if it is your opinion that the Holy Spirit calls another *God* and *Lord*, besides the Father of all things and his Christ."[77]

The dialogical passages that Justin cites here, Ps 110:1 and Ps 45:6–7, are both attributed to the Holy Spirit. Though the language of "person" is not explicitly cited, as it was in *Dial.* 36.6, the emphasis is on the Holy Spirit as the ultimate speaker in what appears to be the theodramatic moment of the Son's enthronement following his ascension into heaven.[78] With respect to Ps 110:1, Justin draws out the implications contained within the fact that the words of the Father to the Son are observed and reported by some third person who references these two "lords." David is thus recounting a theodramatic moment in which the Spirit reports a dialogue between the Father and the Son. Likewise, in Justin's interpretation of Ps 45:6–7, the Spirit is put forward as the ultimate speaker of the biblical text, in this case words that he speaks directly to the Son, as a way of making sense of the passage's reference to two "gods."

The implication is startling: Justin is suggesting that the Scriptures provide access to divine conversations involving not just the Father and the Son but the Holy Spirit as well. As distinguished from the Spirit's usual role of inspiring the Scriptures, the Spirit in these passages participates in the divine theodrama as his own person, and we, the readers of Scripture, are enabled to "overhear" internal conversations within the Godhead. The Spirit even appears to have a distinct role within these intra-divine dialogues: to testify to the lordship and deity of the Father and the Son. As I have argued elsewhere, this "trinitarian testimony" would be a logical outgrowth of the Johannine understanding of the Spirit as the one who provides true testimony regarding Christ (John 15:26).[79] The pneumatological significance of this move has been largely underappreciated given how this particular trajectory would unfold over the following decades and centuries,[80] but for the purposes of this book we can simply note another instance of how prosopological

---

77. *Dial.* 56.14 (trans. Falls).

78. On this passage, see further Slusser, "Exegetical Roots," 466–68; Hughes, *Trinitarian Testimony*, 54–63; *How the Spirit Became God*, 60–64. On the likely theodramatic setting of these verses, see Bates, *Birth*, 160–65.

79. See Hughes, *How the Spirit Became God*, 19–29.

80. See Hughes, *How the Spirit Became God*, 64–76.

exegesis, in this case from the person of the Holy Spirit, contributes to the development of Christology, with the Spirit providing testimony that Christ is truly "Lord" and "God."

Summary

Despite his attempt to explicitly articulate his approach to prosopological exegesis in *1 Apology*, a survey of the entirety of Justin's extant corpus quickly frustrates any attempt to neatly systematize how Justin is going about reading the Old Testament for evidence of speech from the various divine persons. Nevertheless, Justin represents an important advance in our narrative of the relationship of prosopological exegesis to the development of Christology: Justin, after all, is the first to explicitly call out his prosopological approach to biblical interpretation; additionally, Justin provides more examples of prosopological exegesis than any Christian writer before him. And, in so doing, Justin has demonstrated the continued relevance of a prosopological reading of the Old Testament for adding to a Christian understanding of the person and work of Christ (and indeed the Holy Spirit). If, therefore, the Old Testament is such a significant resource for christological reflection, the challenge posed by someone like Marcion, who proposed to jettison the Old Testament in its entirety, can be seen as a much more existential threat to the entire project of early Christian theology. Justin also appears to have been the innovator of the idea that the Holy Spirit could also speak from his own person, paving the way for later trinitarian conversations between Father, Son, and Spirit. In concluding this section, we can briefly summarize our observations in a table that sets out all the instances in which Justin employs a prosopological reading of Old Testament dialogical passages that involve speech to, from, or about the Son; verses in bold reflect places where Justin explicitly interprets these words as intra-divine dialogue:

	From the Father	From the Son	From the Spirit
Divine Pre-Existence	**Gen 1:26** **Gen 3:22** **Ps 2:7b** **Ps 110:3–4**	Ps 2:7a Prov 8:22–36	—
Pre-Incarnate Ministry	—	Exod 3:5	—
Crucifixion	—	**Ps 22:1–22** Isa 50:6–8	—
Death and Resurrection	—	Ps 3:5	—
Ascension, Enthronement, and Reign	**Ps 2:7b–8** Ps 24:10? **Ps 110:1b–c** Isa 42:1–4 Isa 42:6–7 Isa 49:6 Isa 49:8	Isa 65:1–3	Ps 24:10? **Ps 45:6–7** Ps 110:1a

Perhaps, then, in the *Dialogue* we see two sides of an ongoing conversation between the Father and the Son (with an occasional contribution by the Holy Spirit) over the whole sweep of salvation history; these correspondences seem to at least imply that certain moments in this story—creation, crucifixion, resurrection, ascension, and present reign—were somehow marked by speech between these two divine persons, recorded by the inspiration of the Holy Spirit in the pages of Holy Scripture. Can we say, then, more of why these particular quotations were chosen? Or why these particular themes emerged as central? To answer these questions, we will need to examine Justin's use of *testimonia* collections and his understanding of the *regula fidei*.

Weaving the Threads

Given, then, that Justin's use of prosopological exegesis played a meaningful role in his christological reflection, we can now weigh the influence of other factors that may have contributed to shaping this particular approach to biblical interpretation. We will consider first Justin's use of *testimonia* collections as a source for this interpretive method and then weigh the extent to which Justin's use of prosopological exegesis lines up with his understanding of the *regula fidei*.

Justin's Use of *Testimonia*

As noted in an earlier chapter of this book, scholars have demonstrated that early Christians collected and edited sets of quotations from the Old Testament, to which they added their own interpretations, as proof-texts for defending nascent Christian theology. For his part, Justin himself refers to having "found testimonies proclaimed about [Christ] before He came and was made man,"[81] which could perhaps refer to written *testimonia* collections centered upon Christ. In any event, Oskar Skarsaune has convincingly made the case for Justin drawing upon two such major collections of scriptural proof-texts.[82] First, Skarsaune claims, Justin drew upon a "kerygma source" that collected Old Testament passages related to Christ's life and death in order to prove that he was in fact the promised Messiah. Second, Justin made use of a "recapitulation source" that was designed to show how certain Old Testament passages could not refer to any historical king of Israel but must instead be speaking of Christ. Details of Skarsaune's analysis aside, there can be little doubt that Justin made extensive use of *testimonia* collections in composing his writings.

In Skarsaune's reconstruction, Justin's digression on prosopological exegesis in *1 Apol.* 36–45 represents what he calls "the great insertion."[83] As we observed above, the quotations that Justin selects in this section lack a clear logic or consistency (e.g., the inclusion of Ps 22:7–8 with a "fulfillment report" rather than a clear link to the subject of the chapter); as Skarsaune notes, "Even a superficial reading of these chapters of the *Apology* is sufficient to observe that many of the texts adduced are inappropriate as examples of the principles they are said to exemplify." As a result, the most logical conclusion for us to draw is that the texts "seem to derive from testimony clusters which are composed for other purposes."[84] The verses Justin identifies as having been spoken by the Father are clearly drawn from an anti-cultic testimony source.[85] For our purposes, however, the key chapter in this "great insertion" is *1 Apol.* 38, in which Justin provides examples of prosopological speech from the person of the Son. Skarsaune shows that a common source undergirds

---

81. *1 Apol.* 53.2 (trans. Barnard).
82. Skarsaune, *Proof from Prophecy*, 228–42; cf. Nyström, *Apology*, 110.
83. Skarsaune, *Proof from Prophecy*, 157.
84. Skarsaune, *Proof from Prophecy*, 157.
85. Skarsaune, *Proof from Prophecy*, 158.

not only *1 Apol.* 38 but also *1 Apol.* 35 and *Dial.* 97. The emphasis in all of these passages is on Jesus fulfilling prophecy regarding the Messiah's rejection by Israel (Isa 65:2; 58:2), crucifixion (Ps 22:7–8, 16, 18; Isa 50:6–8), and death and resurrection (Ps 3:5).[86] Justin appears to be repurposing this *testimonia* collection as speech spoken by the person of the Son, just as he attempted, somewhat artlessly, at inserting material from an anti-cultic collection as examples of speech from the person of the Father. Not surprisingly, therefore, Justin's actual application of the prosopological method does not come through as clearly in *1 Apology* as it will in his subsequent *Dialogue*.

As for the *Dialogue*, with the likely exception of Justin's excursus on Old Testament theophanies (*Dial.* 56–60) and the extended interpretation of Psalm 22 (*Dial.* 97–106),[87] the quotations that Justin draws upon for his examples of prosopological exegesis appear to be taken from either the "kerygma source" or the "recapitulation source." In Skarsaune's analysis of these *testimonia* sources, it quickly becomes clear that their emphases fall on proving that Jesus was the fulfillment of Old Testament messianic prophecies, albeit not as the kind of messiah that the Jews of Jesus' or Justin's day were anticipating.[88] In other words, the *Dialogue* gives further evidence to the theory that Justin did not have a testimony source that included a systematic collection of examples of prosopological exegesis from the various divine persons; rather, it would appear that Justin himself was responsible for these prosopological readings. The fact that Justin is the first Christian writer to give an explicit account of his prosopological method should alert us to a level of interest in reading the Scriptures through this lens that would naturally entail a more thorough, albeit not always clear and consistent, application of this method to quotations that were pulled from various *testimonia* collections.

Justin's discussion of Old Testament theophanies in *Dial.* 56–60 is a particularly instructive case study. Martin Albl describes how Justin made use of a *testimonia* collection comprising Old Testament quotations that speak of two "Lords" or two "Gods," including Gen 19:24, Ps 110:1, and Ps 45:6–7, all of which Justin cites at *Dial.* 56.12–14.[89] The

---

86. Skarsaune, *Proof from Prophecy*, 80–82, 158.
87. Skarsaune, *Proof from Prophecy*, 210, 227.
88. Cf. Skarsaune, *Proof from Prophecy*, 430.
89. Albl, *Scripture*, 205; cf. Skarsaune, *Proof from Prophecy*, 209. See also my comments on Heb 1:5–14 in the previous chapter of this book. On Gen 19:24, see further Trakatellis, *Pre-Existence*, 65; Skarsaune, *Proof from Prophecy*, 209n62.

fact that this collection includes both dialogical and non-dialogical texts shows that this collection was not assembled on the basis of examples of prosopological exegesis, but simply as verses that spoke of "two powers in heaven." Likely this *testimonia* collection functioned "to establish the divine or 'Lordly' status of the Son of God over against the status of angels."[90] Justin, however, focuses on the dialogical aspect of the passages, showing how in these verses from the Psalter "the Holy Spirit calls another God and Lord, besides the Father of all things and his Christ."[91] Justin, then, has reworked this "two powers" *testimonia* collection to fit his own objectives, which in this portion of the *Dialogue* primarily involved combating the Marcionite attempt to distinguish the true God from the lesser demiurge who created the world.[92] The prosopological interpretation of these verses, however, was more likely aimed at Justin's own Christian community, insofar as Justin was linking the Christians' possession of the Spirit and the giftings of the Spirit with the Spirit's teaching concerning the lordship and divinity of Christ.[93]

In sum, Skarsaune's analysis of Justin's approach to *testimonia* material is instructive for underscoring how Justin's approach to prosopological exegesis may have come about. Insofar as early Christians took over pre-existing Jewish testimony collections, Justin brought to its "climax" the "process of enriching the dossier of Christological proof-texts with more of the traditional Jewish testimonies."[94] Thus, to synthesize with our above observations, we may conclude that Justin adapted, expanded, and repurposed existing *testimonia* collections to generate examples of prosopological exegesis rather than drawing upon an earlier collection of texts that had been organized as the speech of either the Father or the Son. How, then, did Justin go about selecting the kinds of texts that could be interpreted prosopologically, particularly if they were not used by previous Christian authors? Answering this question requires us to consider Justin's understanding of the rule of faith (*regula fidei*).

---

90. Albl, *Scripture*, 206.
91. *Dial.* 56.15 (trans. Falls).
92. So Skarsaune, *Proof from Prophecy*, 210.
93. See further Hughes, *Trinitarian Testimony*, 68–79; cf. Lieu, *Marcion*, 24.
94. Skarsaune, *Proof from Prophecy*, 262.

Justin and the *Regula Fidei*

While the rule of faith as a formal concept is not introduced in extant literature until later in the second century, Justin nevertheless provides us a window into how earlier Christians sought to organize and express central christological beliefs. Several times in his writings, Justin inserts into his arguments something of a brief summary of core christological material that hits on many of the same themes in each instance. To give just one representative example of Justin's statement of this proto-creedal treatment of Christology, Justin writes,

> And when we say also that the Word, who is the First-begotten of God, was born for us without sexual union, Jesus Christ our teacher, and that He was crucified and died and rose again and ascended into heaven, we propound nothing new.[95]

From this and other passages in Justin, we see that the basic shape of his christological narrative is that God the Son pre-existed with the Father, became incarnate by the Virgin Mary as prophesied,[96] engaged in a ministry of teaching and healing,[97] was rejected, crucified, and killed, was dead but was resurrected and ascended into heaven, from whence he now reigns,[98] and will one day return as judge.[99]

This list is quite similar to the eight elements that characterized the early apostolic preaching as suggested by Matthew Bates;[100] the only two elements missing from Justin's formulations are Jesus' burial and his appearances to many after his resurrection, though both of these events are clearly implied from the other items he has listed. Still, if we simply stay with the elements that Justin explicitly articulates in these sections, we can map his proto-creedal formulation onto our above chart of instances of prosopological exegesis as follows:

---

95. *1 Apol.* 21.1 (trans. Barnard). For other, similar statements from Justin, see *1 Apol.* 31.7; 42.4; 46.5; *Dial.* 63.1; 85.2; 126.1. See further Bokedal, "Rule of Faith," 243.
96. Cf. *1 Apol.* 31.7; 46.5; *Dial.* 63.1; 85.2.
97. Cf. *1 Apol.* 31.7.
98. Cf. *1 Apol.* 42.4.
99. Cf. *Dial.* 126.1.
100. See again Bates, *Salvation*, 52.

	From the Father	From the Son	From the Spirit	Rule of Faith
Divine Pre-Existence	**Gen 1:26** **Gen 3:22** **Ps 2:7b** **Ps 110:3–4**	Ps 2:7a Prov 8:22–36	—	Pre-existed with the Father
Pre-Incarnate Ministry	—	Exod 3:5	—	—
—	—	—	—	Born of the Virgin Mary
—			—	Engaged in ministry
Crucifixion	—	**Ps 22:1–22** Isa 50:6–8	—	Rejected, crucified, and killed
Death and Resurrection	—	Ps 3:5	—	Resurrected from the dead
Ascension, Enthronement, and Reign	**Ps 2:7b–8** Ps 24:10? **Ps 110:1b–c** Isa 42:1–4 Isa 42:6–7 Isa 49:6 Isa 49:8	Isa 65:1–3	Ps 24:10? **Ps 45:6–7** Ps 110:1a	Ascended and reigns
—	—	—	—	Will return as judge

Interestingly, four of the five categories for which we identified examples of prosopological exegesis with respect to the Son are echoed in Justin's presentation of the rule of faith, with only the odd example of Exod 3:5, in which Jesus was said to have spoken out of the burning bush to Moses, corresponding to a category (pre-incarnate theophany) excluded from Justin's summary formulations. Looking at this from the other direction, we see that of the seven elements of Justin's emerging *regula fidei*, four correspond with categories for which we identified examples of relevant prosopological exegesis, with only the matters of Jesus' virgin birth, earthly ministry, and second coming absent from the passages interpreted prosopologically. There is, therefore, considerable overlap between the content of Justin's christological summary and the themes reflected in the instances of prosopological exegesis found in his writings. Still, one could imagine still closer alignment between these two threads of early Christology, a phenomenon which we will be keen to identify in subsequent chapters of this book.

Conclusion: Scripting the Son in Justin Martyr

In sum, Justin Martyr offers us an intriguing vantage point from which to view the development of Christology through the lens of prosopological exegesis. Here we see prosopological exegesis, developed out of his use of pre-existing *testimonia* collections, employed to advance a high Christology that captures the broad sweep of Christ's role in salvation history, starting with his generation before the creation of the world and proceeding through his enthronement and present reign. Justin's proto-creedal formulations provide some intriguing similarities to his emphases with respect to prosopological exegesis involving the Son, establishing a reference point as we proceed to consider the alignment of these phenomena in the writings of later Christian writers. It is with this in mind, then, that we turn to the next key figure in this particular story of doctrinal and exegetical development: Irenaeus of Lyons.

4

Irenaeus of Lyons

IRENAEUS OF LYONS (CA. 135–200), the famous defender of early Christian orthodoxy, is the next significant milestone in our story of christological development. As bishop of Lyons in what is now France, Irenaeus is best known to history as the author of *Against Heresies*, a compendious refutation of a range of teachings that scholars have traditionally, if imprecisely, referred to as Gnosticism.[1] These so-called gnostics, while likely much more diverse in reality than Irenaeus makes them out to be, seem to have largely shared belief in an expansive cosmology featuring a large number of Aeons, or emanations of the true deity. Irenaeus was familiar with Justin's writings if not actually himself a student of Justin,[2] providing us with a unique opportunity to analyze elements of continuity and discontinuity between how these two early Christian writers sought to use prosopological exegesis, in very different polemical contexts, in support of their search for dialogues involving Christ in the Old Testament.

This chapter will first survey how Irenaeus uses prosopological exegesis in his two extant works, *Demonstration of the Apostolic Preaching* and *Against Heresies*.[3] We will then consider how Irenaeus's reliance on

---

1. On Irenaeus's life and background, see further Minns, *Irenaeus*, 1–13; Lashier, *Irenaeus on the Trinity*, 18–41; on the subject of "Gnosticism," see further King, *What Is Gnosticism?* For an overview of the structure and rhetorical strategy of *Against Heresies*, see Behr, *Irenaeus*, 74–103; Moringiello, *Rhetoric of Faith*.

2. For various proposals on this matter, see Lashier, *Irenaeus on the Trinity*, 22–26; Slusser, "Irenaeus," 515–20.

3. This portion of the chapter builds on my initial analysis of some of these passages in Hughes, *Trinitarian Testimony*, 105–33.

Justin and his use of *testimonia* collections, in concert with his articulation of the *regula fidei*, helped shape Irenaeus's distinctive approach to finding the *vox Christi* in the Old Testament. Given the proximity of these works to one another (ca. 190),[4] this chapter will proceed thematically rather than by separately focusing on each work. As will be demonstrated, Irenaeus follows Justin in using prosopological exegesis to identify intra-divine dialogues in the Old Testament that buttress his christological claims, but he also demonstrates flexibility in using such interpretive readings to reflect the needs of his own anti-gnostic polemic in line with his defense of the rule of faith.

Prosopological Exegesis in the Writings of Irenaeus

In his *Demonstration of the Apostolic Preaching* (abbreviated according to the beginning of its Greek title, *Epideixis*), as he crafts an argument concerning how the Old Testament demonstrates the eternal existence of Christ, Irenaeus makes a direct statement of his approach to what scholars now call prosopological exegesis. As with Justin, Irenaeus's methodological introduction serves us as a starting point from which to analyze his use of this person-centered reading strategy. After quoting Ps 2:7–8, Ps 110:1, and Isa 45:1,[5] Irenaeus comments that because David never received any of what was promised in these dialogical passages, they must in fact be examples of the Father speaking to the Son. As Irenaeus therefore suggests:

> Since the same promise is made by both prophets [that is, David and Isaiah], namely that he would be king, so the words of God are addressed to one and the same, by this, I say, to Christ the Son of God. Since David says, *The Lord said to me* [Ps 2:7], it is necessary to say that since it is not David nor a certain other of the prophets who speaks from himself—for it is not a human being who speaks prophecies—but that the Spirit of God, forming and shaping himself like the persons [*personae*] that have been set forth, was speaking in the prophets, producing

---

4. For the scholarly view that the *Demonstration* was written between the composition of books 3 and 4 of *Against Heresies*, see Hill, *Lost Teaching*, 75–77; Behr, *Irenaeus*, 69. Books 1–3 of *Against Heresies* and the *Demonstration* are therefore dated to the time of Eleutherus (AD 178–189), and the final two books of *Against Heresies* are best dated around or soon after the accession of Victor (AD 189–198).

5. For Isa 45:1 Irenaeus reads "Lord" instead of "Cyrus," a difference of one *iota* in the Greek.

> speech sometimes from Christ and sometimes from the Father. Thus Christ suitably says through David that the Father himself speaks with him, and most reasonably he also says other things through the prophets concerning himself.[6]

Irenaeus then provides an additional example of the Son speaking and quoting the Father's words to him in Isa 49:5–6. What is particularly striking about this introduction to prosopological exegesis, here explicitly invoked with the language of "persons" (Greek *prosōpa*; Latin *personae*), is how similar it is to Justin's. Both Justin and Irenaeus argue that certain dialogical passages should be interpreted as words from the Father or the Son even when these divine persons are not explicitly in view in the original textual setting. Both describe a divine force at work beyond the human prophet in accomplishing this task.

There are, however, some subtle differences: for one thing, Irenaeus clarifies that it is the Holy Spirit, and not the Logos (as at *1 Apol.* 36.1–2), that is responsible for this work of inspiration. Another difference concerns the nature of the quotations themselves: Justin's examples in *1 Apol.* 36–45 included things like rebukes of Israel or prophecies concerning Jesus' passion, but Irenaeus's examples (Pss 2:7–8; 110:1; Isa 45:1; 49:5–6) are all instances of speech from one divine person to or concerning another divine person. This suggests that Irenaeus has further distinguished prosopological exegesis from mere prophecy or standard divine speech by (at least here) emphasizing examples of intra-divine dialogue. In so doing, Irenaeus elevates the contribution of prosopological exegesis to Christology by focusing more precisely on divine speech to, from, or about the Son; in this particular instance, Irenaeus's clear aim is to demonstrate the Son's pre-existence on account of the Father having spoken with him prior to the incarnation, if not in fact before the creation of the world.[7] This approach, as will be discussed further below, naturally follows from Irenaeus's primary intention of defending the *regula fidei* against the gnostic hermeneutic.

Irenaeus, unlike Justin, does not go on to provide specific sets of examples of prosopological speech from each divine person. But with this introduction in place, we can proceed to trace how Irenaeus employs prosopological exegesis from Father, Son, and Holy Spirit across all of his writings.

---

6. *Epid.* 49–50 (AT).
7. Cf. MacKenzie, *Demonstration*, 177.

From the Father

As Irenaeus explains in the above passage (*Epid.* 49), the Holy Spirit sometimes produces speech from the person of the Father. As in the case of Justin's writings, it requires a close reading of Irenaeus's work to identify those instances in which God the Father is speaking prosopologically in an Old Testament text. Those times when the Old Testament identifies "God" in a general sense as speaking to human beings or through the prophets without distinguishing among divine persons are, therefore, not to be considered examples of prosopological exegesis. Likewise, those quotations that Irenaeus likely intends for us to read as dialogue involving divine persons but which are not clearly marked as such, being simply cast as the words of the human prophet, are set aside for the purposes of this study.[8] Having established these parameters, a search of the Irenaean corpus for examples of speech from God the Father returns an intriguing result: every instance of the Father's prosopological speech consists of instructions to the Son (and, occasionally, also the Spirit). These instructions cluster around two themes: the Son's divine pre-existence and the Son's present reign over the gentiles.

Divine Pre-Existence

Irenaeus's favorite verse for demonstrating the Son's pre-existence through the Father's prosopological speech is Gen 1:26. This contrasts with Justin, whose clear preference for Ps 110:3–4 overshadowed his less frequent appeals to Gen 1:26. Irenaeus in fact never interprets Ps 110:3–4 as the words of the Father to the Son anywhere in his corpus. We can locate Irenaeus's frequent appeal to the Father's instructions to the Son (and, as we will see, at times also to the Spirit) to make human beings "in our image" (Gen 1:26) in the context of his polemic against the gnostics and their various cosmogonies. To take just one example from his writings:

> And so the angels did not create or fashion us; nor could the angels have made an image of God; nor could anyone else besides the Word of God; nor could a Power far distant from the Father of all things. Really, God had no need of these things to make the things that he had decreed beforehand with himself, as if he did not have his hands. Surely, the Word and the Wisdom, the Son and the Spirit, were always present with him. Through

---

8. See, e.g., *Haer.* 3.21.7; 4.14.1; 5.12.2; *Epid.* 43; 48; 62; 68; 85.

> these and in these he created all things freely and autonomously. It was these he addressed when he said, *Let us make man to our image and likeness* [Gen 1:26]. He himself took from himself the substance of the creatures, and the exemplar of the things made, and the shape of the ornaments in the world.[9]

Irenaeus is therefore explicitly contrasting the gnostic view of creation as having been carried out by angels or lesser divine beings with his understanding of creation taking place by God the Father through the two "hands" of God: the Son and the Holy Spirit. Interestingly, three out of the five times Irenaeus quotes and prosopologically interprets Gen 1:26, he specifies that God the Father spoke these words to both the Son and the Spirit.[10] This notion of Son and Spirit as the "two hands of God," which he likely adopted from Theophilus of Antioch, has received a good bit of scholarly attention as it is relatively rare among patristic writers, who otherwise see these words as directed exclusively to the Son.[11]

Irenaeus is here asserting, against the gnostics, that creation was a unified action of the Father, the Son, and the Holy Spirit. As for how this instance of prosopological exegesis impacts Christology (and, indeed, pneumatology), the implication is that the Son (and, also, the Holy Spirit) pre-existed before the creation of the world, with the theodramatic setting of this divine conversation occurring before the carrying out of the Father's command to fashion human beings in God's own likeness. Indeed, as Irenaeus hastens to point out, the Son and the Spirit "were always present" with the Father, just as the hands of a person are never separated from the rest of the human body. The case for the Son's divine pre-existence is thereby advanced.

This example is illuminating for our understanding of Irenaeus's exegetical method as it concerns prosopological exegesis and its relevance for the development of Christology. Irenaeus clearly draws on Justin Martyr for his understanding of prosopological exegesis writ large, and yet he feels the freedom to focus on his own emphases in order to buttress his argument in his unique polemical context (in this case, against the gnostic theology of creation). This shows both a

---

9. *Haer.* 4.20.1 (trans. Unger).

10. See also *Haer.* 4.pref.4; 5.1.3. This speech is interpreted as directed only to the Son at *Haer.* 5.15.4 and *Epid.* 55.

11. See further Briggman, *Irenaeus of Lyons*, 104–26. On Irenaeus's use of Gen 1:26 more broadly, see Presley, *Intertextual Reception*, 135–204; Lashier, *Irenaeus on the Trinity*, 170–71, 181–83.

fundamental continuity in the use and purpose of prosopological exegesis while allowing for flexibility in the application of the method, making it a particularly potent tool for the early church fathers.

Present Reign

Again following Justin, Irenaeus sets out examples of the prosopological speech of the Father to the Son concerning the Son's reign over the nations. Irenaeus is less concerned than Justin with Christ having made a new covenant with the gentiles, but nevertheless emphasizes that Christ has been given authority to rule over all the nations and presently reigns as Lord and King.[12]

Key to Justin's understanding of the Father instructing the Son concerning his present reign was his interpretation of Isaiah; Irenaeus picks up and expands upon these references in his own writings. Like Justin, Irenaeus identifies Isa 42:1–4 as the words of God concerning Christ,[13] setting up subsequent chapters of Isaiah as ripe for prosopological exegesis. Thus, Irenaeus reads Isa 49:6 as the words of the Father to the Son:

> *It will be a great thing for you to be called my servant, to establish the tribes of Jacob and to turn back the dispersion of Israel; and I have placed you to be a light for the gentiles, that you may be for salvation unto the ends of the earth* [Isa 49:6].[14]

For Irenaeus, this text proves, among other things, that Christ is Lord and King, though he does not speculate on the theodramatic setting of each aspect of this speech.[15]

Besides Isaiah, Justin drew support for this theme from Psalm 2. Irenaeus likewise quotes from this psalm as an example of the prosopological speech of the Father to the Son. As part of his argument concerning how Christ recapitulates the whole divine economy, Irenaeus asserts a parallel between the twelve tribes of Israel and the "twelve-pillared foundation" of Christ's church; just as Jacob received an inheritance of

---

12. While Irenaeus affirms a future, earthly kingdom, he does not deny Christ's present spiritual rule (*Haer.* 3.12.9). On Irenaeus's chiliasm, see further Osborn, *Irenaeus of Lyons*, 138–40; Hill, *Regnum Caelorum*, 11–20.

13. *Haer.* 3.11.6.

14. *Epid.* 50 (AT).

15. *Epid.* 51–52. See also Irenaeus's citation of Isa 45:1 at *Epid.* 49. On the key passage of *Epid.* 50–51, see further below on prosopological exegesis from the Son.

sheep of various colors, so Christ's inheritance is humankind, people from all nations: "So the Father promised [Christ], saying, *Ask of me and I will make the nations your inheritance, and the ends of the earth your heritage* [Ps 2:8]."[16] The theodramatic setting is the time of Christ's ascension, as he is enthroned as King over all the earth and finally receives his inheritance. That this refers to Christ's present reign is confirmed by how Irenaeus interprets Ps 2:7–8 elsewhere, as Irenaeus states that these verses show that Christ "is before all, and that He rules over the nations, and judges all men and the kings who now hate Him and persecute His name," and that Christ "both is called and indeed is the Son of God and King of the nations."[17]

Finally, Irenaeus uses Psalm 110 to advance his understanding of the Son's present rule. As noted previously, Justin's presumed theodramatic setting for this psalm was somewhat unclear, though on the whole it appears that he used this text more to assert the Son's divine pre-existence than to explain the Son's present rule. Irenaeus, however, quotes it to emphasize the Son's present reign over the nations. For example, in an important passage on how Christ is truly called both God and Lord in the Scriptures, Irenaeus writes:

> Therefore, neither the Lord nor the Holy Spirit nor the apostles would have ever definitely and absolutely named "God" one who is not God, unless he was truly God; nor would they have ever from their own person [*ex sua persona*] called anyone "Lord" except God the Father, who has dominion over all things, and his Son, who received from his Father lordship over all creation, as this passage pronounces: *The Lord said to my Lord: Sit at my right hand, until I make your enemies your footstool for your feet* [Ps 110:1]. Indeed this shows the Father speaking to the Son, who both gave to him the inheritance of the gentiles and subjected all enemies to him.[18]

Here the Latin word *persona* indicates that Irenaeus's original Greek almost certainly read *prosōpon*, marking this as an explicit appeal to prosopological exegesis.[19] Irenaeus's appeal to Ps 110:1 emphasizes Christ receiving his throne, and therefore his inheritance, from the

16. *Haer.* 4.21.3 (trans. Unger).
17. *Epid.* 48–49 (trans. Behr).
18. *Haer.* 3.6.1 (AT).
19. Irenaeus is almost certainly dependent upon Justin at this point; see further Hughes, *Trinitarian Testimony*, 102–5.

Father. Following what was said above about Irenaeus's interpretation of Ps 2:7–8, the most likely theodramatic setting for Ps 110:1 is the Son's present reign. Irenaeus explains his reading when he cites this verse elsewhere, commenting that Mark 16:19, describing Jesus' ascension, "confirms what the prophet has said" in Ps 110:1.[20] Thus Irenaeus's interpretation of Ps 2:7–8 is of one piece with his interpretation of Ps 110:1 in its description of Christ's present reign; the theodramatic moment of both texts is after Christ's ascension.[21]

From the Son

Irenaeus presents a rich panoply of quotations that he interprets prosopologically as the words of the Son. By way of a general comparison with Justin, Irenaeus places less emphasis on the Son's pre-existence through the Son's own words. Whereas Justin placed Prov 8:22–36 on the lips of the Son as a key proof for this theme, Irenaeus does not follow suit; moreover, as discussed above, Irenaeus uses Psalm 2 for the purposes of explaining the Son's present rule more than for supporting belief in the Son's pre-existence. Instead, Irenaeus tends to use prosopological exegesis from the person of the Son to focus on the Son's pre-incarnate theophanic ministry, incarnate ministry, crucifixion, and present reign over the nations.

Irenaeus does, quite helpfully, give us one sustained example of prosopological exegesis at *Epid.* 50–51 from the person of the Son that, at least in Irenaeus's interpretation, is comprehensive in its attention to many of these themes. Given its significance, it is worth setting out this passage in full:

---

20. *Haer.* 3.10.6 (trans. Unger). Incidentally, this is an important early witness to the so-called "longer ending" of Mark.

21. See also Irenaeus's appeal to this verse at *Haer.* 2.28.7; *Epid.* 48. While not explicitly invoking prosopological exegesis, Irenaeus's interpretation of Ps 110:1 at *Epid.* 85 is interesting as he appears to focus more on a *future* time when all enemies will be subjected to Christ (that is, the final judgment), which contrasts with the *present* subjection of Christ's enemies in passages such as *Haer.* 3.6.1; 3.10.6. Perhaps Irenaeus has 1 Cor 15:24–28 in mind, which has Christ presently possessing a kingdom but the final subjection of all things, such as death, is deferred until the end. On this passage in Paul, Fee writes, "Christ's rule, which by implication began with his resurrection (or subsequent ascension), *must continue* until Ps 110:1 is fulfilled" (*First Epistle to the Corinthians*, 755, italics original).

> So, in a very fitting manner Christ says, by David, that the Father Himself speaks with Him, and most properly does He say still other things concerning Himself through the prophets, just as, amongst others, by Isaias, in this way, *And now thus says the Lord, who fashioned me from the womb to be His servant, to gather Jacob and to gather Israel to Him; and I shall be glorified before the Lord, and my God will be a strength to me; and He said: It will be a great thing for you to be called my servant, to establish the tribes of Jacob and to turn back the dispersed of Israel. I have placed you as a light to the nations, that you may be for salvation unto the ends of the earth* [Isa 49:5–6].
>
> For here, firstly, from that text is that the Son of God pre-existed, that the Father spoke with Him, and caused Him to be revealed to men before His birth; and then, that it was necessary for Him to be begotten, a man amongst men; and that the same God Himself fashions Him from the womb, that is, that He would be born of the Spirit of God; and that He is Lord of all men, and Saviour of those who believe in Him, Jews or others, for the Jewish people are called "Israel" in the Hebrew language, from the patriarch Jacob, who was the first to be called "Israel," and he calls all men "the nations"; and that the Son calls Himself the servant of the Father, because of His obedience to the Father, for also among men every son is a servant of his father.[22]

This passage is particularly revealing for our purposes. *Epideixis* 50 begins by looking back to Ps 2:7–8, quoted in *Epid.* 49, as an example of Christ reporting the Father's speech to himself at an earlier time.[23] The fact that Irenaeus picks up on the change in speakers in Ps 110:1 and Ps 2:7 demonstrates his careful attention to these more subtle features of Old Testament dialogical passages as part of his person-centered reading strategy.

Irenaeus then introduces Isa 49:5–6 in *Epid.* 50 as a further example of the Son speaking through the prophets before then quoting the words of the Father to him. From these two verses, Irenaeus identifies a basic christological narrative, which he unpacks in *Epid.* 51. This interpretation includes the following elements of the Son's work in salvation history:

---

22. *Epid.* 50–51 (trans. Behr).

23. Psalm 110:1 and Isa 45:1 may both also be in view, but the only quotation that precisely fits the description of Christ, by David, telling of how the Father speaks concerning him is Ps 2:7–8.

The Son of God
1. pre-existed and had pre-existent conversations with the Father,
2. was revealed to men before his incarnation,
3. became incarnate as a man, and
4. is Lord and Savior of all nations.

Irenaeus does not, however, explicitly link his commentary to specific phrases in these verses. We can, however, reconstruct most of Irenaeus's logic. In his reading of Isa 49:6, Irenaeus finds the dialogical character of the text to be determinative: these words are to be understood as spoken by the Father to the Son before the incarnation (as necessitated by Irenaeus's placement of "the Father spoke with him" before the second point), words that are now being quoted by the Son. The existence of this first point logically requires the existence of the third point, even if the precise textual correspondences (presumably centered on the Father's "fashioning" of the Son "from the womb") are loose, as indicated by Irenaeus not citing particular phrases in the text in the first half of *Epid.* 51. By contrast, the fourth point is clearly the main thrust of Isa 49:6, in which the Son is quoting the words of the Father to him; Irenaeus references "Israel" and "the nations" from that verse in his interpretation in the second half of *Epid.* 51.

This leaves the second point, Christ having been revealed to men before his incarnation, as the most tenuous connection to the actual text of Isa 49:5–6. Perhaps the simplest solution is to see the prophets' announcement of Christ in texts such as this as what Irenaeus means by Christ being "revealed" to men prior to his incarnation. But a more thorough examination of how Irenaeus finds Christ in the Old Testament across all of his writings suggests a still further possibility: that Christ's pre-incarnate revelation came through a series of theophanies recorded in the Old Testament, a theme that will be explored in more detail below. Let us now consider how these points correspond to how Irenaeus uses prosopological exegesis from the person of the Son elsewhere in his writings.

Divine Pre-Existence

Apart from Isa 49:5–6, Irenaeus does not use prosopological exegesis to place much emphasis on the Son's pre-existent conversations with the Father. It is possible that the Son's words in Ps 2:7 and Ps 110:1, which report the Father's words to the Son, could be further examples of pre-existent divine dialogue, but as observed above, Irenaeus identifies the Son taking his seat at the right hand of the Father as the primary theodramatic moment for at least Ps 110:1. Justin's key text for prosopological speech from the person of the Son proving his pre-existence, Prov 8:22–36, is instead interpreted by Irenaeus as the words of the Holy Spirit. Indeed, in contrast to the majority of Christian interpreters both before and after him, Irenaeus took the character of Wisdom to refer not to Christ but to the Holy Spirit.[24] When compared with Irenaeus's interest in these other categories of prosopological exegesis from the Son, therefore, the theme of divine pre-existence gets relatively short shrift.

Pre-Incarnate Ministry

Where Irenaeus does place a surprising amount of emphasis, then, is on the Son's pre-incarnate theophanic ministry. Likely building on New Testament texts such as 1 Cor 10:4 and Jude 5, Justin had placed the words spoken to Moses from the burning bush on the lips of the pre-incarnate Christ.[25] Justin, however, did not develop this emphasis on Old Testament theophanies as a source for christological reflection to the extent that Irenaeus does. Indeed, Irenaeus's first instinct in interpreting any Old Testament theophany is to identify the pre-incarnate Christ as the divine person prophetically (though not, as Justin appears to have believed, physically) interacting with human beings in these accounts.[26]

Having identified the pre-existent Son as the recipient of divine speech and an agent of creation in Genesis 1, Irenaeus next finds the pre-incarnate Christ in a theophany in Genesis 3. As Irenaeus writes in a comment on the story of Jesus healing a man born blind (John 9:1–12):

> No, the same one [the Word] who in the beginning fashioned Adam and to whom the Father said, *Let us make man after our image and likeness* [Gen 1:26], refashioned the sight for the

---

24. See, e.g., *Haer.* 4.20.3; see further Briggman, *Irenaeus of Lyons*, 126–36; Lashier, *Irenaeus on the Trinity*, 172–73. On the relevance of Proverbs 8 to early christological controversies more generally, see Treier, *Proverbs and Ecclesiastes*, 49–57.

25. See again 1 *Apol.* 62.3.

26. On Irenaeus's christological interpretation of the Old Testament theophanies, see further Lashier, *Irenaeus on the Trinity*, 125–30. For a helpful analysis of such instances through the framework of "reciprocal immanence," see Briggman, *God and Christ*, 107–15.

blind man, who descended from Adam, when in the last times he manifested himself to men. For this reason Scripture points out what would happen in the future, when Adam had hidden himself because of the disobedience. It says that the Lord came, toward evening, and called out to him, and said, *Where are you?* [Gen 3:9]. This means that in the last times the same Word came to call man, thereby he reminded him of his deeds, in which he was living when he hid himself from God.[27]

Here Irenaeus directly connects Gen 1:26 with the creation of Adam by the Son (and not the Father, contra Michelangelo) and then identifies the Son as the divine person who walked in the garden (Gen 3:8) and called out to Adam (Gen 3:9). This same Son would later speak with Abraham, condemn Sodom and Gomorrah, and appear to Jacob in a dream, albeit without Irenaeus quoting any dialogue he attributes to the Son.[28]

The primary example of the Son speaking as part of a theophany, however, is the burning bush episode with Moses. By frequency, this is Irenaeus's favorite Old Testament passage to place on the lips of the Son; near the very beginning of his *Demonstration*, Irenaeus announces that "the Word says to Moses, *I Am HE-WHO-IS* [Exod 3:14]."[29] Indeed, the entirety of this speech is assigned to the Son. When Irenaeus quotes Exod 3:7–8, he ascribes these words to the pre-incarnate Son: "So the Word of God was accustomed from the beginning to ascend and descend for the sake of the salvation of those who were ill."[30] Likewise, Irenaeus identifies "the Word" as the speaker to Moses from the burning bush: "This is what the Word said to Moses from the bush: *But I know that Pharaoh the King of Egypt will not let you go unless compelled by a mighty hand* [Exod 3:19]."[31]

Perhaps unsurprisingly, then, Irenaeus extends this line of interpretation to the theophany at Mt. Sinai later in Exodus. The instructions for how to build the tabernacle and its furniture, for instance, are described as the speech of "the Word" to Moses.[32] Similarly, it was "the Word" who instructed Moses in response to his desire to see God's

---

27. *Haer.* 5.15.4 (trans. Unger); cf. *Epid.* 12.
28. See, e.g., *Haer.* 3.6.1; *Epid.* 24; 44–45.
29. *Epid.* 2 (trans. Behr). See further MacKenzie, *Demonstration*, 53.
30. *Haer.* 4.12.4 (trans. Unger); cf. *Epid.* 46.
31. *Haer.* 4.29.2 (trans. Unger).; cf. *Haer.* 3.6.2; 4.20.9. "The Word" is translating the Greek term "Logos," for which see Lashier, *Irenaeus on the Trinity*, 117–47.
32. *Epid.* 9; cf. Exod 25:40.

glory.³³ The theophanies in Genesis and Exodus, therefore, are prime sources for Irenaeus to find not just types but also examples of speech from the pre-incarnate Christ.

This raises the question, though, of why Irenaeus was so insistent on identifying Christ as the subject of these theophanies. At some level, Irenaeus must have been following Justin in distinguishing between two divine persons: God the Father, "who is not seen by the world," and God the Son, who is at times localized in a particular time and space, "who was always with mankind."³⁴ Irenaeus also, however, uses the theophanies to emphasize their prophetic character, claiming that in so interacting with human beings even before his incarnation, the Son was "demonstrating in advance, by types, things to come."³⁵ As Jackson Lashier points out, the logic here is likely less about the transcendence of the Father as contrasted with the mediating ability of the Logos; instead,

> the Logos is the subject of the theophanies because he is the same subject who is incarnated in Jesus Christ and the incarnation is a continuation of the work of revelation that started in the beginning of the economy—it is always the work of the Logos/Son, no matter the time of the economy, to reveal God/Father.³⁶

After all, in a polemical context in which the gnostics had stressed the utter transcendence of God, such that all divine activity in this world is actually the work of lesser, mediating beings, Irenaeus was concerned not to present the Son as an inferior power to the Father. Thus Irenaeus argues, "For man, of himself, cannot see God. But when he wills, he can be seen by men; namely, by whom he wills, when he wills, and in what manner he wills, because God is all-powerful."³⁷ The Son mediates, but is not inferior to, the Father.

The divine theophanies do not include any examples of intra-divine dialogue, but they nevertheless appear to be an important form of prosopological exegesis for Irenaeus. Why this particular theme did not ultimately find its way into the standard christological summaries of the early church is a topic we will consider in more detail below.

---

33. *Haer.* 4.20.9; cf. Exod 33:20–22. See further Lashier, *Irenaeus on the Trinity*, 127.
34. *Epid.* 45 (trans. Behr).
35. *Epid.* 46 (trans. Behr).
36. Lashier, *Irenaeus on the Trinity*, 130.
37. *Haer.* 4.20.5 (trans. Unger).

Incarnate Ministry

Irenaeus twice uses prosopological exegesis from the person of the Son to speak directly about Christ's incarnate, earthly ministry prior to his crucifixion. This category does not appear in Justin's writings, suggesting it is an innovation by Irenaeus, though the relatively minor emphasis placed on this theme indicates its relative lack of significance for Irenaeus.

First, in the context of describing the incarnation, Irenaeus makes the following comment about why Jesus is rightly called Christ:

> He was anointed by the Spirit of God His Father, as He Himself says of Himself, by Isaias, *The Spirit of the Lord is upon me, because He has anointed me, to bring good tidings to the poor* [Isa 61:1]. And he is called "Saviour," from this, that He was the cause of salvation to those who at that time were freed by Him from all kinds of sickness and from death.[38]

Of course, Jesus himself quotes these words in his sermon at Nazareth (Luke 4:18), but Irenaeus chooses not to cite the words of Jesus from the Gospel but rather describes them as spoken by the Son through the prophet Isaiah. The implication is that the Father's anointing of Christ was always the plan for the Son's incarnate ministry, such that the Son could speak of this anointing as a present reality even from the temporal perspective of Isaiah.[39] As Irenaeus explains elsewhere, these words of the Son through Isaiah reveal God as Trinity: there is "the Father who anoints, and the Son who is anointed, and the Ointment, which is the Spirit."[40]

The second instance of this theme comes in the context of an unusual reading of the account of Lot and his daughters in Gen 19:30–38 as a type of the incarnation of Christ.[41] In his interpretation of this passage, Irenaeus points to the incarnate ministry of Christ as the time when he poured out the Holy Spirit for the forgiveness of sins. With Matt 11:19 as his central text, Irenaeus looks back to the Old Testament for the *vox Christi* speaking prophetically concerning his incarnation. Thus, Irenaeus identifies Christ as saying, "While associating with us in this life," that "*I*

---

38. *Epid.* 53 (trans. Behr).

39. See Irenaeus's citation of Isa 61:1 at *Haer.* 3.9.3.

40. *Haer.* 3.18.3 (trans. Unger). Lashier observes that "despite the functional distinctions necessitated in the act of anointing, Irenaeus's metaphor implies a prior unity" (*Irenaeus on the Trinity*, 219).

41. *Haer.* 4.31.1.

lay down and have taken a sleep [Ps 3:5]," and, "*And my sleep was pleasant to me* [Jer 31:26]."[42] Here Irenaeus helpfully clarifies that the theodramatic setting of these words that the Son speaks in the Psalter and Jeremiah is "in this life," that is, at the time of Christ's incarnate ministry.

While Irenaeus, like other early Christian writers, is generally content to quote prophecies that speak of Christ's incarnate ministry prior to his passion, these two examples of prosopological exegesis in support of this theme demonstrate the continued flexibility of this person-centered reading strategy in connecting the Old Testament to the words of Christ.

Crucifixion

Moving ahead to the climax of Christ's incarnate ministry, his crucifixion, Irenaeus returns to familiar passages cited by Justin. While this point was not explicitly stated in Irenaeus's interpretation of Isa 49:5–6, Jesus' death, resurrection, and ascension are of course the key points that drive the Christ-narrative forward.

Like Justin, Irenaeus finds Psalm 22 to be a key text for prophesying Christ's crucifixion in the Old Testament. For example, Irenaeus quotes portions of Ps 22:14–20 as referring to various aspects of the crucifixion account.[43] What is left unclear, however, is the extent to which we should be confident that Irenaeus is formally marking this as prosopological exegesis. Irenaeus introduces these quotations as the words of David, and though Behr's translation reads that in these quotations "He [that is, Christ] lucidly signifies His Crucifixion,"[44] it is unclear if the subject of the third-person singular verb should switch to refer to Christ rather than still refer to David. A prophetic-typological, rather than truly prosopological, reading may more likely be in view here.[45]

In contrast, Isaiah continues to be Irenaeus's preferred source for finding instances of prosopological exegesis from the person of the Son. As concerns Christ's crucifixion, Irenaeus writes:

> And this is why the Word says by the prophet Isaias, foretelling the things that would come to pass—for this reason were they prophets: because they related things to come—so, in this

---

42. *Haer.* 4.31.2 (trans. Unger).
43. *Epid.* 79–80.
44. *Epid.* 79 (trans. Behr).
45. See also the quotations of Ps 69:21 at *Epid.* 82 and of Hab 3:2 at *Haer.* 3.16.7.

way the Word says by him that, *I am not disobedient and do not contradict; I placed my back to the scourging, and my cheeks to the blows, and my face I did not turn from the shame of the spittle* [Isa 50:5–6]. So, by means of the obedience by which He obeyed unto death, hanging upon the tree, He undid the old disobedience occasioned by the tree.[46]

While the human prophet Isaiah is in view, the Son is clearly marked as the ultimate speaker of these words, identifying this as a clear instance of prosopological exegesis. Given the past tense, the theodramatic setting of the speech must be after the crucifixion; the addressee would appear to be the Father, given the focus on the Son's obedience, though this is not explicitly marked in the text.

Death and Resurrection

As with the crucifixion, Christ's resurrection from the dead was not explicitly mentioned in Irenaeus's interpretation of Isa 49:5–6, but it is a necessary precondition for Christ's reign over the nations. Irenaeus only uses prosopological exegesis from the Son on one occasion to comment on Christ's resurrection. This passage is worth quoting in detail for the further testimony it gives to Irenaeus's prosopological method:

> And again David speaks in this way about the death and resurrection of Christ, *I lay myself down and slept, I awoke, for the Lord has received me* [Ps 3:5]. David did not say this concerning himself, for he is not raised after dying, but the Spirit of Christ, who was also in the other prophets, now says by David concerning Him, *I lay myself down and slept, I awoke, for the Lord has received me* [Ps 3:5]—he calls death "sleep," because He arose.[47]

As noted above, Irenaeus elsewhere uses prosopological interpretation to identify Ps 3:5a as the words of Christ concerning his incarnation (with "sleep" referring to physical rest);[48] in this instance he uses the full verse as an example of Christ speaking concerning his resurrection from the dead (with "sleep" referring to physical death). Here Irenaeus

---

46. *Epid.* 34 (trans. Behr); cf. *Epid.* 68, where a version of Ps 73:14 is also quoted and interpreted prosopologically along similar lines. The citation of Isa 57:1 at *Haer.* 4.34.4 may also contribute to this theme, though it is not, at least as an isolated verse apart from its broader context, a dialogical passage.

47. *Epid.* 73 (trans. Behr).

48. See *Haer.* 4.31.2.

clearly contrasts David as the earthly prophet with Christ as the ultimate speaker to whom the speech ultimately refers. Though Irenaeus does not provide any hints as to the theodramatic setting of this quotation, Christ appears to be looking back on his death and resurrection after those events, with the Father the most likely audience for the Son's speech, although this is again not indicated explicitly in the text.

Present Reign

Just as Irenaeus identified many examples of the Father's prosopological speech with reference to the Son's present reign, so too Irenaeus finds several instances of Old Testament dialogue that he interprets as the Son's own speech about his present rule over the nations. As noted above, Irenaeus has Christ reporting the Father's speech to him concerning his reign in Ps 2:7b–8 and Isa 49:6.[49]

One important consequence of Christ's present reign that Irenaeus uses prosopological exegesis to highlight is the filial adoption of believers. The Son, Irenaeus writes, is God "of those to whom he says, *I have said: You are gods and all sons of the Most High* [Ps 82:6]."[50] As Irenaeus remarks elsewhere when he later quotes this verse, in this passage the Son is "speaking of his gift of grace" to those who have "received the gift of adoption."[51] Here Christ directly addresses believers in this time of his present reign, reassuring them of how he has given them imperishability and immortality. As Irenaeus continues, Christ also addresses unbelievers, those who reject his reign, in the present time. Thus, "to those who have not received the gift of adoption, but who despise the incarnation of the pure generation of the Word of God," Christ speaks the words of Ps 82:7: "*Nevertheless, you shall die like men.*"[52]

Christ's present reign is also likely alluded to when Irenaeus writes, "And through Solomon he [that is, Christ] says, *By me kings reign and the rulers decree what is just; by me princes are exalted, and by me the nobles govern the earth* [Prov 8:15–16]."[53] This is an unusual example insofar as Irenaeus consistently identifies the Holy Spirit, and the not the Son, as the

49. *Epid.* 49–50.
50. *Haer.* 3.6.1 (AT).
51. *Haer.* 3.19.1 (trans. Unger). On this passage, see further Lashier, *Irenaeus on the Trinity*, 75.
52. *Haer.* 3.19.1 (trans. Unger).
53. *Haer.* 5.24.1 (trans. Unger).

speaker of Prov 8:22–36.[54] While this verse is an understandable one to place on the lips of the Son concerning his present rule over the nations, one wonders if Irenaeus was sufficiently attentive to his pattern of identifying Wisdom with the Holy Spirit elsewhere. In any event, the theodramatic setting is after the Son's ascension, with no addressee specified.

Finally, Irenaeus, in a catena of Scriptures that speak of a second "Lord" or "God" besides the Father, describes the Son as the one "who came to men by a manifestation of Himself. He it is who said, *I have shown myself to those who did not seek for me* [Isa 65:1]."[55] The emphasis here is on the gentiles having been incorporated by Christ into his church.[56] The theodramatic setting is again after the Son's ascension, with Irenaeus again neglecting to identify an addressee for this speech. Irenaeus thereby uses prosopological exegesis to demonstrate that Christ is King over all the earth.

From the Spirit

Irenaeus follows Justin in identifying the Holy Spirit as being able to speak from his own person according to the principles of prosopological exegesis. This is most clearly seen in *Haer.* 3.6.1, which was discussed above but is worthy of further study to understand how Irenaeus understood the (at least theodramatic) personhood of the Holy Spirit:

> Therefore, neither the Lord nor the Holy Spirit nor the apostles would have ever definitely and absolutely named "God" one who is not God, unless he was truly God; nor would they have ever from their own person [*ex sua persona*] called anyone "Lord" except God the Father, who has dominion over all things, and his Son, who received from his Father lordship over all creation, as this passage pronounces: *The Lord said to my Lord: Sit at my right hand, until I make your enemies your footstool for your feet* [Ps 110:1]. Indeed this shows the Father speaking to the Son, who both gave to him the inheritance of the gentiles and subjected all enemies to him.[57]

The Spirit is introduced at the beginning of the passage as a potential speaking person in his own right, which then sets the stage for Irenaeus's

54. For an attempt to explain this oddity, see Lashier, *Irenaeus on the Trinity*, 172n83.
55. *Haer.* 3.6.1 (trans. Unger).
56. Cf. the interpretation of Isa 65:1 at *Epid.* 92.
57. *Haer.* 3.6.1 (AT).

prosopological interpretation, which understands the Holy Spirit to be recording the words of the Father ("the Lord") to the Son ("my Lord"). Like Justin, Irenaeus reads Ps 110:1 as an example of the Spirit testifying to the divinity and the lordship of the Father and the Son, though Irenaeus has removed any mention of David as the human author of Ps 110:1, placing further emphasis on the theodramatic, and not prophetic, setting of the text. The flexibility of prosopological exegesis can again be observed; while both Justin and Irenaeus interpret this verse prosopologically, Justin employs it as evidence of there being multiple divine persons, while Irenaeus instead includes it to buttress his claims regarding the unity of God. The theodramatic setting is clearly indicated as after Christ's ascension to the right hand of the Father, who has given the Son the inheritance of the gentiles and placed all enemies beneath his feet.

Irenaeus continues to follow Justin insofar as he quotes Gen 19:24 and Ps 45:6–7 in this passage. With respect to the latter, Irenaeus writes that in the words of Ps 45:6–7 we discover that "the Spirit has designated both of them with the name of 'God'—the Son who is anointed and the Father who anoints."[58] In sum, therefore, Irenaeus, like Justin, presents the Holy Spirit as speaking from his own person in order to testify to the divinity and lordship of the Father and the Son.[59] The theodramatic setting is also in the time of Christ's present reign, for the Son has already been given his eternal throne.

Summary

Irenaeus provides evidence that Justin's quest to identify within the Old Testament examples of speech from various divine persons continued to evolve even as it largely followed the patterns of Justin's initial work. While Justin may have been the first to explicitly describe his prosopological approach to biblical interpretation, Irenaeus demonstrates the flexibility of this mode of exegesis as he uses many of the same texts Justin had used in different polemical contexts. For Irenaeus, the threat posed by Gnosticism could be responded to, at least in part, from the Old Testament itself, with instances of prosopological exegesis continuing to contribute to an orthodox understanding of the person and work of Christ. In concluding this section, we can briefly summarize Irenaeus's

58. *Haer.* 3.6.1 (AT).

59. See further Hughes, *Trinitarian Testimony*, 110–14; *How the Spirit Became God*, 66–68.

prosopological readings in a table that sets out all the instances in which Irenaeus proposes a prosopological reading of Old Testament dialogical passages that involve speech to, from, or about the Son. As before, verses in bold reflect places where Irenaeus explicitly interprets these words as intra-divine dialogue:

	From the Father	From the Son	From the Spirit
Divine Pre-Existence	**Gen 1:26**	Isa 49:5	—
Pre-Incarnate Ministry	—	Gen 3:9 Exod 3:7–8, 14, 19 Exod 25:40 Exod 33:20–22	—
Incarnate Ministry	—	Ps 3:5a Isa 61:1 Jer 31:26	—
Crucifixion	—	Ps 73:14 Isa 50:5–6	—
Death and Resurrection	—	Ps 3:5	—
Ascension, Enthronement, and Reign	**Ps 2:7b–8** **Ps 110:1b–c** Isa 42:1–4 Isa 45:1 **Isa 49:6**	Ps 2:7a Ps 82:6–7 Prov 8:15–16 Isa 65:1	Ps 45:6–7 Ps 110:1a

While acknowledging the differences pointed out over the course of this chapter, the substantial similarities between this table and the table summarizing Justin's use of prosopological exegesis in the previous chapter of this book affirm the continued importance of this reading strategy for the fashioning of Christology. Again, multiple stages of salvation history are in view, reinforcing our claim that the basic outline of the Son's story —from his divine pre-existence to his present reign—are recorded in the Scriptures' account of divine speech involving Father, Son, and Holy Spirit. To further analyze and appreciate Irenaeus's distinctive contribution, we turn next to the subject of Irenaeus's use of *testimonia* collections and his presentation of the *regula fidei*.

92   SCRIPTING THE SON

Weaving the Threads

We have established that, like Justin before him, Irenaeus employed prosopological exegesis to develop and defend his understanding of the person and work of Christ according to the specific needs of his theological context. We can now consider the extent to which *testimonia* collections and the *regula fidei* played a meaningful role in shaping Irenaeus's particular approach to prosopological exegesis.

Irenaeus's Use of *Testimonia*

Scholars have demonstrated the high likelihood that Irenaeus, like Justin before him, made use of written *testimonia* collections.[60] What makes an analysis of Irenaeus's use of such collections challenging, however, is that it is sometimes unclear where Irenaeus is following Justin himself, Justin's reading of a *testimonia* source, or the *testimonia* source independently.[61] Undoubtedly, Irenaeus is dependent on Justin in key passages concerning prosopological exegesis, such as at *Haer.* 3.6.1, which exhibits specific lexical, thematic, and scriptural (Ps 110:1; Gen 19:24; Ps 45:6–7) parallels to Justin's *Dial.* 56.14, a passage that is almost certainly Justin's own creation.[62] What, though, of other examples of prosopological exegesis in Irenaeus's work? A careful examination of Irenaeus's likely sources can provide some illumination regarding his use of *testimonia* collections and how it relates to prosopological exegesis.

In his examination of Irenaeus's *Demonstration of the Apostolic Preaching*, Martin Albl observes that the second half of the work (42b–100) proceeds according to a creedal sequence. Albl concludes that Irenaeus drew on a "wealth of *testimonia* sources," including Justin, the Epistle of Barnabas, Justin's sources, and even some *testimonia* collections that he used independently.[63] In these chapters, Irenaeus only infrequently uses prosopological exegesis. A brief examination of a few

---

60. See, for example, the references provided in Albl, *Scripture*, 112–18.

61. Skarsaune (*Proof from Prophecy*, 435) indicates that Irenaeus often depends on Justin, but does at times make direct use of Justin's sources.

62. This section focuses on Christ as the subject of Old Testament theophanies, which scholars have argued is a prime example of Justin's own original exegesis, though it is likely that Ps 110:1, Ps 45:7, and Gen 19:24 had circulated together in a "two powers" collection of proof-texts. See further Hughes, *Trinitarian Testimony*, 66–67. Albl (*Scripture*, 205) also sees *Epid.* 47–49 as dependent upon *Dial.* 56–60.

63. Albl, *Scripture*, 116.

of these instances can help distinguish which of these sources Irenaeus favors for identifying examples of prosopological exegesis.

First, in *Epid.* 68, Irenaeus quotes several Old Testament prophecies about Jesus' suffering and death. He initially cites Isa 52:13—53:5, which is a non-dialogical prophecy, and then proceeds to prosopologically interpret a rendering of Ps 73:14 as well as Isa 50:6 as spoken from the person of the Son. Irenaeus then pivots to return to another non-dialogical passage (Lam 3:30) and then, in *Epid.* 69–70, resumes his quotation of Isaiah 53. Irenaeus is at minimum dependent to some extent on Justin; not only do Justin and Irenaeus both begin quoting at Isa 52:13 to prove that the Old Testament predicted Christ's suffering and death,[64] but both also interpret Isa 53:8 as speaking of Christ's ineffable origin.[65] What is more difficult to account for, though, is Irenaeus's insertion of Ps 73:14 and Isa 50:6. While Justin never quotes the former, he does quote the latter, like Irenaeus interpreting it prosopologically from the person of the Son in his overview of prosopological exegesis.[66] As argued above, Justin's "great insertion" describing his prosopological method is almost certainly his own creation, drawing texts from *testimonia* collections that were likely composed with other ends in mind. Irenaeus's collection of scriptural "proofs" related to Christ's suffering and death in *Epid.* 68 is thus probably Irenaeus's own expansion of Justin's work, though we cannot rule out Irenaeus using a *testimonia* collection as the source of these supplementary verses.

Second, in *Epid.* 73, Irenaeus places Ps 3:5 on the lips of the Son as a prosopological interpretation supporting his claim that Christ's resurrection was prophesied in the Old Testament. Justin likewise prosopologically interpreted Ps 3:5 from the person of the Son to refer to Christ's death and resurrection in the context of his excursus on prosopological exegesis.[67] Irenaeus, however, uses it in what was almost certainly its original context in a collection of proofs concerning Christ's resurrection from the dead, following quotations of Isa 57:1–2 and Ps 21:4 in *Epid.* 72. Again, Irenaeus follows Justin in being sensitive to the dialogical nature of passages such as this, and he thus inserts the obvious prosopological

---

64. See again *1 Apol.* 50–51.

65. *1 Apol.* 51.1; *Epid.* 70. See further Albl, *Scripture*, 117n101.

66. See again *1 Apol.* 38.3. Isaiah 50:6 also appears within a collection of scriptural proofs for Christ's suffering at *Barn.* 5.14, though the author does not make explicit a prosopological reading.

67. See again *1 Apol.* 38.4; *Dial.* 97.1.

interpretation. And yet Irenaeus also demonstrates flexibility with his use of his prosopological method; he elsewhere uses Ps 3:5 as an instance of prosopological speech from the Son on the subject of his incarnation, with "sleep" referring not to physical death but to mere physical rest.[68] Given the lack of a corresponding interpretation in Justin or other early Christian sources, it is likely that this is a case of a more novel use of this verse for Irenaeus's own prosopological purposes. In this case, writing against the gnostics, Irenaeus was likely motivated to defend the orthodox teaching that Christ's incarnation was the true union of God and humanity.[69] This demonstrates how Irenaeus was able to both mirror Justin's prosopological readings closely in some places and make new uses of this reading strategy for his own changing context.

Finally, in *Epid.* 92, Irenaeus quotes Isa 65:1. Like Justin, Irenaeus interprets these words prosopologically from the person of the Son concerning his present reign over the gentiles. As Skarsaune observes, this quotation follows the standard LXX text; Justin, however, in citing this passage twice, follows a non-standard text, presumably from a *testimonia* collection.[70] Irenaeus has therefore retained Justin's prosopological interpretation of Isa 65:1 even as he follows a different version of the text.[71] This fits a general pattern in which Justin's non-LXX quotations are either not found in Irenaeus or have been changed to conform to an LXX version of the text. Skarsaune suggests that examples such as this demonstrate that "this does not speak for an intensive use of Justin's sources."[72]

These examples suffice to demonstrate what should be self-evident in reading through our analysis of Irenaeus's use of prosopological exegesis as described in the first part of this chapter: that Irenaeus is primarily dependent on Justin for his approach to this person-centered reading strategy. It is possible that Irenaeus occasionally draws on existing *testimonia* collections, whether the same ones used by Justin or other ones altogether, but the balance of the evidence would seem to suggest that when it comes to prosopological exegesis, Irenaeus has adapted, expanded, and repurposed Justin's approach for his own polemical ends. There is no evidence for an underlying *testimonia* collection of passages

---

68. *Haer.* 4.31.2.

69. On this aspect of Irenaeus's anti-gnostic theology, see further Lashier, *Irenaeus on the Trinity*, 218.

70. *Dial.* 24; *1 Apol.* 49.

71. Skarsaune, *Proof from Prophecy*, 449.

72. Skarsaune, *Proof from Prophecy*, 435.

grouped by divine speaker. Again, however, the question remains: *why* was Irenaeus committed to this particular reading strategy? Here we turn to the topic of Irenaeus's relationship with the *regula fidei*.

Irenaeus and the *Regula Fidei*

By way of broad context, Irenaeus, in combating the gnostics, contrasts what he identifies as the orthodox *regula fidei* (which he generally prefers to call "the rule of truth" or simply "the rule") with the *regula* of the gnostics.[73] One of Irenaeus's main claims throughout his *Against Heresies* is that the Word of God is "always the self-same."[74] Thus, the gnostics cannot accept the Christ of the New Testament while rejecting the Old Testament when Christ himself claimed that he stood in continuity with the Old Testament, "fulfilling" the Law and the Prophets (Matt 5:17). In fact, Irenaeus insists, only a true spiritual disciple, who has received the one true Spirit of God, rightly understands the divine economy as expressed in the orthodox *regula fidei*.[75] This divine economy, which can be thought of as God's plan of salvation for the human race across each and every stage of God's relationship with humankind, is thus closely related to the rule of faith: while the *regula fidei* gives the essential content of the Christian narrative, the divine economy provides the manner or sequence in which that content is arranged, centering it on how Christ recapitulates, or "sums up," the entire divine economy.[76] Many of Irenaeus's extant works revolve around the defense of this understanding of the divine economy as the correct expression of the Christian rule of faith.

Crucially, Irenaeus's defense of the orthodox rule of faith against the gnostics hinged in part on the issue of prosopological exegesis. The gnostics, in fact, were notable for interpreting various portions of the Scriptures—including certain dialogical passages—through the lens of their own cosmology.[77] As Irenaeus himself points out, the Valentinians assigned biblical prophecies to various speakers: "One portion they hold

---

73. On Irenaeus's terminology, see further Ferguson, *Rule of Faith*, 17–19; for the function of Irenaeus's rule of faith within his theological framework more broadly, see Laing, *Irenaeus*, 117–29.

74. *Haer.* 4.35.2 (trans. Unger).

75. See further *Haer.* 4.33.1, 7; Hughes, *Trinitarian Testimony*, 137–45.

76. See further, e.g., *Haer.* 1.10.1; Osborn, *Irenaeus of Lyons*, 74–140; Behr, *Asceticism and Anthropology*, 34–85; Hughes, *Trinitarian Testimony*, 134–37.

77. See Presley, "Irenaeus," 167.

was spoken by the Mother, another by the offspring, and still another by Demiurge."[78] Thus, as Stephen Presley has observed, Irenaeus is not "as enamored" with prosopological exegesis as Justin and Tertullian were because of how it was abused by his gnostic opponents. Yet Irenaeus "recognizes that any prosopological methodology requires certain theological assumptions," leading him to "take a step back from the methodological discussions to defend the theological framework underlying the very procedure itself."[79] In other words, for Irenaeus, the theological confession of the Father and the Son as "God" and "Lord," as indicated by the *regula fidei*, in fact *precedes* any exegetical decisions to identify various speaking persons in Old Testament texts. Irenaeus thus shares with the gnostics an understanding that "the theological framework an exegete brings to the text naturally shapes the method of identifying speakers in a given text."[80] He differs from them, of course, in insisting that his theological framework, the rule of faith, is the true and accurate summary of the apostolic preaching, and as such Irenaeus gives a high degree of attention to describing this rule and supporting it with prosopological readings of the Old Testament.

Irenaeus, it has been noted, "gave the earliest full listings of the main items" of the *regula fidei*.[81] Irenaeus gives several summaries of the apostolic teaching; to take just one succinct example:

> They [that is, the many nations of the barbarians who believe in Christ] believe, namely, in one God the Creator of heaven and earth and of all things which are in them, and in Christ Jesus the Son of God, who, because of His surpassing love toward the creature He fashioned, accepted to be born of the Virgin. And so, by Himself He united man with God, suffered under Pontius Pilate, rose again, was taken up in glory and will come in glory as Savior of those who are saved and as Judge of those who are judged, hurling into eternal fire those who disfigure the truth and the condemners of His Father and of His own coming.[82]

As indicated by these and other descriptions of the *regula fidei*,[83] Irenaeus's basic christological narrative encompasses the following elements:

78. *Haer.* 1.7.3 (trans. Unger).
79. Presley, "Irenaeus," 166.
80. Presley, "Irenaeus," 171.
81. Ferguson, *Rule of Faith*, 3.
82. *Haer.* 3.4.2 (trans. Unger).
83. See also *Haer.* 1.10.1; 1.22.1; 5.20.1; *Epid.* 6. On Irenaeus's various statements of

the Son of God pre-existed with the Father, became incarnate for our salvation by being born of a virgin, engaged in an earthly ministry,[84] suffered and died, was resurrected, ascended into heaven to reign over the world,[85] and will come again to judge the world. This list closely matches the set of items in Justin Martyr's narrative; Irenaeus, however, elides from his summaries of the apostolic teaching details about Jesus' earthly ministry of teaching and healing that Justin sometimes included. We can visually depict the alignment between Irenaeus's use of prosopological exegesis and his presentation of the rule of faith as follows:

	From the Father	*From the Son*	*From the Spirit*	*Rule of Faith*
Divine Pre-Existence	**Gen 1:26**	Isa 49:5	—	Pre-existed with the Father
Pre-Incarnate Ministry	—	Gen 3:9 Exod 3:7–8, 14, 19 Exod 25:40 Exod 33:20–22	—	—
—	—	—	—	Born of the Virgin Mary
Incarnate Ministry		Ps 3:5a Isa 61:1 Jer 31:26		Engaged in ministry
Crucifixion	—	Ps 73:14 Isa 50:5–6	—	Rejected, crucified, and killed
Death and Resurrection	—	Ps 3:5	—	Resurrected from the dead
Ascension, Enthronement, and Reign	**Ps 2:7b–8** **Ps 110:1b–c** Isa 42:1–4 Isa 45:1 **Isa 49:6**	Ps 2:7a Ps 82:6–7 Prov 8:15–16 Isa 65:1	Ps 45:6–7 Ps 110:1a	Ascended and reigns
—	—	—	—	Will return as judge

---

the rule of faith, see further Johnson, *Jesus Christ*, 33–47.

84. To use Irenaeus's language, the Word of God "became a man amongst men, visible and palpable" (*Epid.* 6; trans. Behr).

85. On Christ's present reign, see *Epid.* 52; 83–85; 88.

Five of the six categories for which Irenaeus provides examples of prosopological exegesis from or concerning the person of the Son are also found in his rule of faith. The sole outlier, as was the case with Justin, is Christ's pre-incarnate ministry. The fact that Irenaeus finds this such a compelling category for the Son's prosopological speech would lead us to expect that his summary of the christological narrative would therefore include a line about how he "was always with mankind."[86] The fact that Irenaeus does not add such a line likely suggests how seriously he takes the faithful transmission of this summary of the apostolic teaching which he received and which did not include such a point.

Looking at the chart from the other direction, we can observe that five of the seven elements of Irenaeus's *regula fidei* correspond to categories for which Irenaeus has provided examples of prosopological speech that is somehow related to the Son. This is a greater degree of continuity than we observed with Justin, who did not give examples of prosopological speech related to the Son's virgin birth, earthly ministry, and second coming. Irenaeus has thus succeeded in providing an example of prosopological exegesis for one of these three missing categories—the Son's earthly ministry—via texts related to the incarnate Son's anointed ministry (Isa 61:1) and need for physical rest (Ps 3:5a; Jer 31:26). While Irenaeus speaks often of Christ's virgin birth[87] and second coming,[88] his support texts do not include instances of prosopological exegesis.

Conclusion: Scripting the Son in Irenaeus

As we have seen, Irenaeus provides us with a further vantage point from which to view how prosopological exegesis contributed to the development of Christology. We again find that Irenaeus, like Justin, uses prosopological exegesis to advance a high Christology, tracing the Son of God's pre-existence with the Father through his present reign. As was the case with Justin, the major christological themes that surfaced in an analysis of Irenaeus's use of prosopological exegesis have considerable overlap with the elements of his rule of faith, even as Irenaeus often selects different verses than Justin or uses them to make different points. Given Irenaeus's anti-gnostic context, it seems that Irenaeus's *regula fidei* is to some extent

---

86. *Epid.* 45 (trans. Behr).
87. See, for example, *Epid.* 32–33; 53–54; *Haer.* 1.10.1; 3.4.2; 3.19; 3.21–22.
88. See, for example, *Epid.* 41; *Haer.* 1.10.1; 3.4.2; 5.27.

driving his selection and use of passages he interprets prosopologically, passages that he draws from a variety of sources, but especially from Justin. Having established a baseline pattern with Justin and Irenaeus, we now turn to Tertullian to assess the extent to which these threads continued to be woven together in like fashion as we move forward yet another generation in time to the early third century.

5

Tertullian of Carthage

TERTULLIAN OF CARTHAGE (CA. 160–215), the fiery North African apologist, is the next critical figure for our story of christological development through prosopological exegesis. Often considered a founder of Latin Christianity, Tertullian is simultaneously known for his immense contributions to trinitarian theology and for his embrace of the heretical charismatic and rigorist movement known as the New Prophecy (often called Montanism).[1] The author of some thirty-one extant treatises across a variety of genres, Tertullian continues to fascinate and repel, no doubt in his own day as in ours. On account of clear parallels among texts, scholars believe Tertullian made use of the writings of Justin and Irenaeus in his own work,[2] allowing another opportunity to analyze elements of continuity and discontinuity with respect to prosopological exegesis and its contributions to early Christology. As we will see, Tertullian follows Justin and Irenaeus in using prosopological exegesis as a means of advancing his christological position, but outstrips either of his predecessors in both the quantity of instances and in the clarity of purpose he brings to his use of the method.

This chapter will review how Tertullian explains his approach to prosopological exegesis in his treatise *Against Praxeas* before surveying the entirety of his use of this person-centered reading strategy with respect

---

1. On Tertullian's life and background, see further Barnes, *Tertullian*, 1–29; Wilhite, *Tertullian*, 17–27; on the subject of Montanism, see Trevett, *Montanism*. Though "Montanism" is an anachronistic term used to describe pejoratively those who followed the "New Prophecy," I use it in this chapter as the term more familiar to most readers.

2. See, e.g., Evans, *Praxeas*, 31; Waszink, "Tertullian's Principles," 21.

to the Son across all of his writings.³ Per the organization of prior chapters, we will then assess Tertullian's use of *testimonia* collections and his understanding of the *regula fidei* to measure how these factors may have contributed to Tertullian's particular approach to prosopological exegesis. As will be demonstrated, Tertullian dramatically elevates the centrality of this reading method in order to advance his preferred Christology against the views of the Marcionites and the modalistic monarchians, reinforcing the core christological narrative handed down in the *regula fidei* and preparing the way for later trinitarian orthodoxy.

Prosopological Exegesis in the Writings of Tertullian

Tertullian's most important statement of his understanding of prosopological exegesis is found in his treatise *Against Praxeas*. Like Justin and Irenaeus, Tertullian provides a general introduction to this person-centered reading method from which we can then expand our analysis to the entirety of his extant corpus.

In *Against Praxeas*, Tertullian is arguing against a view that some scholars term modalistic monarchianism, which maintained that Father, Son, and Spirit were merely different modes or aspects of a single divine person.⁴ In *Prax.* 11, Tertullian appeals to a close reading of Scripture, and in particular its dialogical passages, for evidence of the existence of multiple divine persons:

> All the Scriptures disclose both the demonstration and the distinction of the Trinity; from them also is deduced our rule: the person speaking and the person spoken to cannot be considered one and the same, because neither perversity nor deceit are consistent with God, so that, although it was himself to whom he was speaking, nevertheless he speaks to another and not to his own self.⁵

The Latin word translated "person" is *persona*, corresponding with the word *prosōpon* in Greek usage and formally marking this section as introducing what scholars today call prosopological exegesis. Still, Tertullian's understanding of *persona* differs in slight but crucial ways from

---

3. This portion of the chapter builds on my initial analysis of some of these passages in Hughes, *Trinitarian Testimony*, 157–81.
4. See further, e.g., Evans, *Praxeas*, 6–18.
5. *Prax.* 11.4 (AT).

how Justin and Irenaeus used the term *prosōpon*. While the Greek term likely continued to carry echoes of its origins in a theatrical context and could thereby be used against him by the modalistic monarchians, the Latin term *persona* is consistently used by Tertullian to describe "the effective manifestation of a distinct being," communicating something true about God's own inner life.[6] It may also have a legal undertone, insofar as *persona* could be used to describe "one who has an existence and a status and rights of his own as well as relations and obligations in respect of others."[7] Thus, with his use of *persona* Tertullian is aiming at drawing the notion of divine personhood out of a literary context and instead applying it to describe the inner workings of the Godhead; in so doing, Tertullian laid the foundation for the orthodox understanding of the Trinity as "one substance in three persons."[8] This point alone demonstrates the incredible significance that prosopological exegesis has for trinitarian theology more broadly.

As he continues in *Prax.* 11, Tertullian proceeds to give several examples of such prosopological speech, identifying Isa 42:1 and Isa 49:6 as the words of the Father to or concerning the Son, Isa 61:1, Ps 71:18, and Ps 3:1 as the words of the Son to or concerning the Father, and Ps 110:1, Isa 45:1, and Isa 53:1–2 as the words of the Spirit to or concerning the other two divine persons; these examples will all be analyzed in more detail below. More significant for the purposes of this introduction is Tertullian's summary conclusion:

> Thus in these passages, however few, the distinction of the Trinity is clearly set forth. For there is the Spirit himself who speaks, the Father to whom he speaks, and the Son of whom he speaks. Likewise the rest, which are spoken sometimes by the Father concerning the Son or to the Son, sometimes by the Son concerning the Father or to the Father, sometimes by the Spirit, establish each person as distinct.[9]

---

6. Osborn, *Tertullian*, 137.

7. Evans, *Praxeas*, 14.

8. See further Evans, *Praxeas*, 46; Bates, *Birth*, 28. For references to scholarly literature on the term *persona* in later trinitarian thought, see the references in Hughes, *Trinitarian Testimony*, 161–62.

9. *Prax.* 11.9–10 (AT). On this crucial chapter of *Against Praxeas*, see further Hughes, *Trinitarian Testimony*, 157–61; Andresen, "Zur Entstehung," 18–25; Slusser, "Exegetical Roots," 464–66; Bates, *Hermeneutics*, 185–86.

There are several notable features of Tertullian's framing of prosopological exegesis in *Prax.* 11. First, Tertullian distinguishes between two types of prosopological exegesis with respect to the Father and the Son: each is capable of speaking directly "to" or indirectly "concerning" the other divine person, with both kinds of divine speech thereby placed under the umbrella of prosopological exegesis. Second, the Spirit is here clearly portrayed as capable of speaking from his own *persona*, a point that I have argued elsewhere is exceedingly important for the development of early Christian pneumatology.[10] Third, this passage reflects further continuity and discontinuity with Tertullian's most significant predecessors. On the one hand, Tertullian's selection of quotations in this introduction has more in common with examples found in Irenaeus than those in Justin. On the other, Tertullian's more expansive definition of prosopological exegesis more closely matches Justin's introduction, insofar as Irenaeus's introduction to the subject indicated that he sought to emphasize examples of intra-divine dialogue. Beyond clear areas of similarity with both Justin and Irenaeus, the different polemical context and novel choice of several verses not previously used by his predecessors show that Tertullian also demonstrates discontinuity with respect to his prosopological method. Fourth, Tertullian seems to be describing something of a "hermeneutical spiral" regarding how prosopological exegesis informs his trinitarian theology. As Michael Slusser comments on this portion of *Against Praxeas*, "It is difficult to say which came first, the exegesis of experience or the exegesis of Scripture."[11] Indeed, while Tertullian's received trinitarian faith, as expressed in the *regula fidei* and as liturgically enacted in, for instance, baptism into the threefold name (cf. Matt 28:19), doubtlessly shaped his approach to interpreting these dialogical passages, the actual results of his prosopological method clearly inform his trinitarian theology. Thus, this chapter will seek to establish how Tertullian used prosopological exegesis with respect to the person of the Son to advance a hermeneutic that would conform to orthodox teaching.

Having analyzed the broad strokes of Tertullian's introduction to prosopological exegesis, we can now investigate how Tertullian applies this method across all his writings. While most of these instances are found scattered throughout either *Against Praxeas* or the final two

---

10. Hughes, *How the Spirit Became God*, 71–74.
11. Slusser, "Exegetical Roots," 476.

books of his *Against Marcion* (both likely ca. 210), Tertullian's use of prosopological exegesis across at least six of his writings means that the organization of this section will again proceed thematically rather than by individual work.

From the Father

As Tertullian's general comments on prosopological exegesis make clear, the Father at times speaks as a distinct divine person in a way that can be categorized apart from those more common references to what "God" said through the prophets without distinguishing among divine persons. As observed in *Prax.* 11, Tertullian indicates that the Father's prosopological speech consists of dialogical passages in which the Father speaks to or concerning the Son. A complete survey of Tertullian's writings demonstrates that Tertullian makes far more extensive use of prosopological exegesis from the Father than either Justin or Irenaeus before him. This enables Tertullian, then, to use the Father's prosopological speech in order to advance an even broader range of christological claims.

Divine Pre-Existence

While Justin favored Ps 110:3–4 as his key example of the Father's prosopological speech to demonstrate the Son's pre-existence, and while Irenaeus selected Gen 1:26 as his favorite text for this purpose, Tertullian greatly exceeds both of his predecessors in the sheer scope of his selection of texts on this theme. We can divide Tertullian's approach to the Father proving the Son's divine pre-existence through prosopological exegesis into three sub-themes: the Son's generation from the Father, the Son's presence at creation, and the Son's preparation for the incarnation.

GENERATION FROM THE FATHER

Key to Tertullian's understanding of the Son's generation from the Father is Ps 45:1, which he interprets prosopologically as the words of the Father concerning the Son on five occasions,[12] with Ps 2:7 and Ps 110:3 often added as supporting texts. All three of these verses are interpreted

---

12. *Herm.* 18.3; *Marc.* 2.4; 4.14; *Prax.* 7.1; 11.2.

together in *Prax.* 7 as Tertullian seeks to show that the Scriptures distinguish between the Father and the Son:

> Thus does He make Him equal to Him: for by proceeding from Himself He became His first-begotten Son, because begotten before all things; and His only-begotten also, because alone begotten of God, in a way peculiar to Himself, from the womb of His own heart—even as the Father Himself testifies: *My heart, says He, has emitted my most excellent Word* [Ps 45:1]. The Father took pleasure evermore in Him, who equally rejoiced with a reciprocal gladness in the Father's presence: *You are my Son, today have I begotten You* [Ps 2:7]; *even before the morning star did I beget You* [Ps 110:3].[13]

In speaking of the Son's generation from the Father, Tertullian first appeals to Ps 45:1. While Ps 45:6–7 was an important example of prosopological speech from the Father to the Son in Heb 1:8–9,[14] we find here another instance of additional parts of a psalm or passage used elsewhere as a source of prosopological speech also being interpreted in the same manner. Following a line of interpretation that can be traced back to Theophilus of Antioch, Tertullian reads the *logos* of Ps 45:1 as "the Word" (that is, God the Son) rather than simply "the word" (that is, the subject matter) of the psalm itself.[15] Critically, here and elsewhere Tertullian interprets the verb in Ps 45:1 as referring to the Son being begotten, and not created, which will of course become a major sticking point in later christological debates.[16] Thus, we again see prosopological exegesis linked with an important christological innovation, with Ps 45:1 functioning as a verse that speaks to the manner of the Son's generation from the Father.

The language of the Son being "begotten" in Ps 2:7 and Ps 110:3 makes those natural verses for Tertullian to select to support his understanding of the Son's generation from the Father.[17] While the earlier Christian tradition maintained that Ps 2:7 and Ps 110:3 could be interpreted prosopologically,[18] the theodramatic setting was not explicitly

---

13. *Prax.* 7.1–2 (trans. *ANF*, modernized).

14. Cf. *Dial.* 56.14; *Haer.* 3.6.1. In those passages, however, the Holy Spirit is identified as the true speaker of this dialogue, reflecting the two "gods" spoken of in Ps 45:7.

15. Evans, *Praxeas*, 227.

16. See also *Prax.* 11.2; *Herm.* 18.3; *Marc.* 2.4; 4.14.

17. See also Tertullian's prosopological interpretation of Ps 2:7 at *Prax.* 11.3 and *Marc.* 4.22.

18. For Ps 2:7, see again, e.g., Heb 1:5; 5:5; *Dial.* 88.8. For Ps 110:3, see again, e.g.,

noted by earlier authors. Tertullian, however, specifies that these verses were spoken by the Father to the Son before the creation of the world; any sense that this verse is commenting on Jesus' birth from the womb of the Virgin Mary[19] has been supplanted by a focus on the Son being begotten from the "womb" of the Father's own heart. With the emphasis on dialogical passages at the heart of Tertullian's argument in *Against Praxeas*, it is not surprising that prosopological exegesis would form the backbone of this and other aspects of Tertullian's pre-existent Christology. And as Ernest Evans notes, Tertullian's careful use of "person" (*persona*) in this passage has christological significance in and of itself: "*Persona* here seems to combine the dramatic with the metaphysical sense" such that "the Son, as well as the Father, is a *persona*, as being distinct from, yet in relation with, another *persona*."[20] Trinitarian theology thus emerges in part through prosopological exegesis.

Presence at Creation

Tertullian also uses prosopological exegesis to assert that the Son existed before the creation of the world insofar as the Son played a key role in the work of creation. Typical is the following claim from *Prax.* 12, still in the context of demonstrating how the Scriptures distinguish between the Father and the Son:

> If you are still offended by the plurality of the Trinity, on the ground that it is not combined in simple unity, I ask you how it is that one only single person speaks in the plural, *Let us make man after our image and likeness* [Gen 1:26], when he ought to have said, Let me make man after my image and likeness, as being one only single person. Also in what follows, *Behold, Adam is become as one of us* [Gen 3:22], he is deceptive or joking in speaking in the plural while being one and alone and singular. . . . Nay rather, because there already was attached to him the Son, a second Person, his Word, and a third Person, the Spirit in the Word, for that reason he spoke in the plural.[21]

Dial. 63.3; 83.4; *1 Apol.* 45.4.
   19. As at *Dial.* 63.3.
   20. Evans, *Praxeas*, 229.
   21. *Prax.* 12.1–2 (trans. Evans).

Again it is dialogical passages, interpreted prosopologically, that form the basis of Tertullian's defense of the distinction between Father and Son (and Spirit) at creation. Tertullian's frequent appeal to Gen 1:26 in this regard thus follows Irenaeus's precedent.[22]

Somewhat more unusual, then, is Tertullian's appeal to Isa 44:25–26 later in *Against Praxeas*. Having interpreted Isa 44:24 as the words of the Son (for which see below), Tertullian proceeds to suggest that the Father "immediately speaks concerning the Son" these verses in which the Son, on the basis of his presence at creation, is characterized as God's exclusive, authorized agent of revelation.[23] While none of Tertullian's predecessors interpreted any portion of Isaiah 44 prosopologically, probably in light of the fact that Tertullian is mistranslating the Greek word *paidos* as "Son" instead of the preferable "servant," its proximity to other important dialogues in Deutero-Isaiah that were ascribed to either the Father or the Son made this an obvious place to identify further dialogue that could be interpreted as spoken by the Father to or concerning the Son.

Preparation for Incarnation

A final, minor grouping of instances of prosopological exegesis from the person of the Son that speak to the Son's pre-existence cluster around the theme of what we might speak of as the Father preparing the way for the Son's incarnation, something that appears to be a unique innovation of Tertullian.

We see this most clearly in a passage from Tertullian's *Against the Jews*, in which he is setting out prophecies concerning Christ's birth and ministry. Tertullian here makes the common Christian claim that, because the Scriptures say that no human can see God and live, any Old Testament theophanies must be appearances of the pre-incarnate Christ. Having identified the pre-incarnate Christ as the speaker to Moses at Sinai (Exod 23:20–21; see further below), Tertullian next notes how this text is echoed by the prophet Malachi; just as Christ called Joshua an "angel," so too "the Spirit, speaking in the person of the Father, calls the forerunner of Christ, John, a future 'angel,' through the prophet: *Behold*,

---

22. See also *Res.* 6.4; *Marc.* 2.4; 5.8. In all of these other instances, the Father's words are directed to the Son alone.

23. *Prax.* 19.4 (trans. Evans).

I send my angel before Your—that is, Christ's—*face, who shall prepare Your way before You* [Mal 3:1]."[24]

Tertullian is clearly signaling his use of prosopological exegesis by distinguishing "the Father" as the specific divine person speaking in this text and by introducing the technical term "person" (*persona*). While we might expect Tertullian to simply read this as a generic prophecy from "God," Tertullian, wishing to call attention to the Son as fulfilling Old Testament prophecies, establishes the Son's words concerning Joshua as parallel to the Father's words concerning Christ, the new Joshua.[25] The theodramatic setting is unclear, but it must be before the incarnation, providing another piece of evidence for the claim that God the Son at least pre-dated the incarnation, if not creation writ large. We see therefore an instance of the Father speaking concerning the Son in the context of the Father's plans regarding the incarnation.

This may perhaps explain three other unusual instances of prosopological exegesis in Tertullian's *Against Marcion*. In one passage, Tertullian is expositing the story of Jesus sending out the seventy-two in Luke 10 when he comes to the verse in which Jesus tells the seventy-two, upon their return, that he has given them the power to tread on serpents and scorpions (Luke 10:19), which Tertullian takes primarily to refer spiritually to demons. As Tertullian comments,

> This power the Creator conferred first of all upon His Christ, even as the ninetieth Psalm [ninety-first in the MT] says to Him: *Upon the asp and the basilisk shall You tread; the lion and the dragon shall You trample under foot* [Ps 91:13].[26]

Tertullian thereby reads Ps 91:13 as the words of the Father to the Son in what appears to be a novel use of prosopological exegesis. While the theodramatic setting is undefined, given the future tense of the dialogue the most likely setting is before the incarnation, or perhaps even before the creation of the world.

In a second instance, in the context of demonstrating that the Psalter and Isaiah predicted Christ's suffering, Tertullian cites portions of Isaiah 52–53 as prophecies concerning the Son's humiliation. This sets up Tertullian to make the following claim:

---

24. *Adv. Jud.* 9.23 (trans. *ANF*, modernized).

25. As Tertullian and other early Christian writers were quick to point out, Joshua and Jesus are forms of the same name.

26. *Marc.* 4.24 (trans. *ANF*, modernized).

> Similarly the Father addressed the Son just before: *Inasmuch as many will be astonished at You, so also will Your beauty be without glory from men* [Isa 52:14]. For although, in David's words, *He is fairer than the children of men* [Ps 45:2], yet it is in that figurative state of spiritual grace, when He is girded with the sword of the Spirit, which is verily His form, and beauty, and glory.[27]

Tertullian thus marks Isa 52:14 as an example of the Father's prosopological speech to the Son concerning the incarnation. As in the previous instance, the future tense of the dialogue suggests the theodramatic context is prior to the incarnation, and perhaps even before the creation of the world. Tertullian then demonstrates how a christological interpretation of Ps 45:2, focusing on Christ's beauty, can be reconciled with this text from Isaiah, contrasting Christ's physical body with his spiritual grace.[28]

In the same way, then, we can understand another instance of this theme in which Tertullian identifies God the Father speaking concerning the Son. As Tertullian writes,

> The heretic, too, may discover that this gentleness of Christ [cf. Luke 9:51–56] was promised by the selfsame severest Judge. *He shall not contend*, says He, *nor shall His voice be heard in the street; a bruised reed shall He not crush, and smoking flax shall He not quench* [Isa 42:2–3].[29]

Here the Father (the "Judge") speaks, still in the future tense, concerning the Son's incarnate ministry. The audience of the speech is, however, undefined, though a time prior to the incarnation would be the most reasonable theodramatic setting of these words. As opposed to those instances in which the Father speaks prosopologically to the Son (indicating the Son's presence in this divine conversation prior to the incarnation), the Father's speech merely concerning the Son does little on its own to advance the notion of the Son's pre-existence; only when combined

---

27. *Marc.* 3.17 (trans. *ANF*, modernized).

28. Though Tertullian has just used prosopological exegesis in this passage, and has interpreted Ps 45:1 as the words of the Father to the Son elsewhere (*Prax.* 7.1; 11.2; *Herm.* 18.3; *Marc.* 2.4; 4.14), he does not take the logical leap of interpreting Ps 45:2 prosopologically, instead attributing it to "David's words." Perhaps this reflects Tertullian's concern for shifts in tenses, as in Isa 52:14 the Father's words are in the future tense, and in Ps 45:1 the Father's words are in the past tense; the present tense of Ps 45:2 matches neither of these established tenses and could thus threaten the theodramatic logic of his interpretation.

29. *Marc.* 4.23 (trans. *ANF*).

with the fact of the Son's pre-existence, established elsewhere, can such an instance be said to contribute to this christological point.

In any event, even comparing this single theme of the Son's pre-existence to writers before him, the breadth and novelty of Tertullian's prosopological method as a means of defending his Christology is already coming into focus. This phenomenon will remain constant as we proceed through additional categories of analysis.

Present Reign

Tertullian follows Justin and Irenaeus in identifying examples of the Father speaking prosopologically to the Son concerning the Son's present reign over all the earth. While Tertullian repeats many of the interpretations found in the writings of his predecessors, he dramatically expands the number of instances of such speech, showing the critical importance of this theme for Tertullian's Christology.

Tertullian's clearest statement of what he means by Christ's present reign is found in his treatise *Against the Jews*. In the course of making his argument that the promised Christ of the Old Testament has indeed already come, Tertullian draws in a quotation from Isaiah:

> *Thus says the Lord God to my Christ the Lord, whose right hand I have holden, that the nations may hear Him: the powers of kings will I burst asunder; I will open before Him the gates, and the cities shall not be closed to Him* [Isa 45:1]. Which very thing we see fulfilled. For whose right hand does God the Father hold but Christ's, His Son—whom all nations have heard, that is, whom all nations have believed—whose preachers, the apostles, are pointed to in the Psalms of David: *Into the universal earth*, says he, *is gone out their sound, and unto the ends of the earth their words* [Ps 19:4]. For upon whom else have the universal nations believed, but upon the Christ who is already come?[30]

While not technically an instance of prosopological exegesis as we have defined it in this book, insofar as the speaker and audience are not ambiguous in the original context of the verse (at least in this text of Isa 45:1), we see Tertullian's logic clearly: Christ currently reigns at God's right hand, and the proof of this present reign is what Paul calls "the obedience of faith for the sake of his name among all the nations" (Rom

---

30. *Adv. Jud.* 7.2–3 (trans. *ANF*, modernized). As with Irenaeus, for Isa 45:1 Tertullian reads "Lord" instead of "Cyrus," a difference of one *iota* in the Greek.

1:5). This present reign was indicated in both Isaiah and the Psalter, whether prosopologically or as direct prophecy, and Tertullian makes much of it throughout his writings.

Tertullian's favorite text for this theme, unsurprisingly, is Ps 2:7–8. As we have seen above, Tertullian at times uses Ps 2:7 in isolation to prove the generation of the Son from the Father; when combined with Ps 2:8, however, it is wielded as a proof of the Son's present reign. Typical of Tertullian's approach to Ps 2:7–8 is this passage from his treatise *Against Marcion*:

> Look at all nations from the vortex of human error emerging out of it up to the Divine Creator, the Divine Christ, and deny Him to be the object of prophecy, if you dare. At once there will occur to you the Father's promise in the Psalms: *You are my Son, this day have I begotten You. Ask of me, and I shall give You the Gentiles for Your inheritance, and the uttermost parts of the earth for Your possession* [Ps 2:7–8]. You will not be able to put in a claim for some son of David being here meant, rather than Christ; or for the ends of the earth being promised to David, whose kingdom was confined to the Jewish nation simply, rather than to Christ, who now embraces the whole world in the faith of His gospel.[31]

The parallels to Tertullian's argument in *Adv. Jud.* 7.2–3 are obvious; Christ reigns at God's right hand, as evidenced by the nations coming to faith in Christ as Lord and King.[32] The theodramatic setting is undefined; the future tense suggests this passage's usefulness as a support for Christ's pre-existence (perhaps explaining why Ps 2:7 was used in this manner elsewhere in Tertullian's writings), but nevertheless Tertullian in this instance is using these verses to support the specific christological point that Christ now rules over all the earth.

Tertullian's second favorite text for this theme is, again unsurprisingly, Ps 110:1. Tertullian uses a prosopological interpretation of this verse to support his description of Christ's present reign by combining it with other key texts on this theme:

> In [God's] gift, too, are *the riches of the glory of His inheritance in the saints* [Eph 1:18], who promised such an inheritance in the call of the Gentiles: *Ask of me, and I will give You the Gentiles for Your inheritance* [Ps 2:8]. It was He who *wrought in Christ His*

---

31. *Marc.* 3.20 (trans. *ANF*, modernized).
32. See also Tertullian's prosopological interpretation of Ps 2:7–8 at *Adv. Jud.* 12.1; 14.12. Tertullian interprets just Ps 2:8, for the same purpose, at *Marc.* 4.25; 5.17.

> *mighty power, by raising Him from the dead, and setting Him at His own right hand, and putting all things under His feet* [Eph 1:19–22]—*even the same who said: Sit on my right hand, until I make Your enemies Your footstool* [Ps 110:1b–c]. For in another passage the Spirit says to the Father concerning the Son: *You have put all things under His feet* [Ps 8:6].³³

Here Tertullian interweaves his interpretation of Eph 1:18–22 with verses from the Psalter that he interprets prosopologically; interestingly, we even get a somewhat infrequent instance of the Spirit speaking in his own person to the Father concerning the Son (see further below). The clear thrust of the passage from Paul is that the Father has already installed the Son as Lord and King; Ps 2:8 then becomes a demonstration of how the Father "promised" this in advance to the Son and Ps 110:1b–c serves as proof that Ps 8:6 has likewise been fulfilled in Christ. Unlike Justin and Irenaeus, who attribute the full verse of Ps 110:1 to the Holy Spirit, who is quoting the Father speaking to the Son, here Tertullian focuses exclusively on the Father's words to the Son. What is particularly distinctive about Tertullian's use of Ps 110:1, however, is how he also uses it to look forward to the consummation of Christ's present reign, which we will consider in more detail below.

Besides the portions of the Psalter referenced above, Tertullian also reads passages from Isaiah prosopologically as the words of the Father to the Son concerning the Son's present reign. Tertullian's favorite Isaianic text on this theme is Isaiah 42, which is interpreted prosopologically across *Against the Jews*, *Against Marcion*, and *Against Praxeas*. For example, as noted above, when Tertullian provides his overview of prosopological exegesis in *Prax.* 11, his first example of the Father's speech concerning the Son is Isa 42:1.³⁴ Elsewhere, Tertullian reads Isa 42:6 as the words of the Father to the Son and Isa 42:4 as the Father speaking concerning the Son.³⁵ On two instances Tertullian quotes Isa 42:6–7 immediately after quoting Ps 2:7–8, reading both passages as the Father speaking to the Son concerning his present reign over the gentiles.³⁶ A

---

33. *Marc.* 5.17 (trans. *ANF*, modernized); cf. 4.41 for a similar reading of Ps 110:1; see also the christological interpretation of Ps 24:10 earlier in *Marc.* 5.17 in making the same point. Tertullian's christological reading of Ps 45:2–5 at *Marc.* 3.14 may also support this theme.

34. *Prax.* 11.5.

35. *Marc.* 5.2.

36. *Adv. Jud.* 12.1–2; *Marc.* 3.20.

further popular Isaianic text for Tertullian is Isa 49:6, which he quotes immediately after Isa 42:1 in his overview of prosopological exegesis in *Prax.* 11 as evidence of the Father speaking to the Son.[37] Here Tertullian follows both Justin and Irenaeus in interpreting this verse prosopologically as the words of the Father to the Son, further underscoring the consistent importance of this verse for early Christian understanding of Christ's reign as extending to the ends of the earth.[38]

Tertullian, however, builds upon the exegetical foundation of his predecessors by pulling in novel verses from Isaiah into his prosopological reading of speech from the Father. Thus, for instance, staying within Deutero-Isaiah, Tertullian follows a prosopological interpretation of Isa 42:6–7 with a quotation of Isa 55:4–5. As a result, Tertullian notes that the Father was speaking concerning those things that "are accomplished through Christ" when the Father spoke of him as "*a prince and commander to the nations* [Isa 55:4]." This sets up a pivot to the Father's direct speech to the Son: "*Nations which know You not shall invoke You, and peoples shall run together unto You* [Isa 55:5]."[39] Tertullian also draws in earlier parts of the book of Isaiah. Thus, the Father speaks concerning Christ through the prophecy of Christ being "*a stone of stumbling and a rock of offense* [Isa 8:14]," and "*a precious stone and honorable* [Isa 28:16]."[40] All the rich prophecies of Isaiah, therefore, become ripe opportunities for Tertullian to find the Father speaking to or concerning the Son.

Future Consummation

As noted above, Tertullian uses Ps 110:1 to comment on Christ's present reign, but at other times he interprets it in a way that emphasizes the future, final consummation of all things. Take, for example, this passage from *Against Praxeas*:

> But to such a degree does [the divine monarchy] abide in its own quality, though a trinity be introduced, that it has even to be restored to the Father by the Son, inasmuch as the apostle writes concerning the last end, *When he shall have delivered up*

---

37. *Prax.* 11.5; see also *Marc.* 4.25; 5.11.
38. See again *Dial.* 121.4; *Epid.* 50.
39. *Marc.* 3.20 (trans. *ANF*, modernized).
40. *Marc.* 5.5–6 (trans. *ANF*, modernized).

> the kingdom to the God and Father. For he must reign until God put all his enemies under his feet [1 Cor 15:24–25], evidently according to the psalm, Sit at my right hand until I make all your enemies the footstool of your feet [Ps 110:1b–c]. But when all things have been made subject to him, except him who has subjected all things to him, then also he himself will be subjected to him who has subjected all things to him, that God may be all things in all [1 Cor 15:27–28].[41]

In this passage, Tertullian interweaves Ps 110:1b–c with 1 Cor 15:24–28 to focus on "the last end." The implication is that while Christ presently reigns (1 Cor 15:24; Ps 110:1b), there is a still future moment in which God will act decisively to defeat all his enemies (1 Cor 15:25; Ps 110:1c). This future-oriented aspect of Ps 110:1 did not receive similar attention from previous writers, who instead used the whole verse to support their claim that Christ is presently reigning over the nations.

When, though, does Tertullian see this "last end" taking place? The answer can be found by looking at the close of *Against Praxeas*, in which Tertullian circles back to this very theme:

> The Son ascended into the higher parts of heaven, as he did also descend into the inner parts of the earth. This is he who sits at the right hand of the Father, not the Father at his own right hand. This is he whom Stephen sees, when he is being stoned, still standing at the right hand of God, as thenceforth to sit, until the Father puts all enemies under his feet. This is he who is also to come again above the clouds of heaven in like fashion as also he ascended.[42]

By alluding to Ps 110:1 and Acts 1:11, Tertullian clearly indicates that the next key moment in redemptive history is the return of Christ, at which time the Father will at last "put all enemies under his feet." The return of Christ, of course, is synonymous with Christ presiding over the final judgment, connecting it to that important element of the *regula fidei*, as we will discuss further below.[43]

This reading is confirmed by an interesting passage in Tertullian's *Against Marcion* in which he is discussing the doctrine of the bodily resurrection in the context of presenting his broader eschatology.[44] Just

---

41. *Prax.* 4.2 (trans. Evans, modernized).
42. *Prax.* 30.4–5 (trans. Evans, modernized).
43. See Osborn, *Tertullian*, 215.
44. On Tertullian's eschatology, see further Osborn, *Tertullian*, 215–19; Hill,

as in his discussion of this topic in *Against Praxeas*, Tertullian bases his commentary on the key Pauline text of 1 Corinthians 15, with his interpretation of 1 Cor 15:25 leading him again to Ps 110:1:

> For the resurrection of the body will receive all the better proof, in proportion as I shall succeed in showing that Christ belongs to that God who is believed to have provided this resurrection of the flesh in His dispensation. When he says, *For He must reign, until He has put all enemies under His feet* [1 Cor 15:25], we can see at once from this statement that he speaks of a God of vengeance, and therefore of Him who made the following promise to Christ: *Sit at my right hand, until I make Your enemies Your footstool* [Ps 110:1b-c]. *The rod of Your strength shall the Lord send forth from Sion, and He shall rule along with You in the midst of Your enemies* [Ps 110:2].[45]

The focus here is on God's eschatological judgment, with Tertullian bringing in Ps 110:2 as a further description of the Son's eschatological rule; later in this chapter, Tertullian also highlights Ps 110:4 to emphasize Christ's eternal priesthood. That Christ has received the role of Lord and King who judges the nations is clarified still later in this same chapter, in which Tertullian comments, "Well, then, there is also another Psalm, which begins with these words: *Give your judgments, O God, to the King* [Ps 72:1], that is, to Christ who was to come as King."[46]

Tertullian thus further expands the scope of a prosopological interpretation of Ps 110:1 (and, additionally, Ps 110:2 and 110:4), with the Father's words to the Son describing not simply Christ's present reign but also his return to judge the earth at the time of the final consummation. Tertullian has thus managed to use a prosopological reading of Psalm 110 to prove the Son's pre-existence, enthronement, and second coming, showing the continued importance of a prosopological interpretation of this psalm for the development of early Christology.

From the Son

Tertullian's overview of prosopological exegesis in *Prax.* 11 includes the following striking claim: "But indeed nearly all the psalms sustain the person [*personam*] of Christ and represent the Son speaking to the Father—that

---

Regnum Caelorum, 27–32.
   45. *Marc.* 5.9 (trans. *ANF*, modernized).
   46. *Marc.* 5.9 (trans. *ANF*, modernized).

is, Christ to God."[47] Tertullian thus expresses the view that those psalms ("nearly all" of them!) in which Christ is identified as the prosopological speaker should be read as speech directed to the Father.

Tertullian indeed consistently follows a christological interpretation of the Psalms.[48] In fact, Tertullian at one point posits that David "sings to us of Christ, and through his voice Christ indeed also sang concerning Himself."[49] As Tertullian recognizes, however, there was some debate about whether Christ is the (prosopological) speaker of an Old Testament text or if it is simply the prophet speaking:

> For whether it was Christ even then, as we hold, or the prophet, as the Jews say, who pronounced these words [in this instance, Isa 50:6] concerning himself, in either case, that which as yet had not happened sounded as if it had been already accomplished.[50]

Interestingly, Tertullian claims that the prosopological interpretation is the true Christian form of exegesis; Marcion, then, is in fact allied with the Jews when he rejects the notion that the Old Testament contains the very words of Christ, not to mention less direct prophecies concerning him.[51] With this overall framework in mind, we can proceed to analyze all of the instances of prosopological speech from the Son in Tertullian's writings. As with the Father's prosopological speech, Tertullian primarily employs this reading strategy in *Against Praxeas* and the latter books of *Against Marcion*, though examples are found in several other writings as well.

Divine Pre-Existence

Following Justin, Tertullian's preferred text for proving the Son's divine pre-existence through the Son's prosopological speech is Wisdom's address beginning at Prov 8:22. As we saw in the previous chapter of this book, Irenaeus instead ascribed these words to the Holy Spirit, obviating their use for Christology; Tertullian, however, restores these verses to their earlier and more common interpretation, again mining them for

---

47. *Prax.* 11.7 (AT).

48. For example, Tertullian (*Marc.* 4.20) claims that Christ "accomplished" Ps 29:3 when he crossed the Sea of Galilee (Luke 8:22), and that Christ's triumph over a multitude of demons (Luke 8:30) fulfilled Ps 24:8.

49. *Carn. Chr.* 20.3 (trans. *ANF*).

50. *Marc.* 3.5 (trans. *ANF*).

51. See, e.g., *Marc.* 3.6–7.

their christological relevance. As such, Tertullian's ability to use prosopological exegesis from the person of the Son to demonstrate the Son's pre-existence is greatly expanded compared to Irenaeus. Typical, then, is the following account from Tertullian in *Against Praxeas*:

> So listen also to Wisdom, established as a second person. First, *The Lord created me as the beginning of his ways for his works' sake, before he made the earth, before the mountains were set in their places; before all the hills he begat me* [cf. Prov 8:22–25]—establishing and begetting, of course, in his own consciousness. Afterwards observe her, by the fact of being separate, standing by him: *When he was preparing the heaven*, she says, *I was present with him, and as he made strong above the winds the clouds on high, and as he made safe the fountains of the earth which is under heaven, I was with him as a fellow-worker, I was she in whose presence he delighted; for daily did I delight in his person* [cf. Prov 8:27–30].[52]

In this passage, Tertullian has demonstrated, against the modalistic monarchians, that the Scriptures speak of a distinct "second person," given the name "Wisdom," who is "the Reason or Discourse of God."[53] As the quotations from Proverbs indicate, this Wisdom pre-existed creation and was present with God at the creation of the world. Who, though, should we understand this Wisdom to be? Tertullian provides an answer in short order: "So also the Son in his own person, under the name of Wisdom, confesses the Father, *The Lord established me as the beginning of his ways for his works' sake; before the hills he begat me* [Prov 8:22]."[54] Thus the Scriptures present the person of the Son speaking in the person of Wisdom. This allows Tertullian to use Wisdom's speech in Proverbs 8 as the basis for his commentary on the Son as the only-begotten of the Father, with Ps 45:1, Ps 2:7, and Ps 110:3 brought in as further Old Testament quotations alongside allusions to New Testament passages such as Col 1:15 and John 1:18. As such, Tertullian concludes, "Whatever therefore the substance of the Word was, that I call a Person, and for it I claim the name of Son: and while I acknowledge him as Son I maintain he

---

52. *Prax.* 6.1–2 (trans. Evans, modernized).
53. *Prax.* 6.1 (trans. Evans).
54. *Prax.* 7.1 (trans. Evans, modernized). As Tertullian notes elsewhere (*Prax.* 19.2), Paul calls Christ "the Wisdom and the Power of God" (1 Cor 1:24), further justifying this linkage.

is another beside the Father."[55] While Tertullian therefore demonstrates continuity in prosopological exegesis in his use of Proverbs 8, it is clear that "he was the first to interpret it with such attention to detail."[56]

Indeed, Tertullian's focus on this passage leads him to identify still further instances of prosopological speech from the Son that he can connect with Wisdom's speech in Proverbs 8. For example, later in *Against Praxeas*, Tertullian again quotes Prov 8:27 as the words of the Son,[57] setting up his claim that it is "the Son's voice which says *I alone have spread out the heaven* [Isa 44:24]" and therefore the Son "who says, *I am the first, and unto things that are to come after, I am he* [Isa 41:4]."[58] Taken together, Tertullian claims, these verses demonstrate precisely what John 1:1 teaches: "Evidently the Word is the first thing of all."[59]

Similarly, in his *Against Hermogenes*, Tertullian ties together verses from Isaiah that he interprets as the prosopological words of the Son on this theme alongside those from Proverbs 8. In this treatise, Tertullian has been concerned to show, contra Hermogenes, that God did not create all things out of pre-existent matter. Therefore, in this context, Tertullian deploys a prosopological interpretation of Wisdom's speech in Prov 8:22–31 to make the point that God, by his Wisdom who is the Word, made all things out of nothing.[60] Tertullian later returns to a prosopological reading of Prov 8:24 and then adds that "of darkness the Lord Himself says by the mouth of Isaias, *I, who formed the light and created darkness* [Isa 45:7]," and that "He says by Isaias, *Because my spirit went forth from me and I have made every breath* [Isa 57:16]," before coming back to the Son's words in Prov 8:28.[61] The polemical thrust of such a reading is amplified at the conclusion of the work:

> But it is not thus that the prophets and apostles tell us that the world was made by God, by merely appearing to and approaching matter. Indeed, they did not even mention any matter but stated that first Wisdom was created, *the beginning of His ways for His works* [Prov 8:22] and that next the Word was also brought forth, *by whom all things were made and without whom*

---

55. *Prax.* 7.9 (trans. Evans).
56. Evans, *Praxeas*, 218.
57. *Prax.* 19.2.
58. *Prax.* 19.5–6 (trans. Evans).
59. *Prax.* 19.6 (trans. Evans).
60. Cf. *Herm.* 18.1; 20.1.
61. *Herm.* 32.2 (trans. Waszink).

nothing was made [John 1:3]. Indeed, *by His Word the heavens were established, and all the hosts of them by His breath* [Ps 33:6]. He is God's right hand, indeed both His hands, by which He worked and built the universe.[62]

While Tertullian's argument has the side effect of rolling back some of Irenaeus's key pneumatological insights,[63] he nevertheless demonstrates an ability to synthesize the creation account in Gen 1:1–3 with the insights of John 1:1–3 by way of a prosopological reading of Prov 8:22–31. In so doing, he increases the scope of what texts could be read prosopologically as the words of the Son, expanding out from Wisdom's speech in Proverbs 8 to encompass portions of Deutero-Isaiah that had traditionally been read as the words of the Father. And by employing a prosopological reading of Proverbs 8 against both Hermogenes and Praxeas, Tertullian continues to show the flexibility of such readings to be applied in varying polemical contexts.

Pre-Incarnate Ministry

Tertullian follows his predecessors in identifying the pre-incarnate Son as the subject of the Old Testament theophanies. In this regard he reflects Irenaeus in more extensively using prosopological exegesis to identify the Son as the speaker to various Old Testament figures. Following a line of argument that can be traced back to Justin, in both *Against Praxeas* and *Against Marcion* Tertullian makes the point that since God the Father is invisible, it must have been the pre-incarnate Son who was made visible to various Old Testament persons. Thus, it was the Son who spoke to Adam the words of Gen 3:9 and spoke to Moses the words of Exod 4:11–12, Exod 23:20–21, and Exod 33:20.[64]

Tertullian is, however, sensitive to potential problems that could emerge from such an approach to making the Son the distinct subject of all the Old Testament theophanies. After all, as Evans writes, "the distinction has in it at least the germs of Arianism" insofar as the invisible Father and the occasionally visible pre-incarnate Son would appear to have

---

62. *Herm.* 45.1 (trans. Waszink).

63. See further Hughes, *How the Spirit Became God*, 87–91.

64. For Adam, see *Prax.* 16.4; *Marc.* 4.20; for Moses, see *Marc.* 4.39; *Adv. Jud.* 9.23; *Marc.* 2.27; 3.16. Without quoting the biblical text, Tertullian also writes that the Son spoke to Balaam (*Marc.* 4.39; cf. Num 22–24).

different natures.⁶⁵ Tertullian therefore adds an important nuance in *Against Praxeas*, namely, that the pre-incarnate Son "was seen in a mirror and an enigma and a vision and a dream," and "not as he really is."⁶⁶ By denying the real corporeal presence of the Son, Tertullian maintains the transcendence of both Father and Son, but "at the cost of surrendering the objective reality of the theophanies."⁶⁷

Tertullian, moreover, surpasses Irenaeus in making explicit how this point impacts his Christology. For example, regarding the pre-incarnate Son's interaction with Adam in the Garden of Eden, Tertullian writes:

> Thus also he already at that time knew human affections, as he was going to take upon himself also man's substances, flesh and soul, asking Adam a question as though he did not know— *Adam, where are you?* [Gen 3:9]—repenting that he had made man, as though he had no foreknowledge; tempting Abraham, as though ignorant what is in a man; angry, and reconciled with the same persons; and all those things which heretics [that is, the Marcionites],⁶⁸ for the destruction of the Creator, seize upon as unworthy of God, ignorant that these things befitted the Son, who was also going to undergo human passions, both thirst and hunger and tears and nativity itself and death itself, for this purpose made by the Father *a little lower than the angels* [Ps 8:5].⁶⁹

Here Tertullian makes an intriguing connection between the Son's pre-incarnate and incarnate states. From the beginning, the Son acted in history because he "was always also learning how as God to company with men, being none other than the Word who was to be flesh," and in so doing was "laying a foundation of faith for us, that we might the more easily believe that the Son of God has come down into the world, if we knew that something of the sort had previously been done."⁷⁰ The pre-incarnate ministry of the Son prepared both the Son and human beings for the incarnation itself; the Son learned to become a man, one might say, in order that man could learn to reach God. Tertullian

---

65. Evans, *Praxeas*, 269.

66. *Prax.* 14.7 (trans. Evans).

67. Evans, *Praxeas*, 272. As Evans points out, this seems to be a development from earlier in Tertullian's writings when he appeared to hold to the pre-incarnate Son having had a real body in each theophany, as at, e.g., *Marc.* 2.27; 3.9; *Carn. Chr.* 6.7 (*Praxeas*, 269).

68. Cf. Evans, *Praxeas*, 284.

69. *Prax.* 16.4 (trans. Evans, modernized). See also *Marc.* 2.27.

70. *Prax.* 16.3 (trans. Evans).

concludes, "From the beginning the whole course of the divine ordinance has come down through the Son."[71] Thus we observe a still further way in which Tertullian's prosopological exegesis advances his Christology through his identification of the Son as the subject of the Old Testament theophanies.

Virgin Birth

One of Tertullian's more novel prosopological interpretations from the person of the Son concerns Christ's virgin birth. Towards the end of his treatise *On the Flesh of Christ*, which aimed at refuting those who denied the reality of Christ's human flesh, Tertullian emphasizes that Christ was truly born of Mary and therefore was born of her flesh. As part of his Old Testament proof, Tertullian turns to the Psalter:

> [David] sings to us of Christ, and through his voice Christ indeed also sang concerning Himself. Hear, then, Christ the Lord speaking to God the Father: *You are He that drew me out of my mother's womb* [Ps 22:9a]. Here is the first point. *You are my hope from my mother's breasts; upon You have I been cast from the womb* [Ps 22:9b–10a]. Here is another point. *You are my God from my mother's belly* [Ps 22:10b].[72]

Tertullian clearly indicates a prosopological interpretation by noting that the words of Ps 22:9–10 are in fact the speech of the Son directed to the Father. Tertullian goes on to interpret the details of these verses as evidence for Christ having taken on real human flesh; for example, Tertullian makes the biological argument that the fact that Mary's "lacteal fountain" was opened insofar as she was able to breastfeed the infant Christ (Ps 22:9b) proves that her womb had contained a true fetus.[73]

Thus, Tertullian's prosopological interpretation of Ps 22:9–10 provides an instance of the *vox Christi* speaking about his own birth from the Virgin Mary. This appears to be a novel use of prosopological exegesis; while Psalm 22 had by Tertullian's time a long history of being interpreted as the words of Christ, the specific application of these two verses to the subject of Christ's miraculous birth demonstrates the

---

71. *Prax.* 16.7 (trans. Evans).

72. *Carn. Chr.* 20.4–5 (trans. *ANF*, modernized); cf. Tertullian's argument at *Prax.* 27.

73. *Carn. Chr.* 20.6 (trans. *ANF*).

continued significance of prosopological exegesis in adapting to meet new christological debates.

Incarnate Ministry

Turning next to the subject of Christ's incarnate ministry, Tertullian again demonstrates his capacity for expanding pre-existing categories of christological themes that he can explore through the lens of prosopological exegesis from the person of the Son. These instances cluster in book 4 of Tertullian's *Against Marcion*, which makes sense insofar as this book is primarily an exposition of Luke's Gospel against the Marcionites who claimed that the Jesus of the New Testament revealed a Father God different from the Yahweh of the Old Testament. In making this case, Tertullian returns to familiar wells, such as Isaiah and the Psalter, but also identifies new verses from less popular books, such as Jeremiah, Hosea, and the Song of Songs.

Tertullian's creativity can be seen with regard to how Christ came to forgive sins. In his commentary on Jesus' healing of the paralytic (Luke 5:16–26), Tertullian claims that Christ in this scene fulfills the prophecies of Isa 35:2–4 and Isa 53:12. Tertullian then transitions to a prosopological interpretation from earlier in the book of Isaiah: "For in an earlier passage, speaking in the person of the Lord himself, he had said, *Even though your sins be as scarlet, I will make them as white as snow; even though they be like crimson, I will whiten them as wool* [Isa 1:18]."[74] Tertullian's move here is surprising; nothing in the source text would suggest that we should read this as anything more than a typical divine prophecy; if anything, we would expect this to be read as the Father speaking concerning the Son's future work of redemption. And yet Tertullian explicitly marks this as the prosopological ("speaking in the person") speech of "the Lord" (one of Tertullian's favored titles for Christ in this work, as distinguished from "the Creator," or the Father), referring to Christ's earthly ministry of extending God's forgiveness to sinners. One wonders, then, how much of the Old Testament speech attributed to "the Lord" (Greek *kyrios*) Tertullian intends for us to read as the prosopological speech of the Son.

The challenges of such an approach become immediately evident in Tertullian's next interpretation of a Gospel pericope, the calling of Levi and the dispute about fasting (Luke 5:27–39). Here Jesus' question about

---

74. *Marc.* 4.10 (trans. *ANF*).

making the wedding guests fast when the bridegroom is among them (Luke 5:34) becomes the basis for pulling together Old Testament verses about bridegrooms that can be applied to Christ. Thus Tertullian identifies Christ as the subject of Ps 19:5–6 before commenting,

> By the mouth of Isaiah He also says exultingly of the Father, *Let my soul rejoice in the Lord; for He has clothed me with the garment of salvation and with the tunic of joy, as a bridegroom. He has put a miter round about my head, as a bride* [Isa 61:10].[75]

This is followed shortly thereafter by a further prosopological reading, this time from the Song of Songs, in which Christ directs his speech at the church: "This spouse Christ invites home to Himself also by Solomon from the call of the Gentiles, because you read: *Come with me from Lebanon, my spouse* [Song 4:8]."[76] Given the immense importance of a christological reading of the Song of Songs for later Christian interpreters, it is significant to note its presence in Tertullian's argument here, though he makes little further use of the Song in such a way.

Tertullian is particularly fond of using prosopological exegesis from the person of the Son to demonstrate that the Old Testament speaks prophetically concerning many of the events in Christ's life. Thus, for instance, Christ speaks regarding his method of teaching in the Psalter: "*I will open*, says He, *my mouth in a parable* (that is, in a similitude); *I will utter dark problems* (that is, I will set forth questions) [Ps 78:2]."[77] Likewise, when Tertullian describes how Christ ascended the mountain to pray (Luke 6:12), he draws a connection with the prophecy of Isa 40:9 before continuing to provide additional prosopological interpretations on the basis of the word "mountain":

> *Therefore, my people shall know my name in that day* [Isa 52:6a]. What name does the prophet mean, but Christ's? *That I am He that speaks—even I* [Isa 52:6b]. For it was He that used to speak in the prophets—the Word, the Creator's Son. *I am present, while it is the hour, upon the mountains, as one that brings glad tidings of peace, as one that publishes good tidings* [Isa 52:7]. . . . Moreover, concerning the voice of His prayer to the Father by night, the psalm manifestly says: *O my God, I will cry in the daytime, and You shall hear; and in the night season, and it shall not be in*

---

75. *Marc.* 4.11 (trans. *ANF*, modernized).

76. *Marc.* 4.11 (trans. *ANF*).

77. *Marc.* 4.11 (trans. *ANF*); cf. 4.25, in which Isa 29:14; 45:3; 44:25 are summoned as prophecies of this feature of Christ's ministry.

vain to me [Ps 22:2]. In another passage touching the same voice and place, the psalm says, *I cried unto the Lord with my voice, and He heard me out of His holy mountain* [Ps 3:4].[78]

Thus Tertullian identifies the "voice" of Christ in both Isaiah and the Psalter, sandwiched around a quotation of a prophecy from Nah 1:15, describing his prayer on the mountainside. Tertullian is clear: the Son of God "used to speak in the prophets," thereby justifying his prosopological method and showing, against the Marcionites, the continuity of Old and New Testaments. In this portion of his treatise, this then sets up still further prosopological interpretations of Isa 43:20, Isa 49:18a, and Isa 49:21 as the words of Christ concerning his ministry's inclusion of gentiles,[79] of Isa 61:1 as Christ speaking concerning his ministry to the poor,[80] and of Isa 32:9–10 as Christ announcing his inclusion of women.[81] These examples further demonstrate Tertullian's inclination to read even seemingly non-dialogical portions of Isaiah as the Son's speech.

Christ's mode of teaching is a final major theme for which Tertullian finds evidence of the Son speaking prosopologically concerning his incarnate ministry. The key verse for Tertullian appears to be Isa 50:4. As Tertullian quotes it in one instance, having surrounded it with thematically similar words of Christ from John's Gospel, "*The Lord gives me the tongue of learning, to know when I ought to speak* [Isa 50:4]."[82] Elsewhere, Tertullian prosopologically interprets Isa 50:4 alongside a verse from Jeremiah, with the Son quoting the words of the Father to him: "*And the Lord said to me, Behold I have put my words in your mouth* [Jer 1:9]."[83] This reading of Jeremiah is quite unusual insofar as the original source text clearly indicates that these words were spoken by God to the prophet himself, a fact that Tertullian has entirely elided from his interpretation. Similarly, when Tertullian twice quotes Isa 50:4 as the words of the Son, he uses these occasions to pull in other quotations (Isa 44:5; Hos 12:4) that would not appear from the source texts to be the most obvious choices

---

78. *Marc.* 4.13 (trans. *ANF*, modernized).

79. *Marc.* 4.13.

80. *Marc.* 4.14; cf. 4.31, where Tertullian gives a similar prosopological interpretation of Isa 58:7; cf. *Prax.* 11.6 in which Tertullian prosopologically interprets Isa 61:1, although without much explanation.

81. *Marc.* 4.19.

82. *Prax.* 23.9 (trans. Evans, modernized).

83. *Prax.* 22.5 (trans. Evans, modernized).

for identifying the Son's prosopological speech.[84] Still, these verses show Tertullian's commitment to a robust and thorough prosopological approach to making his christological points.

Tertullian thus makes frequent use of prosopological exegesis to identify instances of Christ speaking in the Old Testament regarding his earthly ministry, particularly with respect to the events described in Luke's Gospel. The quantity of examples Tertullian provides represents a significant expansion in the scope of the Son's prosopological speech as compared with that of his predecessors.

Crucifixion

Similarly, Tertullian greatly expands the number of passages that he reads prosopologically as the words of the Son concerning the crucifixion. Tertullian's greatest concentration of such examples is found in his *Against the Jews*, in which he demonstrates that the Old Testament not only describes Christ's passion and death but contains Christ's very words about his crucifixion. As Tertullian explains:

> In the psalms, the Spirit Himself of Christ was already singing, saying, *They were repaying me evil for good* [Ps 35:12]; and, *What I had not seized I was then paying in full* [Ps 69:4]; *They exterminated my hands and feet* [Ps 22:16]; and, *They put into my drink gall, and in my thirst they slaked me with vinegar* [Ps 69:21]; *Upon my vesture they did cast the lot* [Ps 22:18]; just as the other outrages which you were to commit on Him were foretold—all which He, actually and thoroughly suffering, suffered not for any evil action of His own, but *that the Scriptures from the mouth of the prophets might be fulfilled* [cf. Matt 26:56].[85]

This catena of citations from the Psalter is followed shortly thereafter with still further examples from Psalm 22:

> If you shall still seek for predictions of the Lord's cross, the twenty-first Psalm [twenty-second in the MT] will at length be able to satisfy you, containing as it does the whole passion of Christ; singing, as He does, even at so early a date, His own glory. *They dug*, He says, *my hands and feet* [Ps 22:16]—which

---

84. *Marc.* 4.39. Hos 12:4 in the LXX can at least be construed as first-person dialogue (unlike in the MT), but the broader context of harsh prophecy against Israel stretches the plausibility of such a reading as Tertullian suggests.

85. *Adv. Jud.* 10.4 (trans. *ANF*).

> is the peculiar atrocity of the cross; and again when He implores the aid of the Father, *Save me*, He says, *out of the mouth of the lion*—of course, of death—*and from the horn of the unicorns my humility* [Ps 22:21]—from the ends, to wit, of the cross, as we have above shown.[86]

What is striking about both of these passages is Tertullian's description of Christ "singing" in the psalms, a term that he uses only sparingly in his writings.[87] When, for instance, he makes similar prosopological appeals to Psalm 22 in *Against Marcion*, this verb is absent.[88] In any event, Tertullian's clear statement that Psalm 22 contains the "whole" passion of Christ is a clear echo of earlier Christian writers such as Justin.[89] Likewise, insofar as Tertullian also prosopologically interprets Isa 50:6 with respect to Christ's crucifixion, he follows well-trodden ground from Justin and Irenaeus.[90]

Other instances of prosopological exegesis on this theme, however, are novel to Tertullian. Thus, in book 4 of *Against Marcion*, Tertullian argues for the reality of Jesus' human body with a criticism of Marcion:

> He did not understand how ancient was this figure of the body of Christ, who said Himself by Jeremiah, *I was like a lamb or an ox that is brought to the slaughter, and I knew not that they devised a device against me, saying, Let us cast the tree upon His bread* [Jer 11:19], which means, of course, the cross upon His body.[91]

Through a eucharistic interpretation of Christ's bread as his body, Tertullian puts forth a still further, and quite unique, prosopological interpretation of the Son speaking concerning his crucifixion.

As Tertullian points out, Christ himself spoke the words of Ps 31:5 from the cross, proving that the Psalter gives us the voice of "the very Christ."[92] Thus, when Tertullian quotes Ps 71:18 and Ps 3:1 as the words of the Son to the Father,[93] though Tertullian does not point out any theological content of these verses apart from the fact that they represent the

---

86. *Adv. Jud.* 10.13 (trans. *ANF*).
87. Cf. *Carn. Chr.* 20.3.
88. See *Marc.* 3.19, in which Tertullian prosopologically interprets Ps 22:16, 21; see also *Marc.* 4.42, which features Ps 22:7–8, 16, 18.
89. Cf. *Dial.* 98.2–5.
90. *Marc.* 3.5; cf. *1 Apol.* 38.1; *Epid.* 34; 68.
91. *Marc.* 4.40 (trans. *ANF*).
92. *Marc.* 4.42 (trans. *ANF*).
93. *Prax.* 11.6.

words of two distinct divine persons, the verses' emphasis on the Son being forsaken and oppressed suggests that they should also be interpreted according to this theme.

Present Reign

A final significant subject of the Son's prosopological speech concerns the Son's reign over the nations. Again, Tertullian wields a surprising variety of passages to develop this theme. The clearest treatment of the Son's speech concerning his reign over the nations is found in book 3 of *Against Marcion*.

In his discussion of how Christ's followers through the ages were foretold to suffer just as Christ himself, Tertullian comments that Psalm 22 paints a picture in which, under Christ's current heavenly lordship, "the brethren of Christ or children of God would ascribe glory to God the Father, in the person of Christ Himself addressing his Father: *I will declare Your name unto my brethren; in the midst of the congregation will I sing praise unto You* [Ps 22:22]."[94] A prosopological reading of Ps 22:22 extends back as early as Heb 2:12, but here Tertullian makes the prosopological reading more explicit, identifying the Son as speaking to the Father in a manner that, in turn, can also be read as being spoken from "the person" of present-day believers. The Son's voice thus becomes not only the voice of the psalmist but the voice of the apostles and succeeding generations of Christians. Presumably, Tertullian's following quotations are then to be read in a similar light: "And a little afterwards He says: *My praise shall be of You in the great congregation* [Ps 22:25]. In the sixty-seventh [MT sixty-eighth] Psalm He says again: *In the congregations bless the Lord God* [Ps 68:26]."[95] The keyword "congregation" becomes the linking element for associating these verses, even as the audience of the speech shifts from the Father to other believers, which can then be read in a similar prosopological light even though no previous author appears to have done so.

As Tertullian proceeds in book 3 of *Against Marcion*, he elaborates on how Christ's present acclamation by the church contrasts with his rejection by and judgment of the Jews. As Tertullian interprets,

---

94. *Marc.* 3.22 (trans. *ANF*, modernized).
95. *Marc.* 3.22 (trans. *ANF*, modernized).

In the fifty-eighth [MT fifty-ninth] Psalm He demands of the Father their dispersion: *Scatter them in Your power* [Ps 59:11]. By Isaiah He also says, as He finishes a prophecy of their consumption by fire: *Because of me has this happened to you; you shall lie down in sorrow* [Isa 50:11].[96]

Given the clear christological resonances of Isa 50:4–9, Tertullian also reading Isa 50:11 as the words of the Son is an unsurprising development. Psalm 59, while not a popular text for prosopological exegesis among earlier Christian writers, nevertheless tracks closely with the theme of God's judgment of his enemies. Tertullian again shows an ability to identify and include additional verses from the Psalter and Isaiah to advance his case for Christ fulfilling the Old Testament Scriptures via prosopological exegesis.[97]

This lengthy analysis of Tertullian's examples of prosopological exegesis from the person of the Son has indeed demonstrated the creativity and comprehensiveness of this fiery North African in wielding this person-centered reading strategy. Tertullian provides far more examples than either of his predecessors, Justin and Irenaeus, though his readings sometimes stretch what a straightforward reading of the Old Testament source text would seem to allow, particularly as the Son's voice in the Old Testament appears at times to drown out any unique role for that of the Father.

From the Spirit

In making his case for the distinction among the three divine persons, Tertullian explicitly identifies the Holy Spirit as a distinct speaking person for the purposes of prosopological exegesis. In a key passage on prosopological exegesis in *Against Praxeas*, Tertullian makes the following claim:

> Consider also the Spirit speaking from a third person (*ex tertia persona*) concerning the Father and the Son: *The Lord said to my Lord: Sit at my right hand, until I make your enemies a footstool for your feet* [Ps 110:1]. Again through Isaiah: *Thus says the Lord to my Lord Christ* [Isa 45:1]. Likewise through the same prophet, to the Father concerning the Son: *Lord, who has believed our report, and to whom is the arm of the Lord revealed? We have*

---

96. *Marc.* 3.23 (trans. *ANF*, modernized).

97. Tertullian also quotes and interprets Ps 59:11 and Isa 50:11 in a parallel passage in *Adv. Jud.* 13.27.

> *announced concerning him: like a young boy, like a root in a thirsty land, also there was no beauty or glory of his* [Isa 53:1–2].[98]

As I have discussed in detail elsewhere, this passage is rich in significance for the development of early Christian pneumatology.[99] For our present purposes, however, we can observe how Tertullian, following Justin and Irenaeus, prosopologically interprets Ps 110:1 as the words of the Holy Spirit. But whereas Justin and Irenaeus had attached Gen 19:24 and Ps 45:6–7 to this verse, Tertullian instead proceeds with prosopological interpretations of Isa 45:1 and Isa 53:1–2.[100] Irenaeus had interpreted Isa 45:1 as the words of the Father without dealing with the somewhat abrupt shift in the source text. Tertullian, though, isolates the introductory clause of Isa 45:1 to draw out the clear parallel to Ps 110:1a. These two examples of the Spirit speaking concerning the Father and the Son then give way to an instance of the Spirit speaking to the Father concerning the Son, with Isa 53:1–2 summoned as the key example. As with the two previous verses Tertullian cited, this one includes two "lords," although in this instance one of the two lords is being directly addressed on the topic of the other. Tertullian does not comment on the christological significance of these verses apart from the fact that they demonstrate the distinction of the three divine persons,[101] but given theological continuity over time there is no reason to doubt that Ps 110:1 and Isa 45:1 speak of the Son's present reign. Isaiah 53:1–2 likewise receives no commentary concerning its theodramatic setting, though it must be after the incarnation, as the Spirit is here speaking to the Father regarding the Son's lack of human beauty. Given that the glorified, incarnate Son is now seated at the right hand of the Father, it is also possible to read this as a statement regarding the Son's present reign, although that emphasis is not in view in Tertullian's argument.

The other handful of instances of prosopological exegesis from the person of the Holy Spirit concerning the Son also support the theme of Christ's present lordship.[102] For example, after identifying Christ as the

---

98. *Prax.* 11.7–8 (AT).

99. See further Hughes, *Trinitarian Testimony*, 163–67; *How the Spirit Became God*, 71–74.

100. Ps 110:1 and Isa 45:1 had previously been quoted together at *Barn.* 12.10–11, although they were not interpreted prosopologically. Tertullian quotes Ps 45:6–7, Ps 110:1, and Gen 19:24 together at *Prax.* 13.1–4.

101. See also Tertullian's citation of Isa 45:1 at *Prax.* 28.11.

102. Similarly, the Spirit calls the Father "Lord" through the quotation of Ps 4:6 at

bridegroom of Ps 19:5–6, Tertullian uses word association to eventually arrive at a prosopological interpretation of Isa 61:10: "For indeed [Christ] counts the church as in himself, concerning which the same Spirit says to him, *You shall place them all on yourself, as an ornament on a bride* [Isa 49:18b]."[103] As Tertullian reads it, in this verse the Spirit explains to the Son how the Son will summon the church to himself; the theodramatic setting is again most plausibly the time of Christ's current reign.

Similarly, when Tertullian comments on Paul's statement in 2 Cor 4:6 concerning the Father giving believers "the knowledge of the glory of God in the face of Jesus Christ," he proceeds via word association to pull in a passage from the Psalter: "To [the Father], the Spirit replies in the psalm by foreknowledge of the future, *The light of your countenance, O Lord, has been shown above us* [Ps 4:6]."[104] As this quotation immediately follows Tertullian's quotation of Isa 49:6 as the words of the Father to the Son concerning the Son's reign over the gentiles, this text is most plausibly read as also speaking of the present revelation of the Son's rule following his ascension and enthronement.[105]

Additionally, in his description of Christ's ascension, Tertullian interprets Ps 2:8 and Ps 110:1 as the words of the Father to the Son before turning to the speech of the Spirit: "And also elsewhere the Spirit says to the Father concerning the Son, *You have subjected all things beneath his feet* [Ps 8:6]."[106] Aligning well with lexical similarities in those two other more popular selections from the Psalter, this verse provides a further testimony to the Son's present reign as the Spirit speaks to the Father about the Son.

This brings us, then, to a final instance of the Spirit's prosopological speech as it concerns the Son that is a bit more oblique, but nevertheless quite interesting. At the close of book 3 of *Against Marcion*, Tertullian's gaze turns to the future, encompassing the millennial kingdom, the destruction

---

Marc. 5.11.

103. *Marc.* 4.11 (AT).

104. *Marc.* 5.11 (AT). Previously (Hughes, *Trinitarian Testimony*, 180), I took the Son as the audience of the Spirit's speech, but I think the better reading is that the Spirit is here speaking to the Father concerning the Son, whom Tertullian identifies as the countenance of the Father.

105. Regarding Christ's countenance, see also Tertullian's christological interpretation of Lam 4:20 at *Prax.* 14.10, which should also likely be understood as the words of the Spirit concerning the Son; Tertullian takes this as a still further example of the Scriptures calling Christ "Lord"; see further Hughes, *Trinitarian Testimony*, 181.

106. *Marc.* 5.17 (AT).

of the world, and the final translation of believers into the eternal heavenly kingdom.[107] In describing this blessed state, Tertullian comments, "Thus the Spirit marvels at those who by that ascent are going to heavenly kingdoms, saying, *They fly, and they are the ones who fly like clouds and like little doves towards me* [Isa 60:8]; that is, simply like doves."[108] In context, this scene presents believers rising to be with Christ for all eternity, and so Christ is at least indirectly in view in this passage. This verse therefore places Christ at the outworking of the final things, and so in that way can be compared with how Tertullian interpreted parts of Psalm 110 as the words of the Father concerning the Son's return as judge even though the language of judgment is not explicit in this text.[109]

Summary

Tertullian further demonstrates how his predecessors' mission to discover from within the Old Testament examples of speech from each of the three divine persons continued to develop, expand in comprehensiveness, and incorporate responses to new theological challenges. While Tertullian clearly follows Justin at times and Irenaeus at others, he is also more than content to go his own way and repurpose existing prosopological texts or identify new ones as necessary for accomplishing his purposes. For Tertullian, this primarily meant arguing against the Marcionites on the one hand and against the modalistic monarchians on the other. Despite the different polemical points directed at each group, Tertullian frequently returned to a common strategy: identify within the Old Testament the voice of Christ (or the voices of the Father and the Spirit speaking to or concerning the Son) in order to demonstrate that

---

107. As Osborn observes, here is where we find the sole reference to "the spectacular millenarianism of Irenaeus" in Tertullian's writings (*Tertullian*, 216). However, Hill maintains that Tertullian "is fusing together the millennialism of Irenaeus with the non-millennialist notion of the descent of heavenly Jerusalem to earth sometime in the near future" (*Regnum Caelorum*, 150). Thus Hill reads Tertullian's approach to the millennium as "strikingly eclectic" (151). On Tertullian's understanding of the timing of the opening of the heavenly kingdom, cf. *An.* 55.

108. *Marc.* 3.24 (AT).

109. As Osborn writes, "The second advent of Christ is pivotal in Tertullian's eschatology, but the four main elements (return of Christ in glory, resurrection of the body, universal judgement and a renewed earth) are not discussed in every place" (*Tertullian*, 215).

Christ, while fulfilling the purposes of the Creator God of the Old Testament, is nevertheless distinct from that Creator God.

Through all of these various examples of prosopological speech, we must remember the christological and even trinitarian significance of Tertullian identifying the Son as a *persona* through this reading strategy. As noted earlier, Tertullian uses the term *persona* to describe "the effective manifestation of a distinct being," using it in such a way to describe not a theatrical mask but rather something about God's own inner life.[110] It is not surprising, then, that Tertullian is the first to use the language of "Trinity" (*trinitas*) to describe how the three *personae* of Father, Son, and Holy Spirit nevertheless eternally exist as one substance (*substantia*). In this way, then, we can affirm with Matthew Bates that "prosopological exegesis contributed decisively to the development of the concept of the Trinity, since it was this way of reading that especially led to the consolidation of 'person' language to express the three-in-one mystery."[111]

In concluding this section, we can summarize Tertullian's prosopological readings in a table that sets out all the instances in which Tertullian proposes a prosopological reading of Old Testament dialogical passages that involve speech to, from, or about the Son. As in previous chapters, verses in bold reflect places where Tertullian explicitly interprets these words as intra-divine dialogue:

	From the Father	*From the Son*	*From the Spirit*
Divine Pre-Existence	**Gen 1:26**	Prov 8:22–31	—
	Gen 3:22	Isa 41:4	
	Ps 2:7b	Isa 44:24	
	Ps 45:1	Isa 45:7	
	Ps 91:13	Isa 57:16	
	Ps 110:3		
	Isa 42:2–3		
	Isa 44:25–26		
	Isa 52:14		
	Mal 3:1		
Pre-Incarnate Ministry	—	Gen 3:9	—
		Exod 4:11–12	
		Exod 23:20–21	
		Exod 33:20	

---

110. Osborn, *Tertullian*, 137.

111. Bates, *Birth*, 7.

	From the Father	From the Son	From the Spirit
Virgin Birth	—	**Ps 22:9–10**	—
Incarnate Ministry	**Jer 1:9b–c**	Ps 3:4 **Ps 22:2** Ps 78:2 Song 4:8 Isa 1:18 Isa 32:9–10 Isa 43:20 Isa 44:5 Isa 49:18a Isa 49:21 Isa 50:4 Isa 52:6–7 Isa 58:7 Isa 61:1 Isa 61:10 Jer 1:9a Hos 12:4	—
Crucifixion	—	**Ps 3:1** Ps 22:7–8 Ps 22:16 Ps 22:18 **Ps 22:21** **Ps 31:5** Ps 35:12 Ps 69:4 Ps 69:21 **Ps 71:18** Isa 50:6 Jer 11:19	—
Ascension, Enthronement, and Reign	**Ps 2:7b–8** **Ps 110:1b–c** Isa 8:14 Isa 28:16 Isa 42:1 Isa 42:4 **Isa 42:6–7** **Isa 49:6** Isa 55:4 **Isa 55:5**	Ps 22:22 Ps 22:25 **Ps 59:11** Ps 68:26 Isa 50:11	Ps 4:6 Ps 8:6 Ps 110:1a Isa 45:1 **Isa 49:18b** **Isa 53:1–2**
Return and Final Consummation	**Ps 110:1b–c** Ps 110:2 Ps 110:4	—	Isa 60:8

As this table demonstrates, Tertullian drastically expands both the scope and the frequency of prosopological exegesis relative to both Justin and Irenaeus. Still, the basic framework remains what we have seen in earlier writers: prosopological exegesis is used to further elaborate upon the story of the Son, from his divine pre-existence through his present reign and now even extending into his return at the final judgment. To explore further the significance of Tertullian's accomplishment, we may now turn to the matter of Tertullian's sources and his understanding of the *regula fidei*.

Weaving the Threads

Given that Tertullian, following Justin and Irenaeus, used prosopological exegesis to advance christological claims across his various theological projects, we can now analyze the extent to which early Christian *testimonia* collections and the *regula fidei* may have shaped or otherwise influenced his more comprehensive and thorough presentation of prosopological exegesis relating to the Son.

Tertullian's Use of *Testimonia*

Again following in the footsteps of his predecessors, Tertullian makes ample use of *testimonia* collections in several of his works, with *Against the Jews*, *Against Marcion*, and *Against Praxeas* containing the most frequent use of such sources.[112] These three works are also the ones that include the highest number of instances of prosopological exegesis, likely reflecting the fact that the themes of these works, which all in some regard focus on how the right interpretation of the Old Testament is essential for Christian orthodoxy, naturally lend themselves to both phenomena.

Unlike his predecessors, however, Tertullian clearly marks his use of *testimonia* sources in a passage touching on the subject of prosopological exegesis. To return again to the key passage of *Prax.* 11, Tertullian introduces the claim that "all the Scriptures disclose both the demonstration and the distinction of the Trinity; from them also is deduced our rule: the person speaking and the person spoken of and the person

---

112. See further Albl, *Scripture*, 126–31. Albl notes that the *testimonia* collections used in *Against the Jews* are essentially repeated in *Against Marcion*, leading to the unusual reality that "ironically, [Tertullian] constantly accuses the anti-Jewish Marcion of taking his positions from the Jews" (*Scripture*, 127).

spoken to cannot be the same."[113] Tertullian then provides a series of examples, all discussed above, in which the Father speaks to or concerning the Son, the Son speaks to or concerning the Father, and the Holy Spirit speaks to or concerning the Father and the Son.[114] Following these quotations, Tertullian makes the following statement:

> These are a few testimonies out of many; for we do not pretend to bring up all the passages of scripture, because we have a tolerably large accumulation of them in the various heads of our subject, as we in our several chapters call them in as our witnesses in the fullness of their dignity and authority.[115]

As Albl observes, the scriptural quotations found in *Prax.* 11 bear the distinctive marks of having been drawn from a *testimonia* collection, a hypothesis confirmed by this statement of Tertullian that he is drawing his sequence of texts from a *testimonia* collection organized by various subject headings.[116] A plausible conclusion to draw from this is that there existed in Tertullian's day a *testimonia* collection that included headings of speech from Father, Son, and Spirit. Presumably, then, this predated Tertullian, but based on our analysis in the previous two chapters it must have post-dated Justin and Irenaeus, placing its composition near the very end of the second century. One plausible explanation of its origins is that it was a later evolution of early "two powers" *testimonia* collections anchored in Ps 110:1, glimpsed in Justin and Irenaeus, that focused on the issue of the distinction between Christ and God. Isaiah 45:1 appears to be the key verse brought in to supplement this point, displacing the previous priority of Ps 45:6–7 and perhaps also Gen 19:24.[117]

The significance of this hypothesis should not be minimized; as argued in previous chapters, Justin and Irenaeus both used *testimonia* collections as sources for quotations, but we found no evidence for an underlying *testimonia* collection containing passages arranged by the divine speaker. With Tertullian, however, we arrive at a new phase of development in which the lines of prosopological exegesis and the creation of *testimonia* collections appear to have converged. Unfortunately, we simply cannot identify the ultimate author of such a collection

---

113. *Prax.* 11.4 (AT).
114. *Prax.* 11.5–8.
115. *Prax.* 11.9 (trans. Albl, *Scripture*, 127).
116. Albl, *Scripture*, 127.
117. See further Albl, *Scripture*, 205, 232.

focused upon prosopological exegesis. Albl, for his part, speculates that Tertullian made use of collections unknown to Justin and Irenaeus that had perhaps been produced "in a school or liturgical setting."[118] It is not inconceivable that Tertullian himself played a role in the composition of such a collection.

Also of interest is Tertullian's use of *testimonia* collections in *Adv. Jud.* 9–14, which contain several examples of prosopological speech from both the Father and the Son. Albl again demonstrates Tertullian's reliance on written *testimonia* collections in this sequence, noting Tertullian's "immense respect for the *testimonia* sources" on account of the fact that "he retains LXX-deviant quotations despite the fact that he is intimately familiar with the LXX: his normal method was to translate his biblical texts directly from the LXX Greek himself."[119] What is particularly fascinating about this section of *Against the Jews* is that the proof-texts are arranged according to a "creedal sequence."[120] The implication, then, is that this particular *testimonia* collection was also arranged according to a creedal sequence. Of course, this section and its underlying source included far more verses than those that could be interpreted prosopologically, suggesting that, unlike in *Prax.* 11, prosopological interpretation was not the focus of the underlying collection. Nor was prosopological exegesis, however, the primary point of interest of this section of *Against the Jews*; here it seems more plausible that Tertullian is simply highlighting the prosopological interpretation inherent in these texts, an interpretation that may not have been commented upon in the original *testimonia* collection.

We find, therefore, that Tertullian draws upon a wide range of *testimonia* collections, at least one of which may have featured passages organized according to the presumed prosopological speaker. Without question, Tertullian's approach to prosopological exegesis built upon previous writers and sources; nevertheless, the sheer scope and comprehensiveness of his use of this reading strategy suggests that he was additionally an innovator in the use of this method. Still, it is difficult to evaluate the originality of any one instance of prosopological exegesis. Take, for example, the novel uses of prosopological exegesis in book 4 of *Against Marcion*. As observed above, over the course of this book Tertullian includes a plethora of instances of the Son's prosopological

---

118. Albl, *Scripture*, 129.
119. Albl, *Scripture*, 129.
120. Albl, *Scripture*, 128.

speech concerning various specific aspects of Christ's earthly ministry, such as how he prayed on the mountain or reached out to the poor and to women. There are no parallels for such interpretations in earlier writers, as we have no extant equivalent of such an in-depth commentary on the Gospel of Luke. Thus when we are confronted with new prosopological interpretations, such as Isa 1:18,[121] we may be tempted to ascribe their creation to Tertullian. But the odd nature of examples such as this, which would appear to read every instance of the words of "the Lord" in Isaiah as referring to the speech of God the Son (despite the problems this creates for when "the Lord" then speaks to the servant in Deutero-Isaiah), could point to the passage being drawn from a *testimonia* collection—perhaps even the one centered on prosopological exegesis that Tertullian describes in *Prax.* 11. That could explain, in other words, why the passage's original context has been obscured.

In any event, Tertullian's writings demonstrate the continued convergence of early Christian *testimonia* collections with prosopological exegesis. As with earlier authors, though, we next need to try and account for why this reading strategy was so significant for Tertullian and those who compiled *testimonia* collections. The fact that at least some of these collections were organized according to a creedal sequence points us to a still further factor, that of the influence of the *regula fidei*, to which we now turn.

Tertullian and the *Regula Fidei*

Tertullian, writing in Latin, "established 'rule of faith' (*regula fidei*) as standard terminology in Latin and for the later Western church" to describe the body of essential Christian teaching.[122] Tertullian set forth his *regula fidei* in direct opposition to Marcion's own claim to possess the true rule of faith,[123] claiming that his alone was given by Christ and the apostles.[124] More controversially, however, Tertullian appears to suggest that the Holy Spirit, as understood as the Paraclete of the Montanists, is

---

121. *Marc.* 4.10.
122. Ferguson, *Rule of Faith*, 22.
123. *Marc.* 1.1; 1.20.
124. *Praesc.* 13.6; 26.9; cf. Ferguson, *Rule of Faith*, 23. On Tertullian's rule of faith, see further Countryman, "Tertullian and the Regula Fidei," 208–14; Evans, *Praxeas*, 189–92.

the one who "proves" this rule. We see this language in one of Tertullian's clearest statements of the *regula fidei* in *Against Praxeas*:

> In truth, as always—and now even more so, being better instructed by the Paraclete, the leader into all truth—we believe that there is indeed one only God, yet under this dispensation (or "economy"), that this one only God has also a Son, his Word, who proceeded from himself, by whom all things were made, and without whom nothing has been made. This one was sent by the Father into the virgin and from her was born man and God, son of man and son of God, and named Jesus Christ. This one suffered, this one died and was buried according to the Scriptures, and was reawakened by the Father and taken up again into heaven to sit at the right hand of the Father, [from whence] he will come to judge the living and the dead. Thereafter he will send from the Father, in accordance with his promise, the Holy Spirit, the Paraclete, the sanctifier of the faith of those who believe in the Father and the Son and the Holy Spirit. That this rule has come down from the beginning of the Gospel . . . he will prove [*probabit*].[125]

Assuming *probabit*, as an active verb, needs a subject, the context points to the Paraclete as the most natural choice, heightening the Montanist character of Tertullian's argument in this passage (and, by extension, in this treatise as a whole).[126] This passage nevertheless gives an important summary of the *regula fidei* as understood by Tertullian. The christological portion of the rule encompasses the following elements: the Son of God pre-existed with the Father, became incarnate by being born of a virgin, suffered, died, and was buried, was resurrected, ascended into heaven to reign, and will come again to judge the world. This statement of the rule is, apart from its setting within a Montanist framework, unremarkable.

Perhaps more interesting, then, is Tertullian's other major statement of the *regula fidei* in his *Prescription against Heretics*:

> The rule of faith which is believed: there is but one God, and he alone is the creator of the world, who by the sending forth of his Word in the beginning brought the universe into being out of nothing; and this Word, called his Son, was seen in various ways in the name of God by the patriarchs, was heard always by the

---

125. *Prax.* 2.1–2 (AT).

126. See further Hughes, *Trinitarian Testimony*, 182–83; *How the Spirit Became God*, 84n28. Other translations render *probabit* in the passive voice ("will be proved"), but in that case we would expect *probabitur*.

prophets, and last of all was brought down into the virgin Mary by the Spirit and power of God the Father, was made flesh in her womb and was born from her as Jesus Christ; thereafter he proclaimed a new law and a new promise of the kingdom of heaven, worked miracles, was nailed to the cross, was resurrected on the third day, was taken up to heaven to sit at the Father's right hand and to send in his place the power of the Holy Spirit to guide believers, and will come again in glory to take the saints into the enjoyment of life eternal and heavenly promises, and to condemn the impious to everlasting fire, both parties being raised from the dead and having their flesh restored.[127]

This statement of the *regula fidei* is quite similar in most respects to the version found in *Against Praxeas*, though it glosses over the specific facts of Christ's death and burial while expanding upon Jesus' miracles and the significance of Christ's ascension and final judgment. The most striking difference, however, is that the version in *Praesc.* 13 includes a line about Christ being seen by the patriarchs, a reference to the pre-incarnate Christ being the subject of the Old Testament theophanies. This does not appear in other early Christian statements of the *regula fidei*, demanding further comment.

Other statements of the *regula fidei* are content, if they mention anything about the Old Testament period, merely to mention that the prophets announced Christ's coming. Even Justin and Irenaeus, who believed that the pre-incarnate Christ was the subject of Old Testament theophanies, did not attach this particular action to the christological narrative of the *regula fidei*. Setting aside any theological issues that may arise from such a christological interpretation of the theophanies, the addition of a "new" item to the *regula fidei* would be particularly problematic insofar as the rule of faith was, as Tertullian himself pointed out, fixed and unchanging.[128] As we will see, therefore, Tertullian's successors would revert to a form of the *regula fidei* more in line with that found in *Against Praxeas*, which does not include the comment on the pre-incarnate Son's appearances to the patriarchs. Indeed, it is interesting that Tertullian's *Prescription against Heretics* was almost certainly written before both *On the Veiling of Virgins* and *Against Praxeas*,[129]

---

127. *Praesc.* 13 (trans. Ferguson, *Rule of Faith*, 6–7); see also *Virg.* 1.3–4, a statement of the rule of faith that does not include the point about the theophanies.

128. Cf. *Virg.* 1.3.

129. While dating Tertullian's works is a tricky endeavor, this basic assumption appears safe; cf., e.g., Barnes, *Tertullian*, 55.

suggesting that Tertullian's initial enthusiasm for including the Old Testament theophanies in the *regula fidei* waned in his later years.

We can visually depict the extent of alignment between Tertullian's use of prosopological exegesis and his presentation of the rule of faith as follows:

	From the Father	*From the Son*	*From the Spirit*	*Rule of Faith*
Divine Pre-Existence	**Gen 1:26** **Gen 3:22** **Ps 2:7b** Ps 45:1 **Ps 91:13** Ps 110:3 Isa 42:2–3 Isa 44:25–26 **Isa 52:14** Mal 3:1	Prov 8:22–31 Isa 41:4 Isa 44:24 Isa 45:7 Isa 57:16	—	Pre-existed with the Father
Pre-Incarnate Ministry	—	Gen 3:9 Exod 4:11–12 Exod 23:20–21 Exod 33:20	—	Was seen by the patriarchs
Virgin Birth	—	**Ps 22:9–10**	—	Born of the Virgin Mary
Incarnate Ministry	**Jer 1:9b-c**	Ps 3:4 **Ps 22:2** Ps 78:2 Song 4:8 Isa 1:18 Isa 32:9–10 Isa 43:20 Isa 44:5 Isa 49:18a Isa 49:21 Isa 50:4 Isa 52:6–7 Isa 58:7 Isa 61:1 Isa 61:10 Jer 1:9a Hos 12:4	—	Engaged in ministry

	From the Father	From the Son	From the Spirit	Rule of Faith
Crucifixion	—	**Ps 3:1** Ps 22:7–8 Ps 22:16 Ps 22:18 **Ps 22:21** **Ps 31:5** Ps 35:12 Ps 69:4 Ps 69:21 **Ps 71:18** Isa 50:6 Jer 11:19	—	Rejected, crucified, and killed
Death and Resurrection	—	—	—	Resurrected from the dead
Ascension, Enthronement, and Reign	Ps 2:7b–8 **Ps 110:1b–c** Isa 8:14 Isa 28:16 Isa 42:1 Isa 42:4 **Isa 42:6–7** **Isa 49:6** **Isa 55:4** **Isa 55:5**	Ps 22:22 Ps 22:25 **Ps 59:11** Ps 68:26 Isa 50:11	Ps 4:6 Ps 8:6 Ps 110:1a Isa 45:1 **Isa 49:18b** **Isa 53:1–2**	Ascended and reigns
Return and Final Consummation	**Ps 110:1b–c** Ps 110:2 Ps 110:4		Isa 60:8	Will return as judge

The overlap is quite striking: all seven elements of the christological narrative supported in Tertullian's writing with prosopological exegesis from or concerning the Son are also found in Tertullian's *regula fidei*. At least in the case of the form of the rule of faith presented in *Praesc.* 13, Tertullian finally includes the element absent from both Justin and Irenaeus's summaries of Christian doctrine even as they made use of this category for prosopological exegesis. As Christ's pre-incarnate ministry does not appear to have been a part of earlier versions of the *regula fidei*, it would appear that Tertullian took quite seriously this particular element of the christological narrative, perhaps reflecting the importance of this theme for anti-Marcionite polemic; the lesser value of this argument in combating modalistic monarchianism likely explains why it drops out of Tertullian's summary of the rule of faith in *Against Praxeas*.

Looking at the chart from the other direction, we can observe that a remarkable seven of the eight christological items in Tertullian's *regula fidei* correspond to categories for which Tertullian has provided examples of prosopological speech that is somehow related to the Son. This is a far greater degree of continuity than we observed with Justin, and also greater than we observed with Irenaeus, whose writings do not include instances of prosopological exegesis related to Christ's virgin birth and second coming. Tertullian does give examples of prosopological speech supporting both of these points but oddly does not seem to have any instances of prosopological speech concerning Christ's resurrection from the dead. Psalm 3:5 had served this role for both Justin and Irenaeus; Tertullian, however, does not seem to ever quote this verse.[130] Still, as the chart makes clear, there is an increasing degree of convergence between the verses that Tertullian interprets prosopologically with respect to the Son and the content of the *regula fidei* that he presents.

Conclusion: Scripting the Son in Tertullian

This chapter has analyzed how Tertullian's use of prosopological exegesis furthered his christological claims. Tertullian, in greatly expanding the scope and depth of his examples of this person-centered reading strategy, continues his predecessors' articulation of a high Christology while providing novel instances of Old Testament texts that could be placed on the lips of the Son or one of the other divine persons to connect these passages with events in the past, present, or future work of Christ. Specifically, Tertullian further underscores the significance of prosopological exegesis by using it to connect the Son's pre-incarnate ministry with his incarnation and to support the classification of Christ's virgin birth and return in judgment as key parts of the christological narrative. And simply by using the term *persona* to describe the Son, Tertullian advances an understanding of the Son as a distinct divine person. The themes that emerge from this analysis show a further convergence between prosopological exegesis, the *regula fidei*, and even the development of early Christian *testimonia* collections. While it goes beyond the available evidence to suggest which of these three threads is most influencing the other two, the fact of this three-way convergence illustrates the consolidation of early "orthodox" Christology around a shared set of priorities. Still,

---

130. Interestingly, Tertullian does quote and prosopologically interpret Ps 3:4 at *Marc.* 4.13.

Tertullian's approach to prosopological exegesis at times can violate the plain sense of the source text or even threaten to deny any voice to the Father, suggesting the need for a still more nuanced and brilliant early Christian exegete to further refine the method's use.

6

Later Developments in the West

WE HAVE OBSERVED THAT Tertullian greatly accelerated a trajectory of christological development that aligned prosopological exegesis with the emerging rule of faith, providing a flexible yet deeply scriptural approach to resolving a myriad of early christological controversies. This achievement helped solidify the notion of "person" (*persona*) as the preferred language for speaking of the distinct divine persons, paving the way for Nicene Trinitarianism. While it would be tempting to conclude this study of early Latin biblical exegesis on this high note, a more honest recounting of theological development in the third century would also detail how, after Tertullian, the importance of prosopological exegesis faded in the West. Indeed, as this chapter will demonstrate, after Tertullian the Latin tradition of the third century shows remarkably less interest in prosopological exegesis. This chapter therefore examines how later Latin writers—including Hippolytus of Rome, Novatian of Rome, and Cyprian of Carthage—approached the matter of prosopological exegesis before concluding with some possible explanations for the decline of this person-centered reading strategy in the West.

Prosopological Exegesis in the Writings of Hippolytus

The enigmatic Hippolytus of Rome (ca. 170–235) presents scholars with serious challenges for reconstructing his life and identifying his authentic works; for the sake of briefly surveying this corpus, we will assume Hippolytus to be the author of the works studied below while acknowledging this remains a contested issue.[1] This set of writings in any event displays a very limited interest in prosopological exegesis, providing a contrast with the earlier Latin theologian Tertullian.

Generally speaking, Hippolytus is content to interpret Old Testament dialogical passages that before him had often been read prosopologically as the mere words of the prophet. For example, in his *Christ and Antichrist*, Hippolytus's interpretation of Revelation 12 connects Rev 12:5 with Ps 110:1. But when he quotes Ps 110:1, he identifies David as the speaker and obscures the dialogical character of Ps 110:1b–c in favor of providing a proof from prophecy.[2]

Particularly intriguing is the fact that, like Tertullian, Hippolytus wrote a treatise against modalistic monarchianism. But whereas Tertullian's *Against Praxeas* is brimming with instances of prosopological exegesis, Hippolytus's *Against Noetus* is devoid of such interpretation. While Hippolytus's treatise is, unlike Tertullian's, directed more narrowly at those monarchians who held to the doctrine of patripassianism (that is, that the Father suffered and died on the cross),[3] there would appear to be no obvious reason that appeals to prosopological exegesis would be any less effective in this context than in Tertullian's. That Hippolytus has any knowledge of prosopological exegesis is only evident from a single instance in the fragmentary remains of his commentaries on the Bible. Assuming the manuscript that ascribes this excerpt to Hippolytus is correct in its attribution of authorship, we here find Hippolytus in his commentary on Gen 49:21–26 interpreting Ps 110:1b as spoken by the Father to the Son following the resurrection.[4]

Despite Hippolytus's proximity in time and space to Tertullian, not to mention their shared concerns in combating modalistic monarchianism, we nevertheless discover Hippolytus has nearly no use for prosopological exegesis. This surprising observation brings us to consider the next major figure in Rome to have left significant theological writings, Novatian.

1. For more on this issue, see further Heine, "Hippolytus," 142–49.
2. *Antichr.* 61.
3. On patripassianism, see, e.g., *Noet.* 1.
4. This fragment is quoted from *ANF* 5.166; the editors note the fragment comes from "a *Commentary on Genesis*, compiled from eighty-eight fathers, which is extant in manuscript in the Vienna Library" (*ANF* 5.163n2). Another fragment, from an *Expository Treatise Against the Jews*, is of more doubtful authorship, but does contain an interesting prosopological interpretation of the Son speaking Ps 69:1–28 and Ps 16:10 concerning his crucifixion and death (*ANF* 5.219–20). Given its uncertain authorship and provenance, however, I have chosen not to analyze it in this section.

Prosopological Exegesis in the Writings of Novatian

The schismatic presbyter Novatian (ca. 200–258), leader of the rigorist party in Rome in the wake of the Decian persecution, is credited as being the first Roman Christian to have penned a distinctly theological treatise.[5] Novatian's *The Trinity* (ca. 245) demonstrates clear points of continuity with Tertullian's *Against Praxeas*, likewise using Scripture and the *regula fidei* to dismiss modalistic monarchianism and other related views that threatened the Son's status as a distinct divine person.[6] The major point of christological development found in this work is Novatian's claim that the Son was not only pre-existent and coeternal with the Father but also eternally distinct from the Father, giving rise to the notion of the "eternal generation of the Son."[7] Given, then, Novatian's dependence on Tertullian and the specific similarities between *Against Praxeas* and *The Trinity* in particular, we would expect Novatian to follow Tertullian in making extensive use of prosopological exegesis. This is not, however, what we actually find when we open Novatian's treatise; Novatian in fact uses prosopological exegesis far more sparingly than did his predecessor Tertullian.

Novatian's most focused use of prosopological exegesis occurs towards the end of the treatise in his refutation of those who denied the real distinction of the Father and the Son. As Novatian argues:

> For who does not acknowledge that the Second Person after the Father is the Son, when he reads what was said by the Father to the Son in view of this relationship: *Let us make men to Our image and likeness* [Gen 1:26]; and after these words it is related: *And God made man, according to the image of God He made him* [Gen 1:27]? Or when he holds in his hands the text: *The Lord poured down on Sodom and Gomorrah fire and sulphur from the Lord out of heaven* [Gen 19:24]? Or when he reads the words addressed to Christ: *You are my Son; this day I have begotten You. Ask of Me and I will give You the Gentiles for Your inheritance and the ends of the earth for Your possession* [Ps 2:7–8]? Or when even that beloved writer says: *The Lord said to my Lord: Sit at my right hand till I make your enemies your footstool* [Ps 110:1]?

---

5. On Novatian's life and significance, see further DeSimone, *Novatian*, 1–9.
6. See further DeSimone, *Novatian*, 14–17; Papandrea, *Novatian of Rome*, 106.
7. See further Papandrea, *Novatian of Rome*, 33–34.

Or when he opens the prophecies of Isaiah and finds it written: *Thus says the Lord to Christ my Lord* [Isa 45:1]?[8]

Here Novatian covers well-trodden ground, noting the divine plural in the creation account (Gen 1:26) before giving the classic "two powers" texts of Gen 19:24 and Ps 110:1, which we have seen linked as far back as Justin.[9] Novatian's appeal to Ps 2:7-8 as the words of the Father to the Son likewise have an impressive pedigree, as seen in previous chapters of this book; the theodramatic setting is unclear, but given interpretive continuity over time the most likely way to interpret the verses is as referring to Christ's present reign. The christological reading of Isa 45:1 follows the misreading of Tertullian, among others.[10] There is, therefore, nothing original in Novatian's argument here.

In fact, what is striking about this passage is how minimal and perfunctory Novatian's appeal to prosopological exegesis comes across to readers acquainted with the method. Novatian does follow Tertullian in bringing the term "person" (*persona*) to bear and explicitly introduces this section as containing "what was said by the Father to the Son"; prosopological exegesis is clearly in view. But the flow of prosopological speech, begun with the quotation of Gen 1:26, is then broken by the citation of non-dialogical passages (Gen 1:27; 19:24) before returning to a prosopological interpretation of Ps 2:7-8, simply introduced as "the words addressed to Christ." The Father is obviously the speaker of these words even though he is not explicitly referenced, but the Father's presence continues to fade from view over the course of the following quotations. Psalm 110:1, when quoted in full with the introductory phrase, had been attributed to the Holy Spirit by Justin, Irenaeus, and Tertullian; Novatian, however, breaks with this pattern of interpretation by assigning the speech to "that beloved writer"—presumably, David. The prosopological character of the dialogue within the verse is left unremarked upon altogether. Similarly, Tertullian identified Isa 45:1 as the words of the Holy Spirit; again, however, Novatian merely attributes the verse to the prophet Isaiah and moves on from the quotation without further comment. Novatian thus presents a very minimal use of prosopological exegesis in this passage, suggesting, perhaps, a discomfort with this method of interpretation.

---

8. *Trin.* 26.3-7 (trans. DeSimone).
9. Cf. *Trin.* 17.4; see also again *Dial.* 127.5.
10. Cf. *Prax.* 11.8.

This hypothesis is backed up by an examination of the rest of the treatise. The prophecies of Christ in Isaiah are generally simply that: the words of Isaiah, the human prophet. Novatian is content to string such verses together without commenting on changes of speaker within the source texts.[11] When quotations of Ps 110:1 and Ps 2:8 are first presented in concert with one another, they are only set forth as proof-texts for the fact that the Old Testament prophesied the coming of Christ.[12] Similarly, when Novatian quotes Ps 45:1, an important passage for articulating his understanding of the Son's generation from the Father, he does not identify the speaker of the text.[13]

In fact, outside of the above passage there is only one clear instance of prosopological exegesis from the person of the Father. In making his case that the Scriptures call Christ "God," Novatian writes, "The prophet Hosea says in the person of the Father: *I will not save them by bow, nor by horses; but I will save them by the Lord their God* [Hos 1:7]."[14] Here prosopological exegesis is explicitly invoked with Hosea being said to have spoken "in the person of the Father," who is here speaking concerning the Son as the exclusive source of salvation for Novatian's audience.[15] Novatian is the first writer to provide an extant prosopological interpretation of this verse, identifying in it evidence of God the Father speaking of another God, the Son, who would be the source of the people's salvation. The theodramatic setting appears to be prior to the incarnation based on the future tense of the verbs. Oddly given his novel selection of this one verse, Novatian omits the large majority of verses that Justin, Irenaeus, and Tertullian had ascribed to the Father, making the selection of just this one verse all the more odd.

In examining how Novatian sets forth the prosopological speech of the Son, we find a similar pattern as that which emerged in the case of the Father. Those passages that had been traditional sources of the Son's prosopological speech, such as the words of the suffering servant in Deutero-Isaiah, are here simply described as the words of the prophet

---

11. See, e.g., *Trin.* 9.6–8.

12. *Trin.* 9.8.

13. *Trin.* 13.1; 15.6; 17.3. Contrast, for example, Tertullian's usage at *Prax.* 7.1, in which Tertullian ascribes this verse to the Father and follows it with further examples of speech from the "person" of the Father with quotations of Ps 2:7 and Ps 110:3.

14. *Trin.* 12.1 (trans. DeSimone).

15. Novatian may also want us to read his quotation of Hab 3:3 later in this chapter (*Trin.* 12.7) as the Father's prosopological speech, but the introductory formula ("he says through Habakkuk the prophet") is too vague to really warrant an emphasis on prosopological rather than prophetic speech.

Isaiah.[16] Like his predecessors, Novatian identifies the pre-incarnate Christ as the subject of the Old Testament theophanies;[17] thus, the Son is the one who speaks to Hagar the words of Gen 21:17–18 and to Jacob across Gen 31–32.[18] While this theme is nothing new, Novatian's emphasis on the Son's pre-incarnate ministry to Hagar and Jacob transcends the usual examples of speaking to Adam and Moses. Novatian's method is to discern the "person" who is the subject of these theophanies by ruling out alternative subjects, such as the Father or an angel.[19] Novatian's focus is more on how this subject is portrayed and less on the specific words that he speaks, thereby diminishing the prosopological thrust of the interpretation.

Outside of these instances, there is only one time that Novatian explicitly invokes prosopological exegesis to find the Son speaking in the Old Testament. In his brief teaching on the Holy Spirit at the end of the treatise, Novatian comments,

> [Isaiah] reiterated the very same thing [that is, that the Holy Spirit abides in Christ] in another passage in the person of the Lord Himself: *The Spirit of the Lord is upon Me, because He has anointed Me; to bring good news to the poor He has sent Me* [Isa 61:1].[20]

By invoking the term "person," Novatian makes clear his knowledge of this person-centered reading strategy, and he selects perhaps the most obvious Old Testament text as his example, given that Christ himself spoke these words during his earthly ministry (Luke 4:18).[21] Novatian's surrounding interpretation, however, seems to suggest that he is emphasizing Christ as the present source of the Spirit by which Novatian's audience can receive eternal salvation. Surprisingly, given his awareness of prosopological exegesis and knowledge of Tertullian's writings, Novatian makes no further attempts at providing such instances of the Son's

---

16. *Trin.* 28.10–12. Similarly, Novatian has the prophet Joel speak the promise of Joel 2:29 even as he acknowledges that Christ is the one through whom the Spirit was "bestowed" (*Trin.* 29.2).

17. E.g., *Trin.* 18.2.

18. For Hagar, see *Trin.* 18.19; for Jacob, see *Trin.* 19.1–14.

19. *Trin.* 18.10.

20. *Trin.* 29.13 (trans. DeSimone).

21. Novatian immediately follows this with a quotation of Ps 45:7 (*Trin.* 29.14), which he attributes to David rather than following his predecessors in reading it as the words of the Spirit to the Son concerning the Father.

prosopological speech. Nor does Novatian ever portray the Holy Spirit as capable of speaking as a distinct divine person.[22]

Novatian's relatively minimal use of prosopological exegesis may be explained in part by his intense interest in the Gospel of John. The Fourth Gospel is the most cited biblical text in *The Trinity*, suggesting that the battle lines over Christology had shifted from controversies over the interpretation of the Old Testament to how to interpret those verses in John's Gospel that could, for example, be used to promote modalism.

Prosopological Exegesis in the Writings of Cyprian

The Carthaginian bishop Cyprian (ca. 210–258), who would have undoubtedly had access to Tertullian's writings in some capacity,[23] makes for an interesting test case for how the earlier Carthaginian's ideas were transmitted over subsequent decades. Having found prosopological exegesis to have played only a very minimal role in the theological writings of Roman writers in the early third century, we might expect Tertullian's influence to have been stronger in his home city of Carthage. While there is some truth to this, we nevertheless also see an overall decline in the method's importance even here. Cyprian, it is worth noting, "does not explicitly state his hermeneutical principles."[24] Articulating a hermeneutical method, with respect to prosopological exegesis or otherwise, appears not to be a priority for Cyprian.

Nevertheless, Cyprian does show some small degree of interest in prosopological exegesis. For instance, Cyprian interprets the words "*I am asleep and my heart is awake* [Song 5:2]" as having been written "in the character of the church."[25] This language clearly invokes prosopological exegesis while providing a novel application of this verse to describe the Christian's constant spiritual devotion to God.[26] Cyprian's use of this method for the sake of Christology is, however, relatively minimal. On one occasion, Cyprian presents the Father as speaking to the Son the words of Ps 110:4 to comment on the Son's present priestly ministry,[27] but that is about the extent of the Father's speech to or concerning the

22. See further Hughes, *Trinitarian Testimony*, 199–200.
23. Wiles, *Working Papers*, 69–70; cf. the more guarded view of Fahey, *Cyprian*, 626.
24. Murphy, *Bishop*, 19; cf. Fahey, *Cyprian*, 624–26.
25. *Dom. or.* 31 (trans. Stewart-Sykes).
26. Here we have another early example of this form of interpretation of the Song of Songs; see again *Marc.* 4.11.
27. *Ep.* 62.4. The numbering of Cyprian's epistles can differ in different editions; I follow the numbering in *ANF*.

Son in Cyprian's writings. In just a single instance, Cyprian has the Son speaking Isa 50:5–6 concerning his crucifixion.[28]

Rather, the primary category across all of Cyprian's works is that of the Son speaking to the church through the words of the Old Testament. Cyprian appears to read Old Testament quotations spoken by "the Lord" as the words of Christ the Lord, and so many prophecies spoken to warn or encourage Israel are re-cast as the words of God the Son to the church. We can consider as illustrative two sets of examples. First, in *Epistle 51*, a letter on whether repentance should be extended to the lapsed, Cyprian presents Christ as the divine speaker of many Old Testament quotations in which Yahweh was speaking through the prophets. Here Cyprian identifies "the Lord"—clearly Christ, the one who also speaks "in his Gospel" and is distinguished from God the Father—as the speaker not just of New Testament passages (such as Matt 7:9–11, Luke 15:7, and Rev 2:20–22) but also Old Testament ones (including Joel 2:12–13, Ezek 18:20, and Deut 24:26).[29] Similarly, in *Epistle 54*, Cyprian writes against heretical schismatics by having Christ condemn and threaten them with punishment through the words of Isaiah (Isa 14:13–16) and Hosea (Hos 8:4; 9:4).[30] This category, in which God the Son rebukes heretics and challenges Christians in the time of his present reign, is therefore another category of prosopological exegesis, one that we will see developed with greater clarity and power by Origen. Somewhat confusingly, the Holy Spirit is at other times the source of such prophetic speech, but given the Spirit's role in inspiring Scripture it is less clear that this should be considered a form of prosopological exegesis.[31] In any event, while Cyprian

---

28. *Ep.* 6.4.

29. *Ep.* 51.22–27.

30. *Ep.* 54.3–5. An additional instance in this letter, at *Ep.* 54.15, cites Sir 16:1–2, but has significant issues in the manuscript tradition (*ANF* 5.545n2). For further examples, the Son ("the Lord") also speaks Song 6:9 (*Unit. eccl.* 4, though there are textual issues with this passage, for which see Brent, *Select Treatises*, 41–44); 1 Kgs 11:31–32, 36 (*Unit. eccl.* 7); Jer 23:16–17, 21–22 (*Unit. eccl.* 11); Isa 40:6 (*Hab. virg.* 6); Joel 2:13 (*Laps.* 36); Isa 58:6 (*Dom. or.* 33); Hos 6:1 (*Dom. or.* 35); Isa 1:2 (*Zel. liv.* 15); Jer 7:16 (*Fort.* 4); Isa 43:1–3 (*Fort.* 10); Isa 66:2 (*Ep.* 17.1); Jer 23:16–17 (*Ep.* 39.5); Ezek 34:3–6, 10–16 (*Ep.* 53.4); Jer 3:15 (*Ep.* 61.1); Ps 50:16–18 (*Ep.* 62.18); Jer 23:28, 30, 32 (*Ep.* 62.18); Jer 3:9–10 (*Ep.* 62.18); Isa 57:6 (*Ep.* 63.1); Exod 22:20 (*Ep.* 63.1); Isa 2:8–9 (*Ep.* 63.1); Ezek 34:4–6, 10, 16 (*Ep.* 66.4); Isa 29:13 (*Ep.* 67.2); Jer 2:13 (*Ep.* 69.1); Mal 2:1–2 (*Ep.* 73.8); Song 4:12–13 (*Ep.* 73.11); Song 6:9 (*Ep.* 75.2); Song 4:12 (*Ep.* 75.2) References to the speech of "the Lord" in *Test.* are even more difficult to discern their intended referent and are therefore not included here. When "the Lord" is identified as the speaker of an Old Testament text without that text being re-spoken to a present-day audience, it would seem this speech would be more that of an inspiring secondary agent (e.g., at *Ep.* 64.1; 67.3–4; 75.9). I take speech by "the Lord God" as referring instead to God the Father.

31. For example, see *Demetr.* 17; 20; *Laps.* 10; 27; *Unit. eccl.* 8; 10; 24; *Hab. virg.* 1;

does not explicitly set out his rationale for why he assigns prophetic words to various speakers in the way that he does, the most natural hypothesis would be that he has "the Lord" (that is, the Son) speak when he reads the text in such a way that the Lord "counsels and teaches us" through the words of the prophet.[32] Unfortunately, however, there are plenty of examples in which God (presumably, the Father) is likewise "instructing" us "by his divine voice."[33] There is, at least as far as I can tell, no discernible pattern for Cyprian's decisions in this regard. In any event, the christological value of these interpretations is negligible: beyond demonstrating that the Son, as a part of his present reign, is speaking to the church in the words of the prophets, there is little attempt by Cyprian to connect any one of these verses to any particular aspect of Christology as such. The net effect is to diminish the Father's voice in the Old Testament, a potential issue with this approach to prosopological exegesis that would require a more astute exegete to solve.

Interestingly, Cyprian does present the Holy Spirit as speaking to the Son in his *Epistle 62*, in which he develops his theology of the Eucharist. For one thing, Cyprian portrays the Spirit as speaking with reference to the Son's future ministry: "And so too in Isaiah the Holy Spirit testifies to the same concerning the passion of the Lord, saying, *Why are your garments red, and your clothing as from the treading of a full and trodden vat?* [Isa 63:2]."[34] As a dialogical passage and one that uses a verb ("testifies") that implies personal agency beyond a functional inspiration of Scripture, this instance could be considered a case of the Spirit speaking to the Son as his own distinct person. Similarly, later in the letter, Cyprian criticizes those whose Eucharist uses water instead of wine, writing, "And the Holy Spirit in the Psalms is not silent about the mystery of this matter, making mention of the Lord's cup and saying, *Your intoxicating cup is exceedingly excellent* [Ps 23:5]."[35] Implied is that the Holy Spirit is speaking these words directly to the Son, making this a matter of intra-divine dialogue. While neither of these instances is a clear-cut example of prosopological exegesis, given Cyprian's

---

Dom. or. 5; 35; *Mort.* 11; 23; *Eleem.* 2; 5; 9; *Pat.* 22; *Zel. liv.* 8; *Fort.* 10; 12; *Ep.* 8.1; 54.5; 54.21. While Downs has argued that such examples should be categorized as prosopological exegesis ("Prosopological Exegesis," 279–93), I have argued elsewhere against such a view based on a more careful distinction between "primary" and "secondary" forms of the Spirit's speech (Hughes, "Spirit and the Scriptures," 35–47).

32. Cf. *Dom. or.* 33 (trans. Stewart-Sykes).
33. Cf. *Demetr.* 6 (trans. Brent).
34. *Ep.* 62.7 (AT).
35. *Ep.* 62.11 (AT).

overwhelming preference for presenting the Spirit as the secondary, inspiring agent of Old Testament speech, they are still the most likely candidates among Cyprian's writings for such a classification.[36]

Most surprisingly, however, is the fact that Cyprian does not apply prosopological readings where we would least expect them. For example, in his *To Quirinius: Testimonies against the Jews*, Cyprian includes Prov 8:22–31 in a catena of Old Testament *testimonia* related to Christ being the firstborn of God and creator of all things.[37] It is certainly implied that the passage refers to Christ, who by extension must be the speaker of this first-person dialogue, but Cyprian pays no attention to the implications of such a reading, instead slotting quotations one after the other without any regard for the dialogical nature of some of the texts.

To Quirinius is, however, a remarkable work with respect to one other feature that we have traced throughout this book: the use of *testimonia*. Though Cyprian does not himself use the term *testimonia* in this work, it is nevertheless the case that scholars have identified it as a "model" *testimonia* collection, featuring some 174 sets of proof-texts corresponding to an equal number of headings.[38] In his introduction to the first book, Cyprian suggests that he himself arranged this "abridged compendium" of *testimonia* from the myriad of "diffuse" sources available to him.[39] As Albl concludes, in at least the first two books of this work "Cyprian seems to have taken over earlier collections, probably reordering material, adding quotations, and conforming the quotations to the current Latin biblical text."[40] To speculate with just one hypothesis, then, it could certainly be the case that a pre-existing *testimonia* collection organized according to the presumed prosopological speaker (such as we suggested was used by Tertullian) has been passed over or pulled apart by Cyprian for his own purposes and interests. After all, Cyprian is here concerned above all with brevity for the purposes of memorization in a catechetical context.[41] The theological nuances and implications inherent in many of these texts are, then, subordinated to this more foundational and simple purpose.

---

36. On the interpretive challenges with these passages, see further Hughes, *Trinitarian Testimony*, 197–98.
37. *Test.* 2.1.
38. See further Albl, *Scripture*, 132.
39. *Test.* 1.pref. (trans. *ANF*).
40. Albl, *Scripture*, 133. See further Skarsaune, "Scriptural Interpretation," 441.
41. See Albl, *Scripture*, 133; cf. *Test.* 1.pref; 3.pref.

Conclusion: Scripting the Son in the Later Latin Tradition

In concluding this chapter, we can again pull together our observations in a table that sets out all the instances in which these Latin writers prosopologically interpret Old Testament dialogical passages that involve speech to, from, or about the Son. As usual, verses in bold are instances in which the passage is dialogue addressed by one divine person to another (intra-divine dialogue):

	From the Father	*From the Son*	*From the Spirit*
Divine Pre-Existence	**Gen 1:26** Hos 1:7	—	—
Pre-Incarnate Ministry	—	Gen 21:17–18 Gen 31—32	—
Crucifixion	—	Isa 50:5–6	—
Ascension, Enthronement, and Reign	**Ps 2:7b–8** **Ps 110:1b-c** **Ps 110:4**	Exod 22:20 Deut 24:26 1 Kgs 11:31–32, 36 Ps 50:16–18 Song 4:12–13 Song 6:9 Isa 1:2 Isa 2:8–9 Isa 14:13–16 Isa 29:13 Isa 40:6 Isa 43:1–3 Isa 57:6 Isa 58:6 Isa 61:1 Isa 66:2 Jer 2:13 Jer 3:9–10 Jer 3:15 Jer 7:16 Jer 23:16–17, 21–22 Jer 23:28, 30, 32 Ezek 18:20 Ezek 34:3–6, 10–16 Hos 6:1 Hos 8:4 Hos 9:4 Joel 2:12–13 Mal 2:1–2	**Ps 23:5** **Isa 63:2**

We observe, then, a decline in interest in prosopological exegesis in the Latin tradition in the decades after Tertullian, especially when we consider that almost all of these instances are Cyprian simply having the Son re-present Old Testament speech to the church during this time of his present reign. There is simply not enough data to bring to a discussion of the use of *testimonia* collections or the influence of the *regula fidei* in these writers beyond what has already been mentioned above. The texts themselves give no explanation for this phenomenon, but one reasonable hypothesis concerns the legacy of the method's greatest proponent, Tertullian. In the decades after Tertullian's death, Montanism (the New Prophecy) appears to have been vanquished; at least one synod declared the movement heretical, and writings from the middle of the third century do not mention the movement or its distinctive themes.[42] This strongly suggests that the tide had turned decisively against Montanism within just a few decades of Tertullian's death, and since Tertullian was at the end of his life an outspoken supporter of the New Prophecy, Tertullian's reputation suffered accordingly. Given Tertullian's enormous contributions to Christian theology, especially with respect to Christology and Trinitarianism, later Latin writers such as Cyprian and Novatian had to be judicious in their approach to Tertullian's work. Indeed, while the basic shape of his *regula fidei* and his understanding of unity and diversity in the Godhead were preserved, it appears that prosopological exegesis, having played its role in advancing the cause of trinitarian theology, was largely jettisoned in favor of new arguments for new times. It would be in the East, then, that prosopological exegesis would make further advances through the writings of Origen.

---

42. On the decline of the New Prophecy, see further Hughes, *Trinitarian Testimony*, 201.

7

Origen of Alexandria

ORIGEN OF ALEXANDRIA (CA. 185–253), the most brilliant exegete of the early church, is an interesting figure to set alongside the theological trajectory we have traced thus far in this book. While Origen is unfortunately best remembered by many today for his supposed act of self-castration and what is viewed as an overly enthusiastic taste for allegorical interpretation, a careful reading of his extant writings reveals a scholar whose command of Scripture, philosophy, philology, and Christian spirituality was (and perhaps in many ways remains) unmatched.[1] Insofar as Origen's exegesis is largely independent of that of Justin, Irenaeus, and Tertullian, instead following a different, Alexandrian trajectory that reaches back to figures such as Clement of Alexandria, Origen provides us with an additional lens by which to study the impact of prosopological exegesis on the making of early Christology.[2] The great challenge in studying Origen, of course, is the sheer quantity of his extant writings; even so, this prolific writer's works that are lost to modern scholars far surpass the enormous amount of material that is still preserved.

This chapter will demonstrate that Origen finds prosopological exegesis to be an important tool in his exegetical toolbox. As we will see, assuming Origen's extant works to be a representative sample of his overall corpus, Origen's approach to prosopological exegesis from the person of the Father is largely conventional, echoing texts referenced in earlier

1. On Origen's life and background, see further Trigg, *Origen*, 3–61. Cf. Eusebius's comments on Origen's supposed self-castration in *Hist. eccl.* 6.8.

2. On Alexandrian Christianity as a distinct "trajectory," see further Heine, *Scholarship*, 26–64; Paget, "Alexandrian Tradition," 478–542.

chapters of this book, while his approach to the Son's prosopological speech shows a great deal of exegetical creativity and christological innovation. After surveying Origen's use of prosopological exegesis across all of his extant writings, this chapter will briefly consider how Origen's use of *testimonia* collections (among other potential sources) and his understanding of the *regula fidei* may have impacted his use of this person-centered reading strategy. In particular, we will find that Origen's use of prosopological exegesis more closely weaves together these three threads of early Christology even as he pursues new avenues of focus, demonstrating a much more methodologically grounded and comprehensive approach to finding the *vox Christi* in the Old Testament.

Prosopological Exegesis in the Writings of Origen

Origen's extant writings do not contain any lengthy passages in which prosopological exegesis is discussed at great length or in which quotations assigned to each divine person are collected. Still, Origen sets out some of his rationale for this person-centered reading strategy in several brief asides throughout his corpus. Take, for example, the following passage in his *Commentary on Romans*, which provides a basic overview of his prosopological method of interpretation:

> As we have observed in the writings of the prophets, not only has the person speaking been suddenly changed without notice, but also the person of those to whom or about whom the discourse is addressed. For instance, sometimes something is said under the *persona* of the Father, sometimes of the Son or of the Holy Spirit, and sometimes even something under the *persona* of the prophet or anyone else you like. And indeed, sometimes the message is directed to the nation of Israel, sometimes to foreign nations or to kings or to thousands of others. It seems to me that the Epistle to the Romans has been written in this way too. At various times the role of the one who is speaking is changed, so that sometimes the spiritual Paul is speaking, as is the case in a great number of passages in the letter. But at other times the fleshly Paul is speaking . . .[3]

---

3. *Comm. Rom.* 2.11.2 (trans. Scheck). For further instances of Origen's attention to shifting *personae*, see also *Comm. Rom.* 2.11.3–5; 5.5.6; 6.9.3–4, 11–12; 6.10.2; 7.16.4; 8.6.2–3, 6, 9.

Ever the careful exegete, Origen goes on to demonstrate that Paul not only takes on different speaking roles in the epistle but also varies the audience to whom he is addressing his discourse. Origen thus extends the need for prosopological exegesis (which he formally invokes with the term *persona*) from interpreting just the Old Testament to include what will eventually become part of the New Testament as well. For our purposes, however, we can observe that Origen, like Justin, Irenaeus, and Tertullian, finds the voices of Father, Son, and Spirit in the dialogical passages of Old Testament writings.[4]

Perhaps Origen's most straightforward statement of how he actually goes about identifying prosopological speech is found in a homily on Psalm 16 that was included in the recently discovered Codex Monacensis Graecus 314, which preserves twenty-nine of Origen's homilies on the Psalms in their original Greek. As Origen begins his analysis of this psalm, he presents this introduction:

> Let us see the Psalm itself. The first thing to be said is that the *persona* [Greek *prosōpon*] in the Psalm is that of our Lord Jesus Christ. In introducing some Psalms, we may or may not speak soundly, identifying the *persona* of the Psalm as Christ Jesus, depending on whether we find it or we apply it, whether we are enlightened or we guess. In the case of some Psalms, though, including this one, we learn the *persona* from Scripture. It has been written in the Acts of the Apostles that a passage of this Psalm, *You will not abandon my soul in Hades, nor will you allow your devout one to see corruption* [Ps 16:10], is spoken in the *persona* of the Savior.[5]

Origen then goes on to quote Acts 2:25–31, in which Peter interprets Ps 16:8–11 with reference to Christ, before continuing with his argument, to which we will return shortly. It is worth pausing here, however, to make some important observations. First, Origen is clear that Christ is the ultimate speaker of at least some of the psalms in the Psalter. As he will make clear elsewhere, however, not all psalms are to be interpreted as spoken from the *persona* of Christ.[6] Indeed, it is often the case that

---

4. For more on Origen's prosopological method, see Rondeau, *Les commentaires patristiques*, 2.39–40.

5. *Hom. Ps.* 15H1.2 (trans. Trigg). Following Trigg, for numbering, I have indicated the number of the psalm (in the LXX, following Trigg's translation) followed by an "H" (for "homily") and then the number of the homily on that psalm and the section number of the reference.

6. E.g., Origen says with respect to Psalm 37 that "the whole Psalm is concerned

the speaking *persona* can change even within a particular psalm, as indicated by shifts from singular to plural voice, requiring careful attention on the part of the interpreter.[7] Thus it is Origen's "custom, in the Psalms and in the prophets, to see who is the *persona* speaking."[8] Second, Origen's comment seems to contrast "finding" and "being enlightened" with "applying" and "guessing." As Trigg understands Origen's point,

> We identify the *persona* speaking the Psalm, or a portion of a Psalm, when we "find" it after "seeking" through prayerful scriptural analysis ultimately enlightened by God. We misidentify the *persona* when we apply the identification arbitrarily based on nothing better than a guess.[9]

There are, therefore, appeals to both good exegetical practices and personal spiritual enlightenment as necessary to rightly discern the voice of Christ in the Old Testament. In so doing, Christians can defeat the schemes of the devil, who seeks to twist and corrupt the Scriptures through wrongly identifying the various *personae* in a scriptural text.[10] To return, then, to Origen's introduction to Psalm 16:

> Explicitly, then, he says in this passage that Jesus would not see corruption and that his soul would not be abandoned in Hades, since he had descended in accord with the plan of salvation; because every region needed the visitation of Christ Jesus, including the place beneath the earth, he descended to Hades. For the one who ascended and the one who descended are the same, so that he might fill all things. But the utterances cited by Peter from the Acts of the Apostles will prove that the Psalm was spoken in the *persona* of the Lord Jesus Christ.[11]

---

with behavior; it is treating our soul, rebuking our sins, and recommending that we live according to the law" (*Hom. Ps.* 36H1.1). Ps 24:7–10 is spoken in the *personae* of various groups of heavenly powers (*Hom. Ps.* 15H2.8).

7. See, e.g., *Hom. Ps.* 74H1.1; 77H1.2–3; *Comm. John* 1.280–88.

8. *Hom. Ps.* 77H1.2 (trans. Trigg).

9. Trigg, *Homilies on the Psalms*, 39n15. See also Trigg, *Homilies on the Psalms*, 13–14, though when Trigg notes that Origen identifies Christ as the speaker of Psalms 15 and 67 (LXX), this should probably instead read Psalms 15 and 77 (that is, MT Psalms 16 and 78). See also *Comm. Rom.* 8.7.5.

10. This, after all, was Satan's strategy in the temptation of Christ; see Origen's comments on this at *Hom. Luc.* 31.4, in which the devil suggests the wrong *persona* for the addressee of Ps 91:11–12.

11. *Hom. Ps.* 15H1.2 (trans. Trigg); see also *Hom. Ps.* 15H2.1.

Thus Peter's speech in Acts 2 provides apostolic justification for prosopological exegesis, and therefore for reading at least some of the Psalms as the voice of Christ. Now, as noted earlier in this book, this New Testament passage makes for a somewhat awkward example of prosopological exegesis; while it seems clear that Peter would have us understand the words of Ps 16:8–11 as the words of Christ, the introductory formula identifies David as the speaker, who "says" these words "concerning [Christ]" (Acts 2:25). This instance of what we might call "unmarked" or "implicit" prosopological exegesis is, I maintain, subtly distinct from the marked, explicit use of prosopological exegesis proper that Origen is suggesting when he says the psalm "was spoken in the *persona* of our Lord Jesus Christ."[12] In any event, Origen's desire to find apostolic precedent for this form of exegesis, combined with his willingness to allow for multiple speaking persons within a given chunk of text, suggests a more carefully refined approach to prosopological exegesis than that of any Christian writer before him.

Indeed, we saw, for example, with Tertullian that it was often unclear how much of God's voice in books such as Isaiah or Jeremiah should be attributed to the Son, potentially threatening to silence the Father and minimize the role of the human prophet in history. Origen, though, is carefully attuned to this problem,[13] and provides some methodological comments that help us understand his reasoning. In the first of his *Homilies on Jeremiah*, Origen tackles Jer 1:5, noting,

> We are aware that some people refer these words, in that they surpass Jeremiah, to our Lord and Savior. And one can see that while many passages which I will cite accord with him and can refer to the Savior, a few of the words said about Jeremiah are troublesome for this interpretation, since they cannot be fitting, in the view of many, for the Savior.[14]

Origen is telling us that there is an exegetical debate regarding the proper addressee of the prophecies of Jeremiah: some hold that God is speaking

---

12. Origen makes a similar argument at *Hom. Ps.* 77H1.2, citing Matt 13:35 as justification for reading Ps 78:2 as the words of Christ. Origen at *Hom. Ps.* 77H1.1 explains the issue of Matthew attributing this passage to Isaiah as the result of an early copyist who was "unaware that Asaph was a prophet" (trans. Trigg). But this seems to be functioning more as a prophetic-fulfillment formula than prosopological exegesis as we have defined it in this book.

13. See, e.g., Origen's discussion at *Comm. John* 2.116–32.

14. *Hom. Jer.* 1.6 (trans. Smith).

to Jeremiah the human prophet, and others maintain that God is speaking to his Son. While Origen admits that many such prophecies could be read as directed to Christ, he is equally adamant that there are likewise many that do not seem to make sense if read as the words of the Father to the Son. The obvious solution, then, would be simply to interpret some verses as being addressed to Jeremiah and others to the Son. Origen, though, will have none of this:

> The person of good sense, however, will find it very troublesome in the context, when he realizes that it is senseless to separate in a series of statements words said either to Jeremiah or to the Savior, and state that these do not belong to Christ but to Jeremiah since they are less than appropriate for Christ, and that these, being greater than Jeremiah, do not belong to Jeremiah but to Christ.[15]

Origen's solution, then, is to read in such a way that *both* Jeremiah and Christ are in view, drawing upon his distinction between the "bodily" (literal) and "spiritual" (allegorical or anagogical) senses of Scripture.[16] This allows Origen to pursue the prosopological line of interpretation while preserving the historical context of the text as well. Such sophistication in exegesis, insofar as Origen allows for multiple senses of the text, is a major advance in early Christian biblical interpretation and will of course be foundational for centuries of Christian theologians and homilists after Origen.[17] To put it in simpler terms, Origen thus demonstrates that a prosopological reading of Scripture need not replace the literal, historical interpretation but can in fact co-exist alongside of it.

It is, perhaps, Origen's attention to the "bodily" and the "spiritual" senses of Scripture that then drives his interest in discerning between the humanity and the divinity of Christ. In what is sometimes called partitive exegesis, Origen at times indicates that we should understand a certain saying of Christ according to his humanity or according to his divinity.

---

15. *Hom. Jer.* 1.6 (trans. Smith). Origen is also careful to note the difficulty in distinguishing between the words of the Father and of the Son; see, e.g., *Comm. John* 2.116. Sometimes, though, the multiple senses of Scripture allow for both the Father and the Son to speak the same words in different contexts or moments in salvation history; see, e.g., Origen's prosopological interpretation of Ps 81:11–12 at *Hom. Ps.* 80H2.6 as the words of Christ at multiple theodramatic moments. For a continuation on this point, see *Hom. Jer.* 14.5. See also *Hom. Jer.* 17.4.

16. *Hom. Jer.* 1.7.

17. For a brief overview of the relationship between the literal and allegorical senses, see Martens, *Origen and Scripture*, 63–66.

For example, in introducing his interpretation of Psalm 16, Origen underscores the importance of keeping this distinction in mind:

> Now, in fact, the things spoken by the *persona* of Christ in the Psalm are understood in accord with his humanity. For *my flesh shall set up a tent in hope* [Ps 16:9] is the voice of a human being, and *you will not abandon my soul in Hades* [Ps 16:10] is the voice of one endowed with a soul.[18]

Or, to take another example, when Origen interprets Christ characterizing himself as woeful in the words of Jer 15:10, Origen insists that Christ speaks this "not to the extent he is God, but to the extent he is man."[19] Such a method can be applied to Christ's sayings in the Gospels as well, but it is questionable whether these readings would count as prosopological exegesis insofar as Christ is the marked speaker and it is only a matter of whether Christ is speaking in a particular instance according to his humanity or according to his divinity.[20] There is some precedent for such an interpretive move, for instance, in Tertullian,[21] but Origen greatly expands this approach even as he avoids what Slusser calls "a static analysis or a division of Christ."[22] The relationship between Christ's humanity and divinity would, of course, become a major point of contention in the fifth century, with the key term *prosōpon* serving as the primary technical term for such christological reflection in the Greek-speaking East.[23]

With these points in mind, we can now proceed to examine some of the examples of prosopological exegesis relating to the Son that are found in Origen's extant writings. We begin, as always, with the speech of the Father with respect to the Son.

---

18. *Hom. Ps.* 15H2.2 (trans. Trigg). See also *Hom. Ps.* 15H2.3; 15H2.10; *Comm. John* 1.191–96.

19. *Hom. Jer.* 14.6 (trans. Smith). Origen connects this with Mic 7:1–2 as additional words of the Son on the theme of Jesus' rejection by the Jews during his incarnate ministry; see also *Hom. Ezech.* 1.5.

20. See, e.g., Origen's reading of Luke 4:4 as the words of Christ "as a man" at *Hom. Luc.* 29.5 (trans. Lienhard).

21. See, e.g., *Prax.* 30, in which Tertullian ascribes the words of Matt 27:46 to Jesus' humanity.

22. Slusser, "Exegetical Roots," 472, and the references therein to Rondeau, *Les commentaires patristiques*.

23. See further Slusser, "Exegetical Roots," 472–75.

From the Father

Within the category of prosopological exegesis from the *persona* of the Father, Origen identifies many of the "traditional" instances of the Father's speech to the Son commented upon by earlier writers, though he does not hesitate to append his own lines of interpretation, as the following analysis will demonstrate.

Divine Pre-Existence

Origen, like many earlier interpreters, reads Ps 45:1 as the words of the Father to the Son, providing occasion for Origen to comment on the Son's pre-existence as the "expression" of God's "intellectual and purposeful power concerning the universe."[24] Besides this, Origen looks to the first chapter of Genesis as a source of the Father's speech to the pre-existent Son. As Origen interprets Gen 1:26, for example,

> This, then, is the image about which the Father said to the Son, *Let us make men according to our image and likeness* [Gen 1:26]. The Son of God is the painter of this image. And because he is such a great painter his image can be obscured by negligence; it cannot be destroyed by malice. For the image of God always remains, even if you yourself draw "the image of the earthly" over it in yourself.[25]

Here Origen uses a prosopological reading of Gen 1:26 to comment upon the Son's role in the creation of human beings and, therefore, the persistence of the *imago Dei* even after the fall in light of the Son being such a "great painter." While Gen 1:26 is a conventional text to interpret as the words of the Father to the Son, Origen uses it not only to affirm the Son's pre-existence but to develop his anthropology in light of his Christology. Based on this reading of Gen 1:26, then, Origen speculates that perhaps all the commands to create in the first chapter of Genesis were in fact directed to the Son, through whom all things were created (cf. John 1:1–3): "For Christ is perhaps the creator to whom the Father says, *Let there be light* [Gen 1:3], and *Let there be a firmament* [Gen 1:6]."[26] The Son's cre-

---

24. *Comm. John* 1.282 (trans. Heine).
25. *Hom. Gen.* 13.4 (trans. Heine); see also *Comm. Matt.* 12.2.
26. *Comm. John* 1.110 (trans. Heine); see also *Cels.* 2.9; 5.37.

164   SCRIPTING THE SON

ative role is thereby more consistently and comprehensively demonstrated throughout the creation account of Genesis 1.

Incarnate Ministry

One place in which we see Origen do something novel with prosopological speech from the Father is in his interpretation of Isa 49:6, a passage that other authors had used to comment on Christ's present reign insofar as the whole verse talks about God's servant extending salvation to the ends of the earth. Origen, however, picks up on the language of Christ as servant and takes his interpretation in a different direction. Origen comments,

> Everyone who has understood how Jesus was to his disciples, not as the one who is at table, but as the one who serves, since the Son of God took the form of a servant for the freedom of those enslaved to sin, will not fail to recognize how the Father says to him, *You are my servant* [Isa 49:3], and a little further on, *This is a great thing for you, that you are called my servant* [Isa 49:6].[27]

Here Origen explicitly links the Father's words to the Son in Isaiah 49 with Christ's own words concerning himself in Luke 22:27. Continuing to play with the theme of "servant," Origen next draws in Phil 2:6–8 to note that Christ's goodness and divinity were best seen in his incarnation and at the cross; only having become a servant, Origen claims, could Christ become the "light of the gentiles" spoken of in Isa 49:6.[28] There is, therefore, a greater degree of nuance in Origen's interpretation of Isa 49:6 than that found in any earlier author, with Origen linking the nature of Christ's incarnate ministry and atoning death with his eventual rule over the nations.

Present Reign

Again following convention, Origen uses Psalm 2 as an important source of the Father's prosopological speech to the Son. To take just one of his frequent references to Ps 2:7–8, Origen, in a homily on Genesis, observes,

---

27. *Comm. John* 1.230 (trans. Heine).
28. *Comm. John* 1.231–32.

> For Christ, to whom the Father had said, *Ask of me and I will give you the nations for your inheritance and the utmost parts of the earth for your possession* [Ps 2:8], expelling those very angels from the authority and domination which they had among the nations, provoked them to wrath.[29]

While not explicitly commenting on the theodramatic setting of the dialogue, Origen expands on the meaning of its fulfillment with respect to Christ's victory over the powers and principalities of the world (cf. Eph 6:12), suggesting that this text should be read in the context of Christ's ascension to the right hand of the Father to reign over the world.

Psalm 110 is likewise for Origen an important, if traditional, source of prosopological speech from the Father on the theme of Christ's present reign. Again, though, Origen shows a deft touch with the issue of there being both "already" and "not yet" aspects to Christ's reign:

> In accomplishing all these things it was the will of the Father who delivered him up for the ungodly that he was accomplishing rather than his own will, for the Father is good, and the Savior is an image of his goodness. And when he shows kindness to all the world, since God in Christ is reconciling the world to himself, which had formerly become an enemy because of evil, he performs his acts of kindness methodically and orderly, not all at once taking all his enemies as the footstool of his feet. For the Father says to him who is Lord of each of us, *Sit at my right hand, until I make your enemies the footstool of your feet* [Ps 110:1]. These things go on until death, the last enemy, is destroyed by him.[30]

Here Origen points out that Christ, though the rightful king of this world, in his grace and kindness is "not all at once" subjecting all powers to his rule. This christological point flows from his understanding of Christ as an "image" of the Father's goodness. To take another example from Psalm 110, in a homily on Leviticus, Origen interprets Ps 110:4 prosopologically as the words of the Father to the Son, emphasizing the contrast between earthly priests and Christ, the great high priest (cf. Heb 4:14).[31]

In sum, therefore, Origen follows earlier tradition in reading dialogical passages such as Gen 1:26, Ps 2:7–8, Ps 110:1, Ps 110:4, and Isa

---

29. *Hom. Gen.* 9.3 (trans. Heine); see also *Cels.* 4.8; 5.32; *Hom. Num.* 17.5. For examples of Origen interpreting only Ps 2:7 prosopologically as the words of the Father to the Son, see *Comm. John* 1.204; *Hom. Ezech.* 6.3.

30. *Comm. John* 6.295–96 (trans. Heine); see also *Comm. Matt.* 15.23.

31. *Hom. Lev.* 12.1; see also *Hom. Ps.* 15H1.3.

49:6 as the words of the Father to the Son, even as he feels the liberty to use them according to his own purposes. Still, these instances are relatively infrequent with respect to that category of prosopological exegesis in which the Son speaks as his own *persona* in the Old Testament, suggesting that his interests in the method were found primarily in this latter category.

From the Son

For Origen, all of the Old Testament points to Christ. As Origen introduces one of his homilies on Genesis,

> It is written in the prophet speaking in the person of the Lord: *I have used similitudes by the ministries of the prophets* [Hos 12:10]. What this statement means is this: although our Lord Jesus Christ is one in his substance and is nothing other than the Son of God, nevertheless he is represented as various and diverse in the figures and images of the Scriptures.[32]

Origen here uses prosopological exegesis to justify his claim that Christ is set forth throughout the Old Testament in a wide range of types. In concert with his aforementioned distinction between the bodily and spiritual senses of Scripture, this principle allows Origen great flexibility in identifying prosopological speech from the Son in the Old Testament. Indeed, while the Psalter continues to be an important source for discovering instances of prosopological exegesis (as noted above, Origen reads all of Psalms 16 and 78 as spoken from the *persona* of Christ), the prophets become for Origen a particularly important source from which to place new verses on the lips of the Son. Again, Origen is able to do this on account of his distinction between the bodily and spiritual senses of Scripture, as a full accounting of Origen's use of prosopological exegesis from the person of the Son makes clear. As we will see, as was the case with prosopological exegesis from the person of the Father, much of Origen's prosopological exegesis from the person of the Son follows what appears to have become conventional by Origen's time, and yet, in contrast to what we observed with respect to the Father, Origen also selects a large number of new passages that he marks as

---

32. *Hom. Gen.* 14.1 (trans. Heine).

being the speech of the Son, greatly increasing the usefulness and depth of this method in Origen's exegesis.[33]

Divine Pre-Existence

Following convention (apart from the deviation of Theophilus and Irenaeus), the Son speaks as Wisdom in the famous passage from Proverbs 8.[34] There are, however, additional passages that Origen selects to comment on the Son's pre-existence. For instance, in his treatise on prayer, when speaking of God's foreknowledge, Origen insists that the Son also possesses such knowledge of events to come:

> In his observation of the unfolding of things to come, he saw Judas and the sins that he would commit. Thus, even before Judas was born, he could say with full knowledge by the mouth of David: *O God, be not silent in my praise* [Ps 109:1], and so on.[35]

Here Origen offers what would appear to be a novel prosopological interpretation of Ps 109:1 in order to defend his view of the foreknowledge of the Son with respect to Judas's betrayal, with the reference to this occurring before Judas's birth establishing the Son's pre-existence and foreknowledge. Similarly, Origen offers Isa 61:1, Isa 65:1, and Ps 2:6 ("and as many other words as have been recorded in the Psalms in the person of Christ") as evidence that Christ was always in the world, including prior to his incarnation.[36]

An interesting example concerning the Son's pre-existent relationship with the Father and the Spirit is found in Origen's *Commentary on John*, in which he comments that in Isaiah, "Christ admits that he has not been sent by the Father alone, but also by the Holy Spirit (for he

---

33. Given the polyvalency of the term "word/Word" (Greek *logos*), it is often unclear if Origen intends references to the speech of the *logos* to refer to the second person of the Trinity (e.g., Gen 1:20 at *Comm. Matt.* 10.11; 11.11). While I do think Christ is in fact often in view (cf. *Comm. John* 20.398), this strikes me as a separate, albeit related, phenomenon to that of prosopological exegesis as we have studied it in this book. Similar difficulties are found with respect to the word "Lord," and are common not just in Origen but in other writers as well, including Clement of Alexandria. On the difficulties of *logos* for translation and interpretation, see further Trigg, *Origen: Homilies on the Psalms*, 30–31.

34. See, e.g., Origen identifying the Son as the speaker of Prov 8:25 at *Hom. Jer.* 9.4, or of Prov 8:22 at *Comm. Matt.* 17.14.

35. *Or.* 6.5 (trans. O'Meara, modernized).

36. *Comm. John* 6.196 (trans. Heine).

says, *And now the Lord has sent me, and his Spirit* [Isa 48:16])."[37] This provides the basis for Origen to speculate concerning the Trinity and the Spirit's role in sending the Son.

One final example concerns the Son's departure from heaven for the purpose of the incarnation. The Son, Origen writes, left his heavenly home and

> comes into the earthly place and says: *I have left behind my house, I have abandoned my heritage* [Jer 12:7a]. For that was his heritage, the country with the angels, the rank with the holy powers. *I have given my beloved soul into the hands of its enemies* [Jer 12:7b]. He has handed over his soul into the hands of the enemies of the soul.[38]

This rather obscure verse from Jeremiah, then, serves as commentary on the pre-existent Son's heavenly heritage, which he abandoned for the sake of the salvation of humankind.

Pre-Incarnate Ministry

Relative to other writers studied in this book, Origen places far less emphasis on the Son speaking through Old Testament theophanies. For one thing, Origen appears to be less willing to identify all such encounters between God and human beings as manifestations of the pre-incarnate Christ; it is God the Father, for example, who interrogates Adam in the Garden.[39] Even the theophany shown to Moses is attributed to God the Father, and not God the Son.[40] However, as noted above, Origen's quotation of Hos 12:10 emphasizes how the Son spoke through the prophets, which could potentially be considered an example of this category as well; while not a theophany, it is nevertheless an instance in which the Son encountered the people of God before his incarnation.

Incarnate Ministry

As noted above, following convention, Origen places Isa 49:6 on the lips of the Father to describe the Son's incarnate ministry (quoted, in

37. *Comm. John* 2.79 (trans. Heine); see also *Comm. Matt.* 13.18.
38. *Hom. Jer.* 10.7 (trans. Smith).
39. *Comm. Matt.* 10.14.
40. *Comm. Matt.* 12.43.

this passage, by the Son himself). Origen actually expands beyond this conventional verse to read most of Isa 49:1–6 as dialogue spoken by the Son (with Isa 49:3, as with Isa 49:6, being a quotation of the Father's words to him). For example, as noted above, Origen writes that the Isaianic description of Jesus as a servant should point readers to "how Jesus was to his disciples, not as the one who is at table, but as the one who serves."[41] Origen thus connects Jesus' humility during his earthly ministry with his future glory.[42]

Jesus' incarnation as a Jew is emphasized by Origen, who, in arguing that "Christ came from that race, i.e., from the Israelite race, according to the flesh," pulls in a verse from Hosea as the words of the Son to that effect: "*Woe to them because my flesh is from them* [Hos 9:12]."[43] In this way, then, Jesus prophesied that his incarnation as a Jew would lead to his rejection by the Jews and, therefore, his eventual acceptance among the gentiles.

Crucifixion

The Son speaks concerning his rejection and humiliation through the words of familiar passages, such as Ps 22:6, Ps 69:21, and Isa 50:6.[44] In fact, at one point in his *Commentary on John*, Origen indicates that the entirety of Psalm 69 should be read as spoken by the person of Christ.[45] A novel and more popular text for this purpose, however, is drawn from Jeremiah. As Origen states, after introducing Isa 53:7 as a prophecy about Christ, "Here Christ speaks about himself: *Like a lamb without evil who is led to slaughter to be sacrificed I did not know* [Jer 11:19a]."[46] This provides the basis for a christological interpretation of the following verses, which Origen interprets as the Son speaking concerning his betrayal and the subsequent judgment of the Jews (Jer 11:19b–23).[47]

41. *Comm. John* 1.230 (trans. Heine); see also *Comm. John* 1.133–35, 228.
42. *Comm. John* 1.231; cf. Phil 2:8.
43. *Comm. Rom.* 7.13.8 (trans. Scheck).
44. For instance, Origen reads Ps 22:6 as the words of the Son at *Hom. Luc.* 14.8, Ps 69:21 as the words of the Son at *Cels.* 2.37, and Isa 50:6 as the words of the Son at *Hom. Jer.* 19.12.
45. *Comm. John* 10.222. One would be curious to know how Origen would interpret Ps 69:5 from the Son.
46. *Hom. Jer.* 10.1 (trans. Smith). See also *Comm. John* 1.135.
47. *Hom. Jer.* 10.2–5.

Similarly, Origen reads Psalm 27 as from the *persona* of Christ "precisely at the time of his Passion," when, in the midst of the demonic forces arrayed against him (Origen here quotes Ps 2:2), Christ prays the words of Ps 27:1–3.[48] While, as we have seen, Ps 2:7–8 was an enormously important text for christological reflection through prosopological exegesis, the other parts of Psalm 2 were largely untapped for such analysis. Origen, then, manages to connect and harmonize these two psalms in a profound way as he remains attentive to shifts in speakers within a given psalm.[49]

Resurrection from the Dead

Where Origen breaks significant new ground, however, is expanding upon the Son's descent to the place of the dead. To take just one example, Origen uses a new prosopological interpretation in order to make a point about Christ's descent into hell and about human anthropology more generally. As Origen argues in his *Dialogue with Heraclides*, the human being is a composite of a body, soul, and spirit; in order to redeem mankind, Christ assumed all three of these elements of the human person in the incarnation. But Origen observes that when Christ died, he committed his spirit into the Father's hands (cf. Luke 23:46), his body was placed in the tomb (cf. Luke 23:53), and therefore it must have been his soul that descended into Hades (cf. Eph 4:9). This final point Origen proves with a prosopological reading drawn from the Psalter: "*You do not give up my soul to Hades* [Ps 16:10]." As Origen explains, "These three elements were separated at the time of the passion; they were reunited at the time of the resurrection."[50] Perhaps inspired by Acts 2:27, Origen places this verse on the lips of Christ, providing an early defense of the notion that the Apostles' Creed would later summarize with the phrase "*descendit ad*

---

48. *Comm. John* 32.296 (trans. Heine).

49. Additionally, Origen in book 32 of his *Commentary on John* gives substantial attention to the role of Judas within the Passion narrative. Origen (*Comm. John* 32.157–58, 162–68, 285) points out that Jesus at the Last Supper declared Ps 41:9 fulfilled, leading to Judas' exit from the scene to betray Jesus (John 13:18–30). While a prosopological interpretation is clearly implied, it is not explicit, with Origen instead emphasizing the fulfillment of prophecy.

50. *Dial. Herac.* 7 (trans. Daly). See also *Hom. Ps.* 15H1.2; *Comm. John* 6.175; *Cels.* 2.62, in which Origen interprets Ps 16:9–10 as from "the person of Jesus." Cf. *Comm. John* 19.102, 140, as further examples that are likely meant to be read prosopologically, although that is not explicitly in focus in either passage.

inferos,"⁵¹ and also advancing his tripartite view of the human person that would be so influential for his view of scriptural hermeneutics, among other things.⁵² Such is the genius of the great Alexandrian.⁵³

Similarly, Origen insists that the Son taking on human form entailed

> that he might be able to enter that place where death was holding dominion, in accordance with what the prophet also says under the *persona* of [Christ], *And I was reckoned with those who go down to the pit* [Ps 28:1], and again, *What profit is there in my blood when I go down to corruption?* [Ps 30:9].⁵⁴

The theodramatic setting is undefined, but the subject of the speech clearly concerns the Son's death, by which he defeated the power of death. Thus, with reference to Matt 12:29 and Eph 4:8, Origen can write that when Christ

> had bound the strong man and triumphed over him by means of his cross, he even advanced into his house, the house of death in the underworld, and from there he plundered his possessions, that is, he led away the souls which [the devil] was keeping.⁵⁵

In the same fashion, Ps 88:4–5 is summoned to defend his claim that Christ was "among the dead insofar as he was the only free man there; his soul was not left in Hades,"⁵⁶ and Origen places Hos 13:14 on the lips of the Son to comment on how Christ rescues sinners from the power of death.⁵⁷ Christ's harrowing of hell therefore takes on added importance for Origen's understanding of the atonement.

Present Reign

Origen also comments on Christ's ascension via prosopological exegesis, using the familiar passage Ps 24:7–10 in order to describe how those

---

51. This line was likely a relatively late addition to the Apostles' Creed; on this subject, see further Fairbairn and Reeves, *Story of Creeds*, 120–23.

52. See, e.g., *Princ.* 4.2.4.

53. Origen even has the *persona* of those in the underworld speak to Christ the words of Isa 14:10–11 (*Comm. Matt.* 15.27).

54. *Comm. Rom.* 5.10.10 (trans. Scheck). See also *Hom. Jer.* 14.6 (in which the Father is explicitly identified as the audience); *Hom. Ezech.* 1.5.

55. *Comm. Rom.* 5.10.12 (trans. Scheck).

56. *Comm. John* 1.220 (trans. Heine).

57. *Comm. Rom.* 5.1.36.

escorting Christ called for the heavenly guards to lift up their gates. This scene generates a further dialogue that Origen intends for us to read prosopologically:

> When [the heavenly guards] see [Christ's] blood-stained right hand and his whole body filled with the works of prowess [they inquire]: *Why is your apparel red and your garments like the residue of a full wine-vat which has been trampled down?* [Isa 63:2]. To which he answers, *I have crushed them in pieces* [Isa 63:3].[58]

Here Origen provides a creative synthesis of Psalm 24 and Isaiah 63 to generate a dialogue between Christ and the heavenly guards in the context of Christ's ascension.

Also on the subject of the ascension, returning to Ps 2:7–8, Origen is attuned to the shift in speakers in this verse, and thus he can point out the significance of interpreting these words as the Son quoting what the Father had told him at an earlier time. As Origen points out, in these verses the Father "urges the Savior himself to ask that it may be given to him," serving as an example of Christ's own teaching on prayer (cf. Matt 7:7–8).[59] The presumed theodramatic moment is that of Christ's ascension to the Father, when he receives the gentiles as his inheritance.

Origen, when describing the time following Christ's ascension, follows previous writers in presenting the Son speaking concerning the Jews' continued rejection of Christ and the consequent extension of salvation to the gentiles. In addition to conventional texts, such as Isa 65:1, Origen also places more obscure passages, such as Deut 32:21 and 2 Sam 22:44–45, on the lips of the Son.[60] Origen maintains that the gentiles' acceptance of Christ was proclaimed by the Son in words drawn from the Psalter: "*A people whom I have not known have served me* [Ps 18:43]."[61] Again, while the verse chosen is novel, the basic line of interpretation is traditional.

Yet another way in which Origen innovates with respect to the Son's prosopological speech is his identification of texts that he interprets as the Son speaking the words of the Old Testament directly to the church as words of comfort. The governing idea might ultimately be drawn from Heb 2:12–13, in which the author of Hebrews quotes Ps 22:22 and Isa

---

58. *Comm. John* 6.289 (trans. Heine).
59. *Comm. John* 13.5 (trans. Heine).
60. *Cels.* 2.78; see also *Comm. Rom.* 8.6.11 for Isa 65:1.
61. *Comm. Rom.* 7.13.8 (trans. Scheck).

8:18, interpreting these verses as the Son calling believers his "brothers" and the "children" given to him by God. Origen himself, in fact, adopts these same readings of Ps 22:22 and Isa 8:18.[62]

With the idea established, then, that Christ speaks through the Old Testament to believers in Origen's own day, Origen makes similar interpretive moves that appear to be his own innovations. For example, Christ, Origen writes, invites the church to respond to his initial move of coming close to her, placing Zech 1:3 and Jer 23:23 on the lips of the Son.[63] Christ speaks the words of Isa 66:12 to the church, emphasizing his peaceful nature.[64] Christ promises freedom to captives living in darkness in the words of Isa 49:9.[65] And because his followers are themselves "christs," Christ must therefore be the speaker of Ps 105:15, promising his people protection.[66] Christ, in fact, spoke to the church at her birth in the words of Joseph to his son Ephraim on the meaning of his name (Gen 41:52), with Origen suggesting that God increasing Jacob in the land of humiliation images Christ's rule over the church.[67] Indeed, Origen indicates that the entirety of the Song of Songs can be read as dialogue between Christ and the church, here personified as a bride; as he writes, "the appellations of Bride and Bridegroom denote either the Church in her relation to Christ, or the soul in her union with the Word of God."[68] Thus, the words attributed to the Bridegroom in the Song of Songs are placed on the lips of Christ.[69] This use of prosopologi-

62. See, e.g., *Hom. Lev.* 12.2; *Hom. Ps.* 67H1.2; *Hom. Isaa.* 7.1; *Hom. Jer.* 18.6; *Hom. Ezech.* 9.3; *Comm. John* 19.28; *Or.* 15.4.

63. *Hom. Gen.* 1.7. Origen also interprets Jer 23:23–24 as the words of the Son at *Cels.* 5.12; *Comm. John* 6.202.

64. *Hom. Ezech.* 13.4.

65. *Hom. Isaa.* 6.7.

66. *Hom. Ps.* 81H1.1.

67. *Comm. John* 28.223.

68. *Comm. Cant.* 1.1 (trans. Lawson); cf. *Hom. Cant.* 1.1. Interestingly, Methodius, despite being an opponent of Origen, seems to have interpreted the Song in a similar way as Origen based on how he reads Christ as the speaker of Song 2:2; 4:9–12; 6:8–9 (*Symp.* 7.1–4), though Methodius presents Christ as speaking specifically to those who are virgins.

69. In the extant portions of his works on the Song of Songs that survive in Rufinus's Latin translation, Origen has the Son speak Song 1:8–10 (*Comm. Cant.* 2.5–7; *Hom. Cant.* 1.9–10); 1:15 (*Comm. Cant.* 3.1; *Hom. Cant.* 2.4); 2:1–2 (*Comm. Cant.* 3.4; *Hom. Cant.* 2.6); 2:10b–15 (*Comm. Cant.* 3.14–15; *Hom. Cant.* 2.12–13). Origen reads Song 2:1 as the words of the Bridegroom/Son, while English translations such as the ESV identify it as spoken by the Bride. Presumably Origen reads the rest of the Song in this manner, though we lack the extant portion of the commentary or relevant homilies to

cal exegesis to interpret the Song of Songs would come to be a favorite of writers of Late Antiquity and the medieval period, culminating in the works of figures such as Bernard of Clairvaux, indicating the lengthy reach of this trajectory of christological interpretation.[70]

Even those passages originally understood to be Christ speaking concerning his passion, such as Ps 22:14, can now be interpreted as words of warning from the Son to Origen's audience; as Origen comments, reflecting on the details of Jesus' crucifixion and drawing in Paul's image of the body of Christ from 1 Cor 12:12–31: "He did not say this concerning his bodily bones—for they were not scattered—but concerning those neglecting gathering, because body parts of Christ are scattered."[71] This concern with the mystical Body of Christ makes frequent appearance in prosopological exegesis from the person of the Son. To take another example, Origen begins his first homily on Psalm 16 (which, as noted above, is a psalm that Origen ascribes entirely to the Son) with a demonstration of how the first verse actually pertains to Christ praying concerning his own body, the church:

> For I say that [Christ] said this to his Lord and Father about those who are his constituent parts.... Since you are the constituent parts of Christ and, in part, constituent parts, and you are the body of Christ, when he prays and says, *Protect me, Lord* [Ps 16:1], he is speaking about himself as he prays on your behalf.[72]

Thus, a verse that would appear to lend itself to the Son speaking of his passion is instead interpreted in a different theodramatic setting in order to refer to Christ and the church. Likewise, later in this same homily, Origen interprets *"the holy ones who are in his land* [Ps 16:3]" as referring not just to the distribution of the promised land in the Old Testament but also figuratively to the church, which "is already God's land."[73] And thus Origen manages to read the entirety of this psalm as the words of

---

confirm. Origen can even use the Bride's words as a starting point for generating prosopological speech from the Son; e.g., Origen connects Song 2:5c with a prosopological interpretation of Isa 49:2–3 at *Hom. Cant.* 2.8. Cf. *Comm. Cant.* 3.8.

70. On the use of the Song in Late Antiquity, with an emphasis on the Latin tradition, see Shuve, *Song of Songs*; for Bernard of Clairvaux, see, e.g., the collected homilies translated by Evans.

71. *Hom. Ps.* 77H8.3 (trans. Trigg).

72. *Hom. Ps.* 15H1.3 (trans. Trigg). This is a rare instance in which Origen explicitly notes the Son speaking to the Father. Origen goes on to cite Matt 25:35 as further justification for this interpretive move.

73. *Hom. Ps.* 15H1.6 (trans. Trigg).

Christ in this ecclesiological key.[74] Likewise, in his interpretation of Ps 78:1, Origen argues, "If, then, my Savior should say, *Pay attention, my people, to my law* [Ps 78:1], he speaks to Christians, for Christians are the people of Christ."[75] Here the law of the gospel has replaced the law of Moses as the referent of the text in order that Christ can speak with direct relevance to Origen's audience, even as Origen's interpretation then shifts its theodramatic setting to encompass the apostles' response (Ps 78:3–8) to Christ's teaching (Ps 78:2), a response that Christians are now to emulate.[76] So also texts such as Ps 30:9 and Mic 7:1–2, which would seem most naturally to describe Christ's death, can be interpreted as descriptions of Christ "lamenting our sins."[77]

There is, ultimately, a fundamental contrast between those who bear the fruit of the Holy Spirit and those who do not. As Origen summarizes, Christ "also says to all whom he calls to blessedness, *I said: You are gods and all sons of the Most High* [Ps 82:6]. But censuring those who do not wish to be gods or sons of the Most High, he says, *But you will die as human beings* [Ps 82:7]."[78] Interestingly, whereas the source text from the Psalter seems to be speaking to a single group of people, Origen here bifurcates the audience as a way of alluding to Christ's elect as opposed to those who remain outside of Christ.

The net effect of such readings is to make Christ present to Origen's own audience, with the words originally spoken by God through the prophets now being re-contextualized as the words of Christ for the church in Origen's time. Beyond this, however, Origen's stress on Christians as "christs" leads into a further innovative use of prosopological exegesis: Origen's invitation that Christians themselves adopt the *persona* of Christ. In a very interesting passage that invokes the earlier sense of a *prosōpon* as a mask in a theatrical context, Origen makes the following claim:

> Just as those on the stage for plays receive *personae* [that is, *prosōpa*] that they have practiced, now that of a king, now that of a household slave, now of a woman, now of whoever it might be, and it is possible to see in theatrical performances the performers receiving *personae*; such a thing, I think, also occurs on the stage of the world. For all the performers always

---

74. See further *Hom. Ps.* 15H1–2.
75. *Hom. Ps.* 77H1.4 (trans. Trigg).
76. See also *Comm. Matt.* 15.28.
77. *Comm. Matt.* 16.21 (trans. Heine).
78. *Comm. Matt.* 16.29 (trans. Heine).

> receive *personae*; if we would be blessed, we should receive a *persona* like that of God and say: *I have begotten sons and exalted them, but they have rejected me* [Isa 1:2]. Again, if we would be just, we receive the *persona* of Christ, and, while still human beings, we say, *The spirit of the Lord is upon me, for which reason he has anointed me; he has sent me to announce good news to the destitute* [Isa 61:1].[79]

Here Origen connects the use of *prosōpon* in the Greek translation of Ps 82:2 with the sense of actors who assume various *prosōpa* and then, by extension, with the roles that each person plays in this world. The argument is essentially one for the *imitatio Christi*. Christians are, in other words, to act as "little christs," to "put on Christ" (cf. Rom 13:14), and in so doing take Christ's various words as their own, adopting his *persona*. Like Christ, then, Christians are to act upon their anointing with the Holy Spirit and proclaim the gospel (Isa 61:1); perhaps, Origen suggests, they can even take on the *persona* of God in the face of rejection (Isa 1:2). Elsewhere, Origen continues to play with this theme, calling on Christians to take upon themselves the *persona* of Christ, re-speaking for themselves the Son's words from the Psalter.[80] As Origen exhorts his audience, "For the Lord also dwells in you, if you wish, *through everything* [Ps 16:8]. Become his imitator like Paul, and you will find that the Lord is always in you. For you also will say, *It is no longer I that live, but Christ lives in me* [Gal 2:20]."[81] If, Origen argues, Christians are called to imitate Christ such that Christ lives in them, it would be natural for them to speak Christ's words as their own, wielding Christ's own power and authority.[82] What is particularly fascinating is that Origen does not immediately go to the incarnate Christ's words recorded in the New Testament, but to the words that the Son speaks prosopologically in the Old. In such a way, Origen continues to expand the influence and power of prosopological exegesis as it pertains to Christ in the Old Testament, not just for theology but also for application in the lives of his audience.

---

79. *Hom. Ps.* 81H1.3 (trans. Trigg).
80. See, e.g., Ps 16:7–8 at *Hom. Ps.* 15H2.5.
81. *Hom. Ps.* 15H2.5 (trans. Trigg).
82. See, e.g., Origen's interpretation of Psalm 2 at *Comm. Matt.* 12.20; 13.9.

Summary

Origen thus provides thorough evidence that the connection between Christology and prosopological exegesis made deep inroads into the third-century Greek tradition even as its influence appears to have begun to wane in the Latin tradition. While Origen's use of prosopological exegesis shows many similarities with its use among earlier writers, Origen nevertheless brings great creativity to this form of biblical interpretation, particularly insofar as he uses prosopological exegesis to develop the themes of the Son's descent into hell and the ways in which the Son continues to speak to the church in the present day. Origen's suggestion that Christians should themselves adopt the *persona* of the Son is an example of a still further innovative use of prosopological exegesis, this time not for the purpose of polemical struggle or doctrinal definition but for the spiritual formation of individual Christians and congregations. In concluding this section, we can briefly summarize Origen's prosopological readings in a table that sets out all the instances in which he indicates a prosopological reading of Old Testament dialogical passages that involve speech to, from, or about the Son. As before, verses in bold reflect places where Origen explicitly interprets these words as intra-divine dialogue:

	From the Father	*From the Son*	*From the Spirit*
Divine Pre-Existence	**Gen 1:3**	Ps 2:6	—
	Gen 1:6	Ps 109:1	
	Gen 1:26	Prov 8:22	
	Ps 45:1	Prov 8:25	
		Isa 48:16	
		Isa 61:1	
		Isa 65:1	
		Jer 12:7	
Pre-Incarnate Ministry	—	Hos 12:10	—
Incarnate Ministry	**Isa 49:3**	Ps 81:11–12	—
	Isa 49:6	Isa 49:1–2	
		Isa 49:5	
		Jer 15:10	
		Hos 9:12	
		Mic 7:1–2	

	From the Father	From the Son	From the Spirit
Crucifixion	—	Ps 22:6 Ps 27:1–3 Ps 69:1–36 Isa 50:6 Jer 11:19–23	—
Death and Resurrection	—	Ps 16:1–9 **Ps 16:9–10** Ps 28:1 Ps 30:9 Ps 88:4–5 Hos 13:14	—
Ascension, Enthronement, and Reign	**Ps 2:7b–8** **Ps 110:1b–c** Ps 110:4	Gen 41:52 Deut 32:21 2 Sam 22:44–45 Ps 2:7a **Ps 16:1** Ps 18:43 Ps 22:14 **Ps 22:22** Ps 30:9 Ps 78:1–2 Ps 81:11–12 Ps 82:6–7 Ps 105:15 Song 1:8–10 Song 1:15 Song 2:1–2 Song 2:10b–15 Isa 8:18 Isa 49:2–3 Isa 49:9 Isa 61:1 Isa 63:3 Isa 65:1 Isa 66:12 Jer 23:23–24 Mic 7:1–2 Zech 1:3	—

The absence of speech from the Holy Spirit regarding the Son is a striking difference from how Justin, Irenaeus, and Tertullian used prosopological exegesis. It is also intriguing that the Father's prosopological speech is only ever directed towards the Son, while the Son's prosopological speech is only very rarely explicitly directed towards the Father. Still, the evidence summarized in this table demonstrates that Origen used prosopological exegesis to advance his christological claims regarding everything from the Son's divine existence through his present reign.

Weaving the Threads

As has been our pattern thus far in this book, we can now analyze the extent to which Origen's sources and his understanding of the *regula fidei* may have contributed to this particular exegetical approach which proved to be such an important means of advancing Origen's theological vision.

Origen's Use of *Testimonia*

Origen appears to allude to the existence of *testimonia* collections on one occasion in his *Against Celsus*,[83] but this work makes strikingly infrequent use of prosopological exegesis. Instead, the vast majority of prosopological exegesis is found in Origen's homilies and commentaries, with the occasional and sometimes idiosyncratic nature of his interpretations making their origin in a pre-existing *testimonia* collection unlikely. If these interpretations were indeed drawn from such a collection, we would expect to see quotations that are incorrectly attributed, mixed, or linked with other quotations, but instead Origen, particularly in his commentaries and homilies, appears to be starting with the biblical text in view and then providing a prosopological reading as part of his own interpretation. In most cases, then, an underlying *testimonia* collection is an unlikely source for Origen's exegesis.

A better question, perhaps, for exploring Origen's sources for his use of prosopological exegesis is the extent to which his own Alexandrian context shaped his interpretive method. Without texts from the variety of schools that flourished in Alexandria in the second century,[84] which would have predated Origen, we simply cannot say for certain how much of Origen's interpretation is unique to him. It is worth noting, however, that the extant texts we do have, predominantly those from Origen's predecessor Clement of Alexandria, show little in the way of what we would recognize as traditional prosopological exegesis.[85] In

---

83. *Cels.* 3.15.

84. On this subject, see further Heine, *Scholarship*, 48–60.

85. On Clement of Alexandria's use of Scripture more generally, see further Ward, *Clement*.

Clement's *Exhortation to the Greeks* and *Miscellanies*, there are only two clear examples of prosopological exegesis in the entirety of these writings.[86] Meanwhile, in Clement's one other major work, *Christ the Educator*, particularly within book 1, we find that a great number of references to Old Testament Scripture are presented as the words of Christ, the titular "Educator" of this work. How precisely we are supposed to understand the relationship among Christ, the Holy Spirit, the human authors, and the words of Scripture is left largely unclear, as indicated by Clement using a variety of introductory formulas for his citations of Scripture without a clearly articulated or consistent pattern. Perhaps the closest Clement comes to explaining his method is when he writes, "Of old, the Word educated through Moses, and after that through the Prophets; even Moses was in fact a Prophet."[87] Indeed, "Christ the Educator" is most often presented as the speaker of the biblical text when Clement quotes first-person divine speech, either to Moses or to later figures such as David, Solomon, Isaiah, Jeremiah, Ezekiel, and Hosea.[88] In contrast, words of praise to God or prophecies of Christ are often ascribed to the Holy Spirit,[89] and Wisdom often speaks through books such as Proverbs, the Wisdom of Solomon, or Ecclesiasticus;[90] otherwise, in books 2 and 3 most quotations of Scripture are simply attributed to "Scripture." Unfortunately, exceptions to these generalizations complicate any effort to discern an underlying strategy of attribution.

In any event, the question remains whether we should even categorize Clement's presentation of "Christ the Educator" as the speaker

---

86. At *Protr.* 11, Clement describes the Son as having made a promise to the Father through the words of Ps 22:22; at *Strom.* 4.22, Clement writes that "in the person of God it is said to the Lord" the words of Ps 2:8 (trans. *ANF*).

87. *Paed.* 1.11.96. To take just a handful of such examples of Christ the Educator's speech quoted from the Old Testament, see *Paed.* 1.2.5; 1.7.53, 56–61; 1.8.67–70; 1.9.76–82, 84–86; 1.10.90–94; 2.3.28; 2.10.89, 91, 95, 99, 109–10; 2.12.126; 3.2.9–10; 3.3.20; 3.4.27; 3.11.72, 75–76; 3.12.86–87, 89–93.

88. Perhaps the association between Christ and Moses goes back to the belief that Christ was present in the burning bush, a traditional view that Clement endorses at *Paed.* 2.8.75. The Son also judged Sodom (*Paed.* 3.8.44).

89. See, e.g., *Paed.* 1.5.15; 1.7.56; 1.8.73; 1.9.87; 2.1.8; 2.3.30; 2.4.41–42, 44; 2.8.62; 2.10.87, 113; 2.12.126, 129; 3.1.3; 3.11.67. See also *Protr.* 8–9; *Strom.* 2.20, 23; 4.26; 5.4, 14. All of these should be understood as the Spirit speaking as an "inspiring secondary agent"; for this categorization, see further Bates, *Birth*, 164n18; Hughes, "Spirit and the Scriptures," 38–41; *How the Spirit Became God*, 58.

90. See, e.g., *Paed.* 1.8.69, 72; 1.9.75; 1.13.102; 2.1.7–8; 2.3.24, 27; 2.7.54, 58–59; 2.9.79. Wisdom is, of course, identified with the Son by Clement (e.g., *Paed.* 1.2.6).

of Scripture as a form of prosopological exegesis. On the one hand, it is true that the Son is not in view in the source text, and on at least one occasion Clement describes Christ speaking in his own *prosōpon*.[91] On the other hand, Clement does not make any attempts to interpret any of these texts in a way that would imply a divine discourse; the Father and the Son are never portrayed as speaking to one another, a common feature in prosopological exegesis elsewhere. Indeed, the focus is not so much on Christ himself as it is on how Christ's words are meant to impact Clement's audience. Clement appears to be simply transferring the identity of the speaker of most divine instruction (that is, to Moses and the prophets) from God the Father to God the Son.[92] In fact, as a result of this move, God the Father seems to have lost his voice altogether, replaced within the divine economy by Christ, who is even called by Clement "the Creator of the world and of man."[93] Accordingly, in *Christ the Educator* the Son is functioning more as an "inspiring secondary agent" rather than a "primary speaking agent," and so we should not think of these instances as true examples of prosopological exegesis as we have analyzed it in this book.[94]

In fact, those passages which were frequently interpreted prosopologically are not read that way by Clement. Take, for example, Gen 1:26, usually read as the words of the Father to the Son (and potentially also the Spirit). Clement, however, simply introduces the verse as "the original divine command" before commenting, "It is Christ, in fact, who is, in all its perfection, what God then commanded; other men are so only by a certain image."[95] In other words, Clement does not identify Christ as the audience of God's words in Gen 1:26; instead, he makes Christ the *subject* of God's words, the true *imago Dei* from which human beings then derive their own identity. Prosopological exegesis is not in view here, nor is it in other passages where we would expect to find it used.[96]

---

91. *Paed.* 1.7.56, speaking Exod 20:2.

92. Indeed, God the Father appears to have played precisely this role in Clement's *Exhortation to the Greeks*; cf. *Protr.* 10.

93. *Paed.* 3.12.100 (trans. Wood).

94. For the terms "primary speaking agent" and "inspiring secondary agent," see again Bates, *Birth*, 164n18; Hughes, "Spirit and the Scriptures," 38–41.

95. *Paed.* 1.12.98 (trans. Wood).

96. Other examples of Clement not using prosopological exegesis where we would expect to find it include his quotations of Isa 8:18 at *Paed.* 1.5.14 and Ps 45:7–8 at *Paed.* 2.8.65.

In summary, therefore, Origen's overall approach to prosopological exegesis does not appear to be something he learned from Clement of Alexandria. This aligns with Simon Wood's conclusion that Origen "shows only a vague, unacknowledged dependence upon his predecessor, for he retained the broad humanism of Clement, but differed in many points of doctrine and of method."[97] Where then could he have been influenced by this approach to exegesis? Besides from the New Testament or other early Christian writings, the fact that Origen had worked for a time as a *grammatikos*[98] suggests that he would have been intimately familiar with the various steps of ancient interpretation, which as noted earlier in this book would have included the identification of the various speaking persons and addressees in the text, especially when they were unclear. Thus, the innovative readings that Origen presents may in fact have had their genesis in Origen's school, the products of his own instruction and lectures.[99] This attention to the dialoguing characters within a text, after all, was simply a normal part of ancient literary analysis.[100] It would appear, then, that Origen's training in how to interpret texts played a larger role in his interest in prosopological exegesis than the existence of any *testimonia* collection on the subject or any direct predecessor.

Origen and the *Regula Fidei*

Origen provides a number of traditional summaries of the Christian faith at various points in his extant writings. Origen uses a wide range of terms like "the Christian rule," "rule of truth," and "rule of piety" to introduce his accounts of the *regula fidei*, though the existence of key texts only in Latin translation complicates efforts to establish Origen's exact terminology.[101] Origen's summaries, while including all of the basic elements of other such accounts of the *regula fidei*, often also include speculative notions not found in other ones, reflecting "the distinction Origen made between the simple believers, to whom belong the elementary dogmas, and the perfect, to whom belong allegorical

---

97. Wood, *Clement of Alexandria*, viii.
98. See Heine, *Scholarship*, 60; cf. Eusebius's references in *Hist. eccl.* 6.2–3.
99. See Heine, *Scholarship*, 61–64.
100. See again Slusser, "Exegetical Roots," 468–70.
101. See further Ferguson, *Rule of Faith*, 24–29; Johnson, *Jesus Christ*, 93–95.

explanations."[102] The central christological claims of Origen's rule, though, are conventional; a typical passage is as follows:

> [The second article of belief is] that Jesus Christ himself, who came, was born of the Father before all creatures. After ministering to the Father in the foundation of all things, for by him were all things made, in the last times, emptying himself, he became human and was incarnate; being God, when made human he remained what he was, God. He assumed a body like to our own, differing in this respect only, that it was born of a virgin and of the Holy Spirit. And that this Jesus Christ was born and did suffer in truth, and not in appearance, and truly died our common death, and did truly rise from the dead, and after the resurrection, having sojourned for a while with his disciples, was taken up.[103]

This summary of the apostolic teaching highlights Christ's pre-existence, incarnation by being born of the Virgin Mary, suffering, death, resurrection, and ascension. Later Origen describes the final judgment and the resurrection of the dead,[104] but it is interesting that he does not include it within the christological portion of the *regula*. Nowhere does Origen include in a summary of the apostolic teaching any reference to the pre-incarnate Christ appearing to Old Testament patriarchs in theophanies, which lines up with his use (or essentially lack thereof in this case) of prosopological exegesis from the person of the Son in such contexts.

We can visually depict the extent of alignment between Origen's use of prosopological exegesis (at least as found in his extant works) and his presentation of the rule of faith as follows:

---

102. Ferguson, *Rule of Faith*, 42.

103. *Princ.* pref.4 (trans. Behr). On the textual issue related to Christ being "born" of the Father, see Behr, *Origen*, 1.15n15. On Origen's *regula*, see also *Comm. John* 32.183–97.

104. *Princ.* pref.5.

	From the Father	From the Son	From the Spirit	Rule of Faith
Divine Pre-Existence	**Gen 1:3** **Gen 1:6** **Gen 1:26** **Ps 45:1**	Ps 2:6 Ps 109:1 Prov 8:22 Prov 8:25 Isa 48:16 Isa 61:1 Isa 65:1 Jer 12:7	—	Pre-existed with the Father
Pre-Incarnate Ministry	—	Hos 12:10	—	—
Virgin Birth	—	—	—	Born of the Virgin Mary
Incarnate Ministry	**Isa 49:3** **Isa 49:6**	Ps 81:11–12 Isa 49:1–2 Isa 49:5 Jer 15:10 Hos 9:12 Mic 7:1–2	—	Engaged in ministry
Crucifixion	—	Ps 22:6 Ps 27:1–3 Ps 69:1–36 Isa 50:6 Jer 11:19–23	—	Rejected, crucified, and killed
Death and Resurrection	—	Ps 16:1–9 **Ps 16:9–10** Ps 28:1 Ps 30:9 Ps 88:4–5 Hos 13:14	—	Resurrected from the dead

	From the Father	From the Son	From the Spirit	Rule of Faith
Ascension, Enthronement, and Reign	**Ps 2:7b–8** **Ps 110:1b–c** **Ps 110:4**	Gen 41:52 Deut 32:21 2 Sam 22:44–45 Ps 2:7a **Ps 16:1** Ps 18:43 Ps 22:14 **Ps 22:22** Ps 30:9 Ps 78:1–2 Ps 81:11–12 Ps 82:6–7 Ps 105:15 Song 1:8–10 Song 1:15 Song 2:1–2 Song 2:10b–15 Isa 8:18 Isa 49:2–3 Isa 49:9 Isa 61:1 Isa 63:3 Isa 65:1 Isa 66:12 Jer 23:23–24 Mic 7:1–2 Zech 1:3	—	Ascended and reigns

The overlap may not be as consistently clear as was the case with Tertullian, but considerable alignment exists between how Origen uses prosopological exegesis with respect to the Son and the christological content of his *regula fidei*. Of the six elements of the basic christological narrative found in Origen's rule of faith, we have evidence of prosopological speech concerning the Son that aligns with five of these; only the Son's virgin birth is not the subject of any of the Son's prosopological speech, at least in Origen's extant writings. Looking at the chart from the other direction, almost all of Origen's categories for prosopological exegesis from the Son find counterparts in his *regula fidei*; it is not surprising that Origen does not include Christ's pre-incarnate ministry in his *regula fidei*, as the subject plays only a very slight role in his use of prosopological exegesis. Interestingly, Christ's second coming, absent from Origen's formal statements of the rule of faith, is also not a subject connected with his use of prosopological exegesis. Looking at the chart from both directions, then, we find a high level of alignment between Origen's rule of faith and his use of prosopological exegesis.

Conclusion: Scripting the Son in Origen

This chapter has explored how Origen's use of prosopological exegesis served to advance his christological claims. Origen, in making frequent use of this method across his many extant writings, shows the continued utility and flexibility of interpreting the words of the Old Testament as the words of the Son, emphasizing in particular how these words could be represented to Origen's own congregation of "little christs." Origen appears to be indebted for his use of prosopological exegesis not to any *testimonia* collection or to any immediate predecessor such as Clement of Alexandria; rather, his command of the principles of ancient literary analysis would have supplied everything he needed to be attentive to the issue of identifying the true speaker in a given text. As with other early Christian writers, Origen's use of prosopological exegesis with respect to the Son closely aligns with his presentation of the christological portion of the rule of faith. Origen's interest in partitive exegesis and in bringing Christ's words from the Old Testament directly to bear upon his audience provided fodder for future use of this exegetical method in the fourth century, particularly with his Alexandrian successors Alexander and Athanasius. Origen should be recognized, therefore, as a particularly significant figure in the history of this method, bridging the period of ancient Christianity with the church of Late Antiquity, the Middle Ages, and beyond.[105]

---

105. To take just one much later example, Martin Luther continued to read the Psalms through a christological lens, applying prosopological interpretations just like the early church fathers. For instance, Luther writes, "He [Christ] Himself says in Ps 40:8: 'I delight to do Thy will, O My God; Thy law is within My heart'" (*Lecture on Psalm One*, in *LW* 10:13–14).

8

Conclusion: Scripting the Son

As THIS BOOK HAS demonstrated, prosopological exegesis played a significant role in the development of early Christology. Specifically, we have traced how hints of person-centered reading strategies in the Jesus tradition grew into more concrete instances of prosopological exegesis in Hebrews and 1–2 Clement that were used to advance a Christology of the Son's pre-existence and present reign. Building upon this, Justin Martyr became the first Christian writer to explicitly articulate a model of prosopological exegesis as a strategy for deciphering Old Testament dialogues in light of emerging Christian notions of unity and diversity in the Godhead. By expanding and repurposing traditional *testimonia* collections, Justin expanded the use of prosopological exegesis concerning the Son to articulate and defend additional points of the basic christological narrative. Following in Justin's footsteps, Irenaeus of Lyons demonstrated the continued usefulness and flexibility of this method to advance his own christological claims. It would be Tertullian, however, who drastically elevated the significance of prosopological exegesis, both through his use of the language of *persona* to describe the divine persons and on account of the greater depth and thematic range of how he deploys this way of reading Scripture. Some of the shortcomings of Tertullian's approach to prosopological exegesis (and perhaps also Tertullian's Montanist views), however, led to the decline of the method's use in the West in the following decades. As such, Latin writers of the third century, including Hippolytus, Novatian, and Cyprian, were far less interested in this particular approach to reading the Bible.

It would take an exegete of rare brilliance, then, to further refine the use of prosopological exegesis and clarify how an appeal to the multiple senses of Scripture could solve some potential issues with the method's application. And thus Origen made dramatic advances in how prosopological exegesis could be used, not simply to prove elements of the rule of faith but also to provide pastoral words of exhortation and to explore the more mystical elements of the relationship between Christ and the church. In large part because of Origen, prosopological interpretations of certain Old Testament passages became standard fare for the church's exegetical and homiletical approach in subsequent centuries, though that story is better saved for another book.

This book has therefore demonstrated, in line with the scholarly project of retrieving elements of theological exegesis, that Christian doctrine and the interpretation of Scripture were, from the beginning, joined together in a dynamic interplay. In particular, we have observed that early Christian exegetes' attempts to identify the speakers and addressees of dialogical texts in the Old Testament—something any classically trained exegete would seek to establish—in light of their nascent trinitarian convictions generated something that both brought unity to the Scriptures (against, for instance, Marcion) and provided scriptural warrant for key christological claims (against, for example, the gnostics or the modalistic monarchians). This book thereby demonstrates one concrete way in which early doctrines regarding the nature of the Triune God emerged not in opposition to the witness of the Old Testament but rather, to return to the words of C. Kavin Rowe, "precisely because the writers of the New Testament presupposed the authority of the Old Testament and made explicit use of the theological grammar that undergirds the Old Testament's language about the one God."[1] To put it another way, this book's exploration of the contribution of prosopological exegesis with respect to the development of Christology supports Frances Young's claim that "doctrine was generated by the need to make sense of scripture."[2] Pressures emerging from what the early Christians believed to be true about God on the basis of their worship of Christ and their experience of the Spirit, as well as from the language and puzzles of the Scriptures themselves, combined in a mutually reinforcing process

---

1. Rowe, "Biblical Pressure," 299. Rowe points to New Testament texts that posit an ontological identity between Yahweh and Jesus Christ, such as Rom 10:13 and John 20:28 ("Biblical Pressure," 301–3).

2. Young, *Scripture*, 13.

CONCLUSION: SCRIPTING THE SON 189

in which christological claims were increasingly clarified, defended, and applied to Christian life and doctrine more generally.[3]

Having made this theological claim, two applications can be drawn in two potentially unanticipated areas: homiletics and spiritual formation. But just as this book has demonstrated the importance of breaking down barriers between biblical and theological studies, so too barriers between these disciplines and so-called "pastoral" studies must also be torn down in light of the fact that all of the faith is summed up in Christ.

First, Christian preaching needs to recognize that Jesus, on the road to Emmaus, interprets *all* the Scriptures (by which, again, he meant what we call the Old Testament) as about himself (Luke 24:27). This book has demonstrated that the writers of the New Testament and other early Christian literature made a surprising claim (at least to many of our sensibilities) that the Old Testament does not simply point to Christ, nor does it merely contain interesting historical background for the New Testament. On the contrary, Christ is actually present *in* the Old Testament. This book has explored one way in which we can speak of Christ being present in the Old Testament: prosopological exegesis. In this way, dialogical passages in the Old Testament could be read as spoken by, to, or concerning God the Son; thus, the very *vox Christi* can be found not just in the Gospels but throughout the entire canon of the Bible.

How, though, can Christian homilists go about identifying the voice of Christ in the Old Testament? After all, this book traced how, at times, some Christian writers' approach to prosopological exegesis threatened to diminish or even eliminate the voice of the human prophet or even that of God the Father. And the very legitimate insights and challenges of modern historical criticism cannot simply be ignored. What then is a preacher to do? The solution, I suggest, comes from Origen. Origen's distinction between the literal and spiritual senses of the text, which would in the medieval period come to be crystallized as the fourfold sense of Scripture, provides a means by which a text can be engaged on both the literal, historical level as well as the christological, trinitarian one. If, for instance, I were preaching on Psalm 2, my analysis of the psalm's literal sense would focus on its meaning as an ancient Near Eastern enthronement hymn for the Davidic king; I could then pivot with the spiritual sense to discuss how prosopological exegesis provides a means by which we can identify the christological and trinitarian dimensions of the text.

---

3. This point essentially echoes my conclusion about the development of early Christian pneumatology in Hughes, *How the Spirit Became God*, 133–35.

I could, perhaps, explore the typological significance of the Father's words to the Davidic king in Ps 2:7–8, which correspond to the Father's words to the Son at the Son's baptism (as recorded in the Gospels) and then again at the time of Christ's ascension (as read prosopologically), with the very words themselves serving as the true likeness between three very different moments (or four, if we also consider the level of the Father speaking these words to the Son with respect to the Son's eternal generation).[4] In this way, Christian homilists can take seriously Tertullian's claim, echoing that of Christ himself, that "*all* the Scriptures disclose both the demonstration and the distinction of the Trinity."[5] In so doing, I am reinforcing the biblical basis for the christological content of the rule of faith, and indeed of the creeds, that serve as the foundational, authoritative summaries of Christian doctrine. And perhaps most importantly of all, the Old Testament is functioning in a sacramental way, making Christ present among us as we enter into these divine conversations in the context of our gathered worship, culminating in our Eucharistic feast at the King's table.[6]

Second, our identification of the words of Christ in the Old Testament has implications for our spiritual formation into Christ's likeness. As we saw, Origen insisted that both proper exegetical method and spiritual enlightenment are required to truly find the voice of Christ in the Old Testament. Perhaps because of this spiritual component, Origen did not leave prosopological exegesis as a mere theological exercise; rather, we found that Origen used prosopological exegesis to challenge believers to "receive the *persona* of Christ."[7] In other words, having identified the *vox Christi* in Scripture, the true Christian exegete is to pursue the *imitatio Christi*. Because God has called Christians "to be conformed to the image of his Son" (Rom 8:29), this process of believers becoming more like Christ entails being formed into the kinds of men and women who can speak Christ's own words of hope, lament, joy, and sorrow as if they were their own.

4. On typology, see further O'Keefe and Reno, *Sanctified Vision*, 69–88.

5. *Prax.* 11.4 (AT).

6. On preaching as sacramental, see, e.g., Boersma, *Sacramental Preaching*, xx. Reading along with the line of interpretation noted in this book that identifies Psalm 24 as speaking of Christ's ascension, Boersma models such an approach to preaching with a homily on this psalm through a christological lens (*Sacramental Preaching*, 81–93). For further discussion of hermeneutical principles regarding contemporary application of prosopological exegesis, see Bates, *Birth*, 190–202.

7. *Hom. Ps.* 81H1.3 (trans. Trigg).

It is, I suspect, no coincidence that the book of Psalms, the most frequent source of prosopological exegesis from the Son among early Christian writers, has found such a central place in the Christian liturgical and ascetical traditions. In some monastic traditions, most or all the Psalms are prayed every day.[8] My own Anglican tradition has preserved the centrality of praying the Psalms in the Daily Offices of Morning and Evening Prayer. We pray (or sing or chant) the Psalter in some measure because as we do so *we are praying Christ's own words to the Father*. And as we take on the *persona* of Christ by speaking his words, we pray that by the power of the Holy Spirit we would come to take on the *persona* of Christ in every aspect of our lives. Thus, the Psalter not only brings us into hearing range of conversations among Father, Son, and Holy Spirit but also allows us, mysteriously, to participate ever more intimately in the divine life of the Triune God.

To conclude this book, in order to enable us to better enter into these intra-divine dialogues, I have selected some of the most important and interesting examples of prosopological exegesis analyzed in this book to create a "script" for the basic christological narrative of early Christian doctrine.[9] This script also provides a more comprehensive picture of how early Christian exegetes found speech spoken by, to, or concerning the Son in Old Testament dialogues corresponding to every stage of the narrative of salvation history. While it is my own invention, I trust that it is helpful for illuminating the comprehensiveness and creativity of early Christian writers' use of prosopological exegesis as it relates to Christology. Some verses may appear multiple times, reflecting their significance for multiple theodramatic moments.

---

8. See further Peters, *Monkhood*, 108.

9. Given variations in how these verses are cited among early Christian writers, I have decided to simply follow the English translation of the Septuagint found in *The Lexham English Septuagint*, as this (rather than the Hebrew that is the basis of Bibles familiar to most readers) more closely matches the form of the text available to the ancient writers (as throughout this book, however, I continue to use the MT numbering of the Psalms and Jeremiah). The style of this section is indebted to Matthew Bates, as used especially in his *The Birth of the Trinity*. I have provided clarifying words in small-caps to bring out the ancient writers' interpretation when helpful.

Act 1: Divine Pre-Existence

Act 1, Scene 1: Before the Foundation of the World

The Father: "My heart emptied itself in a good word." (Ps 45:1); "I will be like a father to him [the Son], and he will be like a son to me." (2 Sam 7:14)

The Father to the Son: "From the womb, before the morning, I fathered you." (Ps 110:3)

The Son, quoting the Father to the Son: "The Lord [the Father] said to me [the Son], 'You are my son; today I have fathered you.'" (Ps 2:7)

The Son: "The Lord [the Father] created me as the beginning of his ways for his works; before eternity he founded me in the beginning, before making the earth and before making the depths, before the springs of waters came forth, before the mountains were settled, and before all the hills, he produced me." (Prov 8:22–25)

Act 1, Scene 2: At the Creation of the World

The Son: "When he was preparing the heavens, I was there with him, and when he was marking off his own throne upon the winds. And as he was making the clouds above strong, and as he was establishing the unfailing springs of the earth under the heavens, and as he was making the foundations of the earth strong, I was beside him joining it; I was what he delighted in, and every day I rejoiced in his face at all times, when he rejoiced upon completing the inhabited earth, and he rejoiced in the sons of humans." (Prov 8:27–31); "I am the Lord who accomplishes all things; I alone stretched out the heavens and established the earth." (Isa 44:24); "I am the one who prepared the light and made the darkness." (Isa 45:7); "For a spirit will go forth from me, and I have made every breath." (Isa 57:16)

The Father to the Son: "Let light come into being." (Gen 1:3); "Let a firmament come into being in the midst of the water, and let a separator be in the midst of the water." (Gen 1:6); "Let us make humankind according to our image and according to our likeness." (Gen 1:26); "Look, Adam has become like one of us, knowing good and evil." (Gen 3:22)

CONCLUSION: SCRIPTING THE SON   193

Act 1, Scene 3: Before and at the Incarnation

THE FATHER TO THE SON: "You will tread upon snake and serpent, and you will trample down lion and dragon." (Ps 91:13); "The way many will be impressed by you, so your appearance will be despised by people and your glory by the people." (Isa 52:14)

THE FATHER: "He [THE SON] will not cry out or lift up his voice, nor will his voice be heard outside. He will not crush a bruised reed, and he will not extinguish a smoking flax, but he will bring forth justice to truth." (Isa 42:2–3); "But I will have pity on the sons, and I will save them by the Lord, their God [THE SON], and I will not save them by bow or by sword or by war or by horses or by horsemen." (Hos 1:7)

THE SON TO THE FATHER: "You did not want sacrifice and offering, but you restored a body to me. You did not ask a for a whole burnt offering and an offering concerning sin. Then I said, 'Look, I have arrived. In the scroll of the document it has been written concerning me.'" (Ps 40:6–7)

THE SON: "And now the Lord [THE FATHER] sent me and his spirit [THE HOLY SPIRIT] away." (Isa 48:16); "The Spirit of the Lord is upon me, on account of which he [THE FATHER] has anointed me." (Isa 61:1); "I have forsaken my house; I have let go of my inheritance; I have given my beloved soul into the hands of her enemies." (Jer 12:7)

ACT 2: PRE-INCARNATE MINISTRY

Act 2, Scene 1: The Garden

THE SON TO ADAM: "Adam, where are you?" (Gen 3:9)

Act 2, Scene 2: Canaan

THE SON TO HAGAR: "Don't be afraid, because God has heard your child's voice from where he is. Stand up, and take the child and hold him with your hand, for I will make him into a great nation." (Gen 21:17–18)

THE SON TO JACOB: "Jacob! Jacob! I am the God who appeared to you in the place where you anointed a pillar for me and made a vow to me there. Now, then, stand up and go away from this land and go away to the land of your origin, and I will be with you." (Gen 31:11, 13); "Send me away, for the dawn has come. What is your name? No longer will your name be called Jacob, but your name will be 'Israel' because you prevailed with God, and you are mighty with humans." (Gen 32:26–28)

Act 2, Scene 3: Egypt

The Son to Moses: "Do not approach here! Untie your sandals from your feet because the place on which you are standing is holy ground!" (Exod 3:5); "Having observed, I know the suffering distress of my people that is in Egypt, and I have heard their outcry because of their taskmasters. For I know their grief. And I have come down to rescue them from the hand of the Egyptians and to bring them out from that land and lead them into a good and spacious land, into a land overflowing with milk and honey." (Exod 3:7–8); "Who gave a mouth to humankind, and who makes a mute person and a deaf person, a seeing person and a blind person? Is it not I, God? And now go, and I myself will open your mouth, and I will instruct you in what you are about to say." (Exod 4:11–12)

Act 2, Scene 4: Sinai

The Son to Moses: "And look, I myself am sending out my angel before your face, so that he may watch over you along the way, in order that he may guide you to the land that I have prepared for you. Be mindful of yourself and listen to him, and do not disobey him, for he will certainly not put up with you, for my name is on him." (Exod 23:20–21); "See that you make everything according to the pattern shown to you on the mountain." (Exod 25:40); "You cannot see my face, for a human cannot see my face and live. Look, a place beside me! Stand on this rock. And when my splendor passes by, then I will put you into a cleft of the rock, and I will shelter you with my hand over you until I have passed by." (Exod 33:20–22)

Act 2, Scene 5: The Prophets

The Son: "And I will speak to prophets, and I multiplied visions, and I was likened to the hands of prophets." (Hos 12:10)

Interlude: Virgin Birth

The Son to the Father: "For you are the one who drew me out from the womb. You are my hope from the breasts of my mother. Upon you I was cast from the womb. From my mother's belly, you are my God." (Ps 22:9–10)

Act 3: Incarnate Ministry

Act 3, Scene 1: Forgiving Sins

THE SON: "And if your sins are like red, I will whiten them like snow; and if they are like scarlet, I will whiten them like wool." (Isa 1:18)

Act 3, Scene 2: Ministering to the Poor and to Women

THE SON: "The Spirit of the Lord is upon me, on account of which he has anointed me; he has sent me to bring good news to the poor." (Isa 61:1); "Rise up, wealthy women, and listen to my voice; you daughters with hope, hear my words! Make remembrance of this year's day, in pain with hope." (Isa 32:9–10)

Act 3, Scene 3: Teaching

THE SON, QUOTING THE FATHER TO THE SON: "And the Lord [THE FATHER] said to me [THE SON], 'Look, I have placed my words into your mouth.'" (Jer 1:9)

THE SON: "I will open my mouth in parables. I will voice riddles from the beginning." (Ps 78:2); "The Lord [THE FATHER] is giving me a tongue of discipline so that I might know when it is necessary to speak a word." (Isa 50:4)

Act 3, Scene 4: Praying upon the Mountain

THE SON: "With my voice I cried aloud to the Lord [THE FATHER], and he heard me from his holy mountain." (Ps 3:4)

THE SON TO THE FATHER: "O my God, I will cry aloud for days to you, and you will not hear; and during the night, there is nothing for my folly." (Ps 22:2)

Act 3, Scene 5: Need for Physical Rest

THE SON: "I went to bed and fell asleep." (Ps 3:5); "And my sleep was sweet to me." (Jer 31:26)

Act 3, Scene 6: Rejection by the Jews

THE SON: "And my people did not hear my voice, and Israel did not pay attention to me. And I sent them away according to the practices of their hearts." (Ps 81:11–12); "Woe is me! O mother! As whom did you give birth to me? A man condemned and judged by all the land! I did not help, and no one helped anyone." (Jer 15:10)

Act 4: Crucifixion, Death, and Harrowing of Hell

Act 4, Scene 1: Crucifixion

THE SON TO THE FATHER: "Lord, why are the ones afflicting me increased?" (Ps 3:1); "O God, my God, attend to me. For what purpose did you abandon me? But I am a worm and not a person, a reproach of humanity and an object of contempt of the people. All the ones who look at me turn up their nose at me. They speak with their lips; they shake their head, 'He hoped upon the Lord; let him rescue him; let him save him, because he wants him.' For you are the one who drew me out from the womb. You are my hope from the breasts of my mother. Upon you I was cast from the womb. From my mother's belly, you are my God. Do not turn away from me, for affliction is near, because there is no one who helps. Young bulls encircled me. Many fat bulls surrounded me. They opened their mouth against me, as a lion that snatches away and roars. I was poured out like water, and all my bones were scattered. My heart became like beeswax melting in the middle of my belly. My strength was dried up like an earthen vessel, and my tongue has been glued to my throat. You led me into the dust of death. For many dogs encircled me. A gathering of those doing evil surrounded me. They pierced my hands and feet. They can count all my bones; they perceived and gazed upon me. They distributed my garments among themselves, and they cast a lot for my clothing. But you, O Lord, do not delay my rescue; give heed to my help. Rescue my soul from the sword, and my unique one from the hand of a dog. Save me from the mouth of the lion, and my lowliness from the horn of the unicorn." (Ps 22:1, 6–21); "O God, do not forsake me, as long as ever I will announce your strength." (Ps 71:18)

THE SON: "They repay me bad things for good." (Ps 35:12); "And the discipline of the Lord opens my ears, and I do not resist or oppose. I gave my back to the lashes and my cheeks to blows, and I did not turn my face away from the shame of spittings. And the Lord has become a helper to me; on account of this I knew that I was not ashamed." (Isa 50:5–7); "And they gave gall for my food, and they gave me vinegar for my drink. Let their table become before them a trap and a repayment and a stumbling block." (Ps 69:21–22); "But I did not know, like an innocent lamb being led to be sacrificed. They reckoned an evil reckoning against me, saying, 'Come, and let us

CONCLUSION: SCRIPTING THE SON 197

throw wood into his bread and destroy him from the land of the living, and his name will no longer be remembered.'" (Jer 11:19); "The Lord is my light and my savior. Whom shall I fear? The Lord is the protector of my life. From whom shall I fear? When evildoers came up to me to eat my flesh, the ones afflicting me and my enemies, they were weak and fell. If an army is set up against me, my heart will not fear. If a battle rises up against me, in this circumstance I hope in God." (Ps 27:1–3)

ACT 4, SCENE 2: DEATH

THE SON TO THE FATHER: "I will be like those who go down into the pit." (Ps 28:1); "Into your hands I will place my spirit." (Ps 31:5); "What use is there in my blood when I go down into destruction?" (Ps 30:9); "Moreover, my flesh will dwell in hope, because you will not abandon my soul in Hades, nor will you give your holy one to see destruction. You made known to me ways of life. You will make me full of cheer with your face. There are delights at your right side completely." (Ps 16:9–11)

THE SON: "I became as a helpless person, free among the dead." (Ps 88:4–5)

ACT 4, SCENE 3: HARROWING OF HELL

THE SON: "From the hand of Hades I will rescue, and from death I will ransom them." (Hos 13:14)

INTERLUDE: RESURRECTION

THE SON: "I went to bed and fell asleep. I awoke, because the Lord will help me." (Ps 3:5)

ACT 5: ASCENSION, ENTHRONEMENT, AND REIGN

ACT 5, SCENE 1: ASCENSION

THE HEAVENLY PRINCES: "Who is this King of glory?" THE FATHER (OR THE HOLY SPIRIT): "The Lord of mighty powers [THE SON], he is this King of glory!" (Ps 24:10)

THE HEAVENLY PRINCES, TO THE SON: "Why are your clothes red, and your garments as if they came from a trodden winepress?" THE SON: "I crushed them like dirt." (Isa 63:2–3)

Act 5, Scene 2: Enthronement

The Holy Spirit, quoting the Father to the Son: "The Lord [the Father] said to my Lord [the Son], 'Be seated at my right side until I set your enemies as a footstool for your feet.'" (Ps 110:1)

The Father to the Son: "You are a priest for eternity according to the order of Melchizedek." (Ps 110:4)

The Holy Spirit to the Son: "Your throne, O God, is for eternity of eternity. The rod of your kingdom is a rod of uprightness. You loved righteousness and hated lawlessness. On account of this, God, your God [the Father], anointed you with olive oil of great joy beyond your companions." (Ps 45:6–7)

The Holy Spirit to the Father: "You arranged all things under his [the Son's] feet." (Ps 8:6)

The Son to the Father: "I will set out in detail your name to my brothers. In the middle of the assembly I will sing of you." (Ps 22:22); "From you is my praise in the great assembly." (Ps 22:25)

The Father: "Look, I am casting into the foundations of Zion a precious choice stone, a valuable cornerstone into its foundations." (Isa 28:16)

The Son: "I will trust him [the Father]. Look, here I am, along with the children whom God has given me." (Isa 8:17–18)

Act 5, Scene 3: Reign over the Gentiles

The Father to the Son: "You are my son; today I have fathered you. Ask from me, and I will give to you the nations as your inheritance, and as your possession the ends of the earth." (Ps 2:7–8); "I, the Lord God, have called you in righteousness, and I will hold fast onto your hand and strengthen you and make you a covenant for the nation to open the eyes of the blind, to lead those who are bound out from their chains, and those seated in darkness out of prison." (Isa 42:6–7); "It is a great thing for you to be called my child, to establish the tribes of Jacob and to return the dispersion of Israel. Look! I have given you as a covenant for a nation, as a light for the nations so that you may become salvation as far as the end of the earth." (Isa 49:6); "I have listened to you at the acceptable time, and I have helped you in the day of salvation. And I formed you and have given you as a covenant for the nations." (Isa 49:8)

THE FATHER: "Jacob is my child, I will help him; Israel is my chosen one, my soul has accepted him. I have given my spirit upon him [THE SON]; he will bring forth judgment upon the nations." (Isa 42:1); "He will blaze forth and will not be shattered until he brings justice upon the earth, and the nations will hope in his name." (Isa 42:4); "Look! I gave him as a testimony among the nations, a ruler and one who commands the nations." (Isa 55:4)

THE SON: "I became evident to those who did not consult me; I was found by those who did not seek me. I said, 'Look! Here I am,' to a people who have not called upon my name." (Isa 65:1); "God exalted me in the land of my humiliation." (Gen 41:52); "A people whom I did not understand served me." (Ps 18:43); "A people whom I did not know was subject to me. They listened to me in the hearing of an ear." (2 Sam 22:44b, 45b); "By me kings reign, and rulers write righteousness; by me mighty men become mighty, and tyrants control the earth by me." (Prov 8:15–16)

ACT 5, SCENE 4: TEMPORAL JUDGMENT ON ISRAEL

THE SON TO THE FATHER: "Scatter them in your power." (Ps 59:11)

THE FATHER: "[THE SON IS] an obstacle of stone or like a fall from a rock." (Isa 8:14)

THE SON: "I stretched out my hands all day to a people who resisted and opposed, to those who walked in a way that was not good but followed after their sins. This people who provokes me is before me always." (Isa 65:2–3); "They made me jealous against what is not God; they irritated me with their idols, and I will make them jealous against what is not a nation; I will provoke them to wrath against a foolish nation." (Deut 32:21)

ACT 5, SCENE 5: WORDS OF COMFORT FOR THE CHURCH

THE SON: "[I am] saying to those in chains, 'Come out!' and to those in darkness, 'Be revealed!' They will be fed in all the ways, and their pasture will be in all their paths." (Isa 49:9); "Look! I am inclining the glory of the nations toward them like a river of peace." (Isa 66:12)

THE SON, TO THE CHURCH: "Do not be afraid, for I have redeemed you; I have called you by name; you are mine. Even if you pass through water, I am with you, and rivers will not overwhelm you; even if you pass through fire, you will not be burned up; the flame will not burn you up. For I am the Lord your God, the Holy One of Israel who saves you." (Isa 43:1–2); "Pay attention to my law, my people. Bend your ear to the words of my mouth. I will open my mouth in parables. I will voice riddles from the beginning." (Ps 78:1–2); "I said, 'You are gods, and all are children of the Most High.'" (Ps 82:6); "I am a God nearby and not a God far off. Do I not fill the sky and the land?" (Jer 23:23–24); "Turn to me, and I will turn to you." (Zech 1:3); "In the assemblies bless God." (Ps 68:26); "If you do not know yourself, O most beautiful of women, go out in the footsteps of the flocks and tend your goats at the tents of the shepherds. To my mare amongst the chariot horses of Pharaoh I have compared you, my close one. How lovely have your cheeks become, like turtle doves, your neck like necklaces!" (Song 1:8–10); "Look! You are beautiful, my close one. Look! You are beautiful; your eyes are doves." (Song 1:15)

Postlude: Return in Judgment and Final Consummation

The Holy Spirit: "Who are these that fly like clouds and like doves with their young to me?" (Isa 60:8)

The Father to the Son: "Be seated at my right side until I set your enemies as a footstool for your feet. Rule in the midst of your enemies. With you is authority in the day of your power, with the splendor of the holy ones." (Ps 110:1–3a); "You are a priest for eternity according to the order of Melchizedek." (Ps 110:4)

Appendix

Tables of Key Instances of Prosopological Exegesis Pertaining to the Son

Source Abbreviations:

- AF   Apostolic Fathers
- CA   Clement of Alexandria
- CC   Cyprian of Carthage
- H   Hippolytus of Rome
- I   Irenaeus of Lyons
- J   Justin Martyr
- M   Methodius
- N   Novatian
- NT   New Testament
- O   Origen
- T   Tertullian

Table 1: The Speech of the Father (speaking as his own person to or about the Son)

Scripture	Source(s)	Theme(s)
Genesis 1	J, I, T, N, O	Pre-existence
Genesis 3	J, T	Pre-existence
2 Samuel 7	NT	Pre-existence
Psalm 2	NT, AF, J, I, T, N, CA, O	Pre-existence; present reign
Psalm 24	J	Ascension
Psalm 45	NT, T, O	Pre-existence; present reign
Psalm 91	T	Pre-existence
Psalm 102	NT	Present reign
Psalm 110	NT, AF, J, I, T, H, CC, O	Pre-existence; present reign; return as judge
Isaiah 8	T	Present reign
Isaiah 28	T	Present reign
Isaiah 42	J, I, T	Pre-existence; present reign
Isaiah 44	T	Pre-existence
Isaiah 45	I	Present reign
Isaiah 49	J, I, T, O	Incarnate ministry; present reign
Isaiah 52	T	Pre-existence
Isaiah 55	T	Present reign
Jeremiah 1	T	Incarnate ministry
Hosea 1	N	Pre-existence
Malachi 3	T	Pre-existence

Table 2: The Speech of the Son (speaking as his own person)

Scripture	Source(s)	Theme(s)
Genesis 3	I, T	Pre-incarnate ministry
Genesis 21	N	Pre-incarnate ministry
Genesis 31	N	Pre-incarnate ministry

APPENDIX 203

Scripture	Source(s)	Theme(s)
Genesis 32	N	Pre-incarnate ministry
Genesis 41	O	Present reign
Exodus 3	J, I	Pre-incarnate ministry
Exodus 4	T	Pre-incarnate ministry
Exodus 20	CA	Pre-incarnate ministry
Exodus 22	CC	Present reign
Exodus 23	T	Pre-incarnate ministry
Exodus 25	I	Pre-incarnate ministry
Exodus 33	I, T	Pre-incarnate ministry
Deuteronomy 24	CC	Present reign
Deuteronomy 32	O	Present reign
2 Samuel 22	O	Present reign
1 Kings 11	CC	Present reign
Psalm 2	J, I, O	Pre-existence; present reign
Psalm 3	J, I, T	Incarnate ministry; crucifixion; resurrection from the dead
Psalm 16	O	Resurrection from the dead; present reign
Psalm 18	O	Present reign
Psalm 22	NT, AF, J, T, CA, O	Virgin birth; incarnate ministry; crucifixion; present reign
Psalm 27	O	Crucifixion
Psalm 28	O	Resurrection from the dead
Psalm 30	O	Resurrection from the dead; present reign
Psalm 31	T	Crucifixion
Psalm 35	T	Crucifixion
Psalm 40	NT	Pre-existence
Psalm 50	CC	Present reign
Psalm 59	T	Present reign
Psalm 68	T	Present reign
Psalm 69	T, O	Crucifixion
Psalm 71	T	Crucifixion

Scripture	Source(s)	Theme(s)
Psalm 73	I	Crucifixion
Psalm 78	T, O	Incarnate ministry; present reign
Psalm 81	O	Incarnate ministry; present reign
Psalm 82	I, O	Present reign
Psalm 88	O	Resurrection from the dead
Psalm 105	O	Present reign
Psalm 109	O	Pre-existence
Proverbs 8	J, I, T, O	Pre-existence; present reign
Song 1	O	Present reign
Song 2	O, M	Present reign
Song 4	T, CC, M	Incarnate ministry; present reign
Song 6	CC, M	Present reign
Isaiah 1	T, CC	Incarnate ministry; present reign
Isaiah 2	CC	Present reign
Isaiah 8	NT, O	Present reign
Isaiah 14	CC	Present reign
Isaiah 29	AF, CC	Present reign
Isaiah 32	T	Incarnate ministry
Isaiah 40	CC	Present reign
Isaiah 41	T	Pre-existence
Isaiah 43	T, CC	Incarnate ministry; present reign
Isaiah 44	T	Pre-existence; incarnate ministry
Isaiah 45	T	Pre-existence
Isaiah 48	O	Pre-existence
Isaiah 49	I, T, O	Pre-existence; incarnate ministry; present reign
Isaiah 50	J, I, T, CC, O	Incarnate ministry; crucifixion; present reign
Isaiah 52	AF, T	Incarnate ministry; present reign
Isaiah 57	T, CC	Pre-existence; present reign

Scripture	Source(s)	Theme(s)
Isaiah 58	T, CC	Incarnate ministry; present reign
Isaiah 61	I, T, N, O	Pre-existence; incarnate ministry; present reign
Isaiah 63	O	Present reign
Isaiah 65	J, I, O	Pre-existence; present reign
Isaiah 66	CC, O	Present reign
Jeremiah 1	T	Incarnate ministry
Jeremiah 2	CC	Present reign
Jeremiah 3	CC	Present reign
Jeremiah 7	CC	Present reign
Jeremiah 11	T, O	Crucifixion
Jeremiah 12	O	Pre-existence
Jeremiah 15	O	Incarnate ministry
Jeremiah 23	CC, O	Present reign
Jeremiah 31	I	Incarnate ministry
Ezekiel 18	CC	Present reign
Ezekiel 34	CC	Present reign
Hosea 6	CC	Present reign
Hosea 8	CC	Present reign
Hosea 9	CC, O	Incarnate ministry; present reign
Hosea 12	T, O	Pre-incarnate ministry; incarnate ministry
Hosea 13	O	Resurrection from the dead
Joel 2	CC	Present reign
Micah 7	O	Incarnate ministry; present reign
Zechariah 1	O	Present reign
Malachi 2	CC	Present reign

Table 3: The Holy Spirit (speaking as his own person to or about the Son)

Scripture	Source(s)	Theme(s)
Psalm 4	T	Present reign
Psalm 8	T	Present reign
Psalm 23	CC	Present reign
Psalm 45	J, I	Present reign
Psalm 110	J, I, T	Present reign
Isaiah 45	T	Present reign
Isaiah 49	T	Present reign
Isaiah 53	T	Present reign
Isaiah 60	T	Return as judge
Isaiah 63	CC	Present reign

Bibliography

Albl, Martin C. *"And Scripture Cannot Be Broken": The Form and Function of the Early Christian Testimonia Collections.* NovTSup 46. Leiden: Brill, 1999.

Allert, Craig D. *Revelation, Truth, Canon, and Interpretation: Studies in Justin Martyr's Dialogue with Trypho.* VCSup 64. Leiden: Brill, 2002.

Andresen, Carl. "Zur Entstehung und Geschichte des trinitarischen Personbegriffes." ZNW 52 (1961) 1–39.

The Ante-Nicene Fathers: Translations of the Writings of the Fathers Down to AD 325. Edited by Alexander Roberts and James Donaldson. 1885–87. Reprint, Peabody, MA: Hendrickson, 1994.

Armstrong, Jonathan J. "From the κανὼν τῆς ἀληθείας to the κανὼν τῶν γραφῶν: The Rule of Faith and the New Testament Canon." In *Tradition and the Rule of Faith in the Early Church: Essays in Honor of Joseph T. Lienhard, SJ,* edited by Ronnie J. Rombs and Alexander Y. Hwang, 30–47. Washington, DC: Catholic University of America Press, 2010.

———. *The Role of the Rule of Faith in the Formation of the New Testament Canon according to Eusebius of Caesarea.* Lewiston, NY: Mellen, 2014.

Attridge, Harold W. *The Epistle to the Hebrews.* Hermeneia. Philadelphia: Fortress, 1989.

———. "Giving Voice to Jesus: Use of the Psalms in the New Testament." In *Psalms in Community: Jewish and Christian Textual, Liturgical, and Artistic Traditions,* edited by Harold W. Attridge and Margot E. Fassler, 101–12. SBLSS 25. Atlanta: Society of Biblical Literature, 2003.

Barkley, Gary Wayne. *Origen: Homilies on Leviticus 1–16.* FOTC 83. Washington, DC: Catholic University of America Press, 1990.

Barnard, L. W. *Justin Martyr: His Life and Thought.* Cambridge: Cambridge University Press, 1967.

———, trans. *St. Justin Martyr: The First and Second Apologies.* ACW 56. New York: Paulist, 1997.

———. "The Use of Testimonies in the Early Church and in the Epistle of Barnabas." In *Studies in the Apostolic Fathers and Their Background,* edited by L. W. Barnard, 109–35. New York: Schocken, 1966.

Barnes, Timothy David. *Tertullian: A Historical and Literary Study*. Oxford: Clarendon, 1971.
Bates, Matthew W. *The Birth of the Trinity: Jesus, God, and Spirit in New Testament and Early Christian Interpretations of the Old Testament*. Oxford: Oxford University Press, 2015.
———. *The Hermeneutics of the Apostolic Proclamation: The Center of Paul's Method of Scriptural Interpretation*. Waco, TX: Baylor University Press, 2012.
———. *Salvation by Allegiance Alone: Rethinking Faith, Works, and the Gospel of Jesus the King*. Grand Rapids: Baker Academic, 2017.
Beeley, Christopher A., and Mark E. Weedman. "Introduction: The Study of Early Christian Biblical Interpretation." In *The Bible and Early Trinitarian Theology*, edited by Christopher A. Beeley and Mark E. Weedman, 1–23. CUASEC. Washington, DC: Catholic University of America Press, 2018.
Behr, John. *Asceticism and Anthropology in Irenaeus and Clement*. OECS. Oxford: Oxford University Press, 2000.
———. *Irenaeus of Lyons: Identifying Christianity*. CTC. Oxford: Oxford University Press, 2013.
———, trans. *Origen: On First Principles*. Edited by John Behr. 2 vols. OECT. Oxford: Oxford University Press, 2017.
———, trans. *St. Irenaeus of Lyons: On the Apostolic Preaching*. PPS 17. Crestwood, NY: St. Vladimir's Seminary Press, 1997.
———. *The Way to Nicaea*. Vol. 1 of *Formation of Christian Theology*. Crestwood, NY: St. Vladimir's Seminary Press, 2001.
Black, C. Clifton. *Reading Scripture with the Saints*. Eugene, OR: Cascade, 2014.
———. "Trinity and Exegesis." *ProEccl* 19 (2010) 151–80.
Blowers, Paul M. "The *Regula Fidei* and the Narrative Character of Early Christian Faith." *ProEccl* 6 (1997) 199–228.
Boersma, Hans. *Sacramental Preaching: Sermons on the Hidden Presence of Christ*. Grand Rapids: Baker Academic, 2016.
Bokedal, Tomas. "The Rule of Faith: Tracing Its Origins." *JTI* 7 (2013) 233–55.
Boyarin, Daniel. *Intertextuality and the Reading of Midrash*. Bloomington: Indiana University Press, 1990.
Brent, Allen, trans. *St. Cyprian of Carthage: On the Church—Select Treatises*. PPS 32. Crestwood, NY: St. Vladimir's Seminary Press, 2006.
Briggman, Anthony. *God and Christ in Irenaeus*. OECS. Oxford: Oxford University Press, 2019
———. *Irenaeus of Lyons and the Theology of the Holy Spirit*. OECS. Oxford: Oxford University Press, 2012.
Butterworth, G. W., trans. *Clement of Alexandria: The Exhortation to the Greeks, The Rich Man's Salvation, To the Newly Baptized*. LCL 92. Cambridge, MA: Harvard University Press, 1919.
Childs, Brevard. *Biblical Theology of the Old and New Testaments: Theological Reflection on the Christian Bible*. Minneapolis: Fortress, 1992.
Cline, Brandon. *Petition and Performance in Ancient Rome: The Apologies of Justin Martyr*. GSECP 75. Piscataway, NJ: Gorgias, 2020.
Countryman, L. W. "Tertullian and the Regula Fidei." *SecCent* 2 (1982) 208–27.
Daly, Robert J., trans. *Origen: On the Passover; Dialogue with Heraclides*. ACW 54. Mahwah, NJ: Paulist, 1992.

Daniélou, Jean. *The Theology of Jewish Christianity*. Vol. 1 of *A History of Early Christian Doctrine before the Council of Nicaea*. Translated and edited by John A. Baker. London: Darton, Longman & Todd, 1964.

DeSimone, Russell J., trans. *Novatian: The Trinity, The Spectacles, Jewish Foods, In Praise of Purity, Letters*. FOTC 67. Washington, DC: Catholic University of America Press, 1974.

Dively Lauro, Elizabeth Ann, trans. *Origen: Homilies on Isaiah*. FOTC 142. Washington, DC: Catholic University of America Press, 2021.

Dodd, C. H. *According to the Scriptures: The Sub-Structure of New Testament Theology*. London: Nisbet, 1952.

———. *The Apostolic Preaching and Its Developments*. New York: Harper and Row, 1964.

Donovan, Mary Ann. *One Right Reading? A Guide to Irenaeus*. Collegeville, MN: Liturgical, 1997.

Downs, David J. "Prosopological Exegesis in Cyprian's *De opere et eleemosynis*." *JTI* 6 (2012) 279–94.

Dulk, Matthijs den. *Between Jews and Heretics: Refiguring Justin Martyr's Dialogue with Trypho*. RSECW. London: Routledge, 2018.

Edwards, Mark. "Exegesis and the Early Christian Doctrine of the Trinity." In *The Oxford Handbook of the Trinity*, edited by Gilles Emery and Matthew Levering, 80–91. Oxford: Oxford University Press, 2011.

Ehrman, Bart D. *Lost Christianities: The Battles for Scripture and the Faiths We Never Knew*. Oxford: Oxford University Press, 2003.

Evans, Ernest, trans. *Tertullian's Treatise against Praxeas: The Text Edited, with an Introduction, Translation, and Commentary*. Edited by Ernest Evans. 1948. Reprint, Eugene, OR: Wipf & Stock, 2011.

Evans, G. R. *Bernard of Clairvaux: Selected Works*. CWS. Mahwah, NJ: Paulist, 1987.

Fahey, Michael Andrew. *Cyprian and the Bible: A Study in Third-Century Exegesis*. BGBH 9. Tübingen: Mohr Siebeck, 1971.

Fairbairn, Donald, and Ryan M. Reeves. *The Story of Creeds and Confessions: Tracing the Development of the Christian Faith*. Grand Rapids: Baker Academic, 2019.

Falls, Thomas B., trans. *St. Justin Martyr: Dialogue with Trypho*. Revised by Thomas P. Halton. Edited by Michael Slusser. SFC 3. Washington, DC: Catholic University of America Press, 2003.

Fee, Gordon D. *The First Epistle to the Corinthians*. NICNT. Grand Rapids: Eerdmans, 1987.

Ferguson, Everett. *The Rule of Faith*. Cascade Companions 20. Eugene, OR: Cascade, 2015.

Fitzmyer, Joseph A. "'4QTestimonia' and the New Testament." In *Essays on the Semitic Background of the New Testament*, edited by Joseph A. Fitzmyer, 59–89. SBLSBS 5. Missoula, MT: Scholars, 1974.

Gamble, Harry Y. *Books and Readers in the Early Church: A History of Early Christian Texts*. New Haven, CT: Yale University Press, 1995.

Grech, Prosper S. "The Regula Fidei as a Hermeneutical Principle in Patristic Exegesis." In *The Interpretation of the Bible: The International Symposium in Slovenia*, edited by Jože Krašovec, 589–601. JSOTSup 289. Sheffield: Sheffield Academic, 1998.

Hartog, Paul. "The 'Rule of Faith' and Patristic Biblical Exegesis." *TJ* 28 (2007) 65–86.

Hay, David M. *Glory at the Right Hand: Psalm 110 in Early Christianity*. SBLMS 18. Nashville: Abingdon, 1973.

Hays, Richard B. *The Conversion of the Imagination: Paul as Interpreter of Israel's Scripture*. Grand Rapids: Eerdmans, 2005.

———. *Echoes of Scripture in the Letters of Paul*. New Haven, CT: Yale University Press, 1989.

Heine, Ronald E., trans. *The Commentary of Origen on the Gospel of St Matthew*. 2 vols. OECT. Oxford: Oxford University Press, 2018.

———. "Hippolytus, Ps.-Hippolytus and the Early Canons." In *The Cambridge History of Early Christian Literature*, edited by Frances Young et al., 142–51. Cambridge: Cambridge University Press, 2004.

———, trans. *Origen: Commentary on the Gospel according to John, Books 1–10*. FOTC 80. Washington, DC: Catholic University of America Press, 1989.

——— trans. *Origen: Commentary on the Gospel according to John, Books 13–32*. FOTC 89. Washington, DC: Catholic University of America Press, 1993.

———, trans. *Origen: Homilies on Genesis and Exodus*. FOTC 71. Washington, DC: Catholic University of America Press, 1981.

———. *Origen: Scholarship in the Service of the Church*. CTC. Oxford: Oxford University Press, 2010.

Hill, Charles E. *From the Lost Teaching of Polycarp: Identifying Irenaeus's Apostolic Presbyter and the Author of Ad Diognetum*. WUNT 186. Tübingen: Mohr Siebeck, 2006.

———. *Regnum Caelorum: Patterns of Millennial Thought in Early Christianity*. 2nd ed. Grand Rapids: Eerdmans, 2001.

Holmes, Michael W., ed. *The Apostolic Fathers: Greek Texts and English Translations*. Translated by Michael W. Holmes. 3rd ed. Grand Rapids: Baker Academic, 2007.

Hughes, Kyle R. *How the Spirit Became God: The Mosaic of Early Christian Pneumatology*. Eugene, OR: Cascade, 2020.

———. "The Spirit and the Scriptures: Revisiting Cyprian's Use of Prosopological Exegesis." *JECH* 8 (2018) 35–48.

———. "The Spirit Speaks: Pneumatological Innovation in the Scriptural Exegesis of Justin and Tertullian." *VC* 69 (2015) 463–83.

———. *The Trinitarian Testimony of the Spirit: Prosopological Exegesis and the Development of Pre-Nicene Pneumatology*. VCSup 147. Leiden: Brill, 2018.

Jefford, Clayton N. *Reading the Apostolic Fathers: A Student's Introduction*. 2nd ed. Grand Rapids: Baker Academic, 2012.

Johnson, David L. *Jesus Christ and the Rule of Faith: The Confessional Christology of the Early Fathers*. Lexington, KY: Emeth, 2016.

Juel, Donald. *Messianic Exegesis: Christological Interpretation of the Old Testament in Early Christianity*. Philadelphia: Fortress, 1988.

Kelly, J. N. D. *Early Christian Creeds*. 3rd ed. London: Continuum, 1972.

King, Karen L. *What Is Gnosticism?* Cambridge, MA: Harvard University Press, 2003.

Kominiak, Benedict. *The Theophanies of the Old Testament in the Writings of St. Justin*. CUASST 2/14. Washington, DC: Catholic University of America Press, 1948.

Laing, Kenneth. *Irenaeus, the Scriptures, and the Apostolic Writings: Reevaluating the Status of the New Testament Writings at the End of the Second Century*. LNTS 659. London: T&T Clark, 2022.

Lashier, Jackson. *Irenaeus on the Trinity*. VCSup 127. Leiden: Brill, 2014.

Lawson, R. P., trans. *Origen: The Song of Songs: Commentary and Homilies*. ACW 26. Westminster, MD: Newman, 1957.
Lienhard, Joseph T., trans. *Origen: Homilies on Luke; Fragments on Luke*. FOTC 94. Washington, DC: Catholic University of America Press, 1996.
Lieu, Judith M. *Marcion and the Making of a Heretic: God and Scripture in the Second Century*. Cambridge: Cambridge University Press, 2015.
Lindemann, Andreas. "The First Epistle of Clement." In *The Apostolic Fathers: An Introduction*, edited by Wilhelm Pratscher, 47–69. Waco, TX: Baylor University Press, 2010.
Longenecker, Richard N. *Biblical Exegesis in the Apostolic Period*. Grand Rapids: Eerdmans, 1975.
Luther, Martin. *First Lectures on the Psalms I*. Edited by Hilton C. Oswald. Vol. 10 of *Luther's Works, American Edition*. St. Louis: Concordia, 1974.
MacKenzie, Iain M., trans. *Irenaeus's Demonstration of the Apostolic Preaching: A Theological Commentary and Translation*. Aldershot, UK: Ashgate, 2002.
Martens, Peter W. *Origen and Scripture: The Contours of the Exegetical Life*. OECS. Oxford: Oxford University Press, 2012.
Minns, Denis. *Irenaeus: An Introduction*. London: T&T Clark, 2010.
Minns, Denis, and Paul Parvis, trans. *Justin, Philosopher and Martyr: Apologies*. Edited by Denis Minns and Paul Parvis. OECT. Oxford: Oxford University Press, 2009.
Murphy, Edwina. *The Bishop and the Apostle: Cyprian's Pastoral Exegesis of Paul*. SBR 13. Boston: de Gruyter, 2018.
Musurillo, Herbert, trans. *St. Methodius: The Symposium—A Treatise on Chastity*. ACW 27. New York: Newman, 1958.
Nyström, David E. *The Apology of Justin Martyr: Literary Strategies and the Defence of Christianity*. WUNT 2/462. Tübingen: Mohr Siebeck, 2018.
O'Keefe, John J., and R. R. Reno. *Sanctified Vision: An Introduction to Early Christian Interpretation of the Bible*. Baltimore: Johns Hopkins University Press, 2005.
O'Meara, John J., trans. *Origen: Prayer; Exhortation to Martyrdom*. ACW 19. Westminster, MD: Newman, 1954.
Osborn, Eric F. *Irenaeus of Lyons*. Cambridge: Cambridge University Press, 2001.
———. *Justin Martyr*. BHT 47. Tübingen: Mohr Siebeck, 1973.
———. "Reason and the Rule of Faith in the Second Century AD." In *The Making of Orthodoxy: Essays in Honour of Henry Chadwick*, edited by Rowan Williams, 40–61. Cambridge: Cambridge University Press, 1989.
———. *Tertullian: First Theologian of the West*. Cambridge: Cambridge University Press, 1997.
Paget, James Carleton. "The Christian Exegesis of the Old Testament in the Alexandrian Tradition." In *From the Beginnings to the Middle Ages, Part 1: Antiquity*, edited by Magne Sæbø, 478–542. Vol. 1 of *Hebrew Bible/Old Testament: The History of Its Interpretation*. Göttingen: Vandenhoeck & Ruprecht, 1996.
Papandrea, James L. *Novatian of Rome and the Culmination of Pre-Nicene Orthodoxy*. PTMS. Eugene, OR: Pickwick, 2011.
Peters, Greg. *The Monkhood of All Believers: The Monastic Foundation of Christian Spirituality*. Grand Rapids: Baker Academic, 2018.
Pierce, Madison N. *Divine Discourse in the Epistle to the Hebrews: The Recontextualization of Spoken Quotations of Scripture*. SNTSMS 178. Cambridge: Cambridge University Press, 2020.

Pratscher, Wilhelm. "The Second Epistle of Clement." In *The Apostolic Fathers: An Introduction*, edited by Wilhelm Pratscher, 71–90. Waco, TX: Baylor University Press, 2010.

Presley, Stephen O. *The Intertextual Reception of Genesis 1–3 in Irenaeus of Lyons*. BAC 8. Leiden: Brill, 2015.

———. "Irenaeus and the Exegetical Roots of Trinitarian Theology." In *Irenaeus: Life, Scripture, Legacy*, edited by Paul Foster and Sara Parvis, 165–71. Minneapolis: Fortress, 2012.

Rondeau, Marie-Josèph. *Les commentaires patristiques du Psautier Recherches et bilan, 2: Exégèse prosopologique et théologie*. Rome: Pontificium Institutum Studiorum Orientalium, 1985.

Rowe, C. Kavin. "Biblical Pressure and Trinitarian Hermeneutics." *ProEccl* 11 (2002) 295–312.

Sanders, Fred. *The Triune God*. NSD. Grand Rapids: Zondervan, 2016.

Scheck, Thomas P., trans. *Origen: Commentary on the Epistle to the Romans, Books 1–5*. FOTC 103. Washington, DC: Catholic University of America Press, 2001.

———, trans. *Origen: Commentary on the Epistle to the Romans, Books 6–10*. FOTC 104. Washington, DC: Catholic University of America Press, 2002.

———, trans. *Origen: Homilies 1–14 on Ezekiel*. ACW 62. Mahwah, NJ: Newman, 2010.

Segal, Alan F. *Two Powers in Heaven: Early Rabbinic Reports about Christianity and Gnosticism*. SJLA 25. Leiden: Brill, 1977.

Seitz, Christopher R. *The Elder Testament: Canon, Theology, Trinity*. Waco, TX: Baylor University Press, 2018.

Shuve, Karl. *The Song of Songs and the Fashioning of Identity in Early Latin Christianity*. OECS. Oxford: Oxford University Press, 2016.

Skarsaune, Oskar. "The Development of Scriptural Interpretation in the Second and Third Centuries—Except Clement and Origen." In *From the Beginnings to the Middle Ages, Part 1: Antiquity*, edited by Magne Sæbø, 373–442. Vol. 1 of *Hebrew Bible/Old Testament: The History of Its Interpretation*. Göttingen: Vandenhoeck & Ruprecht, 1996.

———. *The Proof from Prophecy: A Study in Justin Martyr's Proof-Text Tradition: Text-Type, Provenance, Theological Profile*. NovTSup 56. Leiden: Brill, 1987.

Slusser, Michael. "The Exegetical Roots of Trinitarian Theology." *TS* 49 (1988) 461–76.

———. "How Much Did Irenaeus Learn from Justin?" StPatr 40 (2006) 515–20.

Smith, John Clark, trans. *Origen: Homilies on Jeremiah; Homily on 1 Kings 28*. FOTC 97. Washington, DC: Catholic University of America Press, 1998.

Stewart-Sykes, Alistair, trans. *Tertullian, Cyprian, and Origen: On the Lord's Prayer*. PPS 29. Crestwood, NY: St. Vladimir's Seminary Press, 2004.

Trakatellis, Demetrius C. *The Pre-Existence of Christ in the Writings of Justin Martyr*. HDR 6. Missoula, MT: Scholars, 1976.

Treier, Daniel J. *Introducing Theological Interpretation of Scripture: Recovering a Christian Practice*. Grand Rapids: Baker Academic, 2008.

———. *Proverbs and Ecclesiastes*. BTCB. Grand Rapids: Brazos, 2011.

Trevett, Christine. *Montanism: Gender, Authority, and the New Prophecy*. Cambridge: Cambridge University Press, 1996.

Trigg, Joseph W. *Origen*. ECF. London: Routledge, 1998.

———, trans. *Origen: Homilies on the Psalms: Codex Monacensis Graecus 314*. FOTC 141. Washington, DC: Catholic University of America Press, 2020.

Unger, Dominic J., trans. *St. Irenaeus of Lyons: Against the Heresies, Book 1*. Revised by John J. Dillon. ACW 55. Mahwah, NJ: Newman, 1992.
———, trans. *St. Irenaeus of Lyons: Against the Heresies, Book 2*. Revised by John J. Dillon. ACW 65. Mahwah, NJ: Newman, 2012.
———, trans. *St. Irenaeus of Lyons: Against the Heresies, Book 3*. Revised by Irenaeus M. C. Steenberg. ACW 64. Mahwah, NJ: Newman, 2012.
———, trans. *St. Irenaeus of Lyons: Against the Heresies, Books 4 and 5*. Revised by Scott D. Moringiello. ACW 72. Mahwah, NJ: Newman, 2024.
Ward, H. Clifton. *Clement and Scriptural Exegesis: The Making of a Commentarial Theologian*. OECS: Oxford: Oxford University Press, 2022.
Waszink, J. H. "Tertullian's Principles and Methods of Exegesis." In *Early Christian Literature and the Classical Intellectual Tradition: In Honorem Robert M. Grant*, edited by William R. Schoedel and Robert L. Wilken, 17–31. ThH 53. Paris: Beauchesne, 1979.
———, trans. *Tertullian: The Treatise against Hermogenes*. ACW 24. Westminster, MD: Newman, 1956.
Welborn, L. L. *The Young against the Old: Generational Conflict in First Clement*. Lanham, MD: Lexington, 2018.
Wiles, Maurice. *Working Papers in Doctrine*. London: SCM, 1976.
Wilhite, David E. *Tertullian the African: An Anthropological Reading of Tertullian's Context and Identities*. Millennium-Studien 14. Berlin: de Gruyter, 2007.
Wilken, Robert Louis. *The Spirit of Early Christian Thought: Seeking the Face of God*. New Haven, CT: Yale University Press, 2003.
Williams, D. H. *Evangelicals and Tradition: The Formative Influence of the Early Church*. Evangelical Ressourcement. Grand Rapids: Baker Academic, 2005.
Williamson, G. A., trans. *Eusebius: The History of the Church*. Revised by Andrew Louth. London: Penguin, 1989.
Wood, Simon P., trans. *Clement of Alexandria: Christ the Educator*. FOTC 23. Washington, DC: Catholic University of America Press, 1954.
Wright, N. T. *The New Testament and the People of God*. Vol. 1 of *Christian Origins and the Question of God*. London: SPCK, 1992.
Yeago, David S. "The New Testament and Nicene Dogma: A Contribution to the Recovery of Theological Exegesis." *ProEccl* 3 (1994) 152–64.
Young, Frances M. *Biblical Exegesis and the Formation of Christian Culture*. Cambridge: Cambridge University Press, 1997.
———. *The Making of the Creeds*. London: SCM, 1991.
———. *Scripture, the Genesis of Doctrine*. Vol. 1 of *Doctrine and Scripture in Early Christianity*. Grand Rapids: Eerdmans, 2023.

Author Index

Albl, Martin C., 11–13, 33–34, 39, 67–68, 92–93, 134–36, 153
Allert, Craig D., 51
Andresen, Carl, 7–8, 23, 102
Armstrong, Jonathan J., 13–14
Attridge, Harold W., 24, 27–28, 31, 33–34, 42

Barnard, L. W., 11, 43, 47–48, 66, 69
Barnes, Timothy David, 100, 139
Bates, Matthew W., x–xi, 5, 7–10, 16–17, 24–33, 35–36, 38, 44, 55, 63, 69, 102, 132, 180–81, 190–91
Beeley, Christopher A., 4
Behr, John, 1–2, 14, 22, 72–73, 78, 80, 83–87, 95, 97–98, 183
Black, C. Clifton, 5
Blowers, Paul M., 14–17
Boersma, Hans, 190
Bokedal, Tomas, 14, 69
Boyarin, Daniel, 11
Brent, Allen, 151–52
Briggman, Anthony, 76, 82

Childs, Brevard, 3
Cline, Brandon, 44
Countryman, L. W., 14–15, 137

Daly, Robert J., 170
Daniélou, Jean, 53–54

DeSimone, Russell J., 146–49
Dodd, C. H., 12, 16–17
Donovan, Mary Ann, 14
Downs, David J., x–xi, 152
Dulk, Matthijs den, 51

Eden, Kathy, ix
Edwards, Mark, ix, 5
Ehrman, Bart D., 2
Evans, Ernest, 100–2, 105–7, 114, 117–21, 124, 137
Evans, G. R., 174

Fahey, Michael Andrew, 150
Fairbairn, Donald, 171
Falls, Thomas B., 2, 52–56, 58–63, 68
Fee, Gordon D., 79
Ferguson, Everett, 13–15, 95–96, 137–39, 182–83
Fitzmyer, Joseph A., 11–12

Gamble, Harry Y., 12–13
Grech, Prosper S., 13

Harris, J. Rendel, 11
Hartog, Paul, 13–14, 16
Hatch, Edwin, 11
Hay, David M., 7
Hays, Richard B., 24, 26, 28

Heine, Ronald E., 145, 156, 163–72, 175, 179, 182
Hill, Charles E., 55, 73, 77, 114, 131
Holmes, Michael W., 38–40
Hughes, Kyle R., x–xii, 7–8, 25–26, 29, 31, 44, 63, 68, 72, 78, 90, 92, 95, 101–3, 119, 129–30, 138, 150, 152–53, 155, 180–81, 189

Irvine, Martin, ix

Jefford, Clayton N., 39
Johnson, David L., 15, 97, 182
Juel, Donald, 22, 24

Kelly, J. N. D., 13–14, 16
King, Karen L., 72
Kominiak, Benedict, 49

Laing, Kenneth, 13, 95
Lashier, Jackson, 72, 76, 82–85, 88–89, 94
Lawson, R. P., 173
Lienhard, Joseph T., 162
Lieu, Judith M., 2–3, 49, 68
Lindemann, Andreas, 37
Longenecker, Richard N., 26, 29
Luther, Martin, 186

MacKenzie, Iain M., 74, 83
Martens, Peter W., 161
Minns, Denis, 48, 72
Moringiello, Scott D., 72
Murphy, Edwina, 150

Nyström, David E., 44, 66

O'Keefe, John J., 5, 16, 58, 190
O'Meara, John J., 167
Osborn, Eric F., 16, 43–44, 77, 95, 102, 114, 131–32

Paget, James Carleton, 156
Papandrea, James L., 146
Parvis, Paul, 48
Peters, Greg, 191

Pierce, Madison N., x–xi, 8, 29–33, 35–36
Pratscher, Wilhelm, 39
Presley, Stephen O., 76, 95–96

Reeves, Ryan M., 171
Reno, R. R., 5, 16, 58, 190
Rondeau, Marie-Josèph, 7, 9, 158, 162
Rowe, C. Kavin, 3, 5, 188

Sanders, Fred, xi, 9
Scheck, Thomas P., 157, 169, 171–72
Segal, Alan F., 53
Seitz, Christopher R., 5, 29–30, 36
Shuve, Karl, 174
Skarsaune, Oskar, 4, 13, 59, 66–68, 92, 94, 153
Slusser, Michael, x, 7–9, 63, 72, 102–3, 162, 182
Smith, John Clark, 160–62, 168–69
Stewart-Sykes, Alistair, 150, 152

Trakatellis, Demetrius C., 49, 67
Treier, Daniel J., 5, 57, 82
Trevett, Christine, 100
Trigg, Joseph W., 156, 158–60, 162, 167, 174–76, 190

Unger, Dominic J., 75–76, 78–79, 82–86, 88–89, 95–96

Ward, H. Clifton, 179
Waszink, J. H., 100, 119
Welborn, L. L., 37
Wiles, Maurice, 150
Wilhite, David E., 100
Wilhite, Shawn J., xi
Wilken, Robert Louis, 5
Williams, D. H., 14
Weedman, Mark E., 4
Wood, Simon P., 181–82
Wright, N. T., 15

Yeago, David S., 5
Young, Frances M., 2, 4, 6, 13–14, 17, 188

Ancient Document Index

Old Testament

Genesis

1	82, 164, 202
1:1–3	119
1:1	23
1:3	163, 177, 184, 192
1:6	163, 177, 184, 192
1:20	167
1:26	53, 58, 65, 70, 75–76, 82–83, 91, 97, 104, 106–7, 132, 140, 146–47, 154, 163, 165, 177, 181, 184, 192
1:27	146–47
3	82, 202
3:8	83
3:9	83, 91, 97, 119–20, 132, 140, 193
3:22	53, 59, 65, 70, 106, 132, 140, 192
19:23–25	62
19:24	53, 59, 67, 90, 92, 129, 135, 146–47
19:30–38	85
21	202
21:17–18	149, 154, 193
31–32	149, 154
31	202
31:11	193
31:13	193
32	203
32:26–28	193–94
41	203
41:52	173, 178, 185, 199
49:10–11	46
49:21–26	145

Exodus

3	203
3:5	49, 65, 70, 194
3:7–8	83, 91, 97, 194
3:14	83, 91, 97
3:19	83, 91, 97
4	203
4:11–12	119, 132, 140, 194
20	203
20:2	181
22	203
22:20	151, 154
23	203
23:20–21	107, 119, 132, 140, 194
25	203
25:40	83, 91, 97, 194
33	203
33:20–22	84, 91, 97, 194
33:20	119, 132, 140

Numbers

22–24	119
24:17	46

Deuteronomy

24	203
24:26	151, 154
32	203
32:21	172, 178, 185, 199
32:43	31

2 Samuel

7	202
7:14	xi, 31, 41, 192
22	203
22:44–45	172, 178, 185, 199

1 Kings

11	203
11:31–32	151, 154
11:36	151, 154

1 Chronicles

17:13	xi

Job

19:26	38

Psalms

1–2	46
2	33, 39, 77, 79, 164, 170, 176, 189, 202–3
2:1–2	33
2:2	170
2:6	167, 177, 184
2:7–8	39, 41, 56, 65, 70, 73–74, 78–80, 88, 91, 97, 111–12, 133, 141, 146–47, 154, 164–65, 170, 172, 178, 185, 190, 198
2:7	x, 30–31, 33–34, 39, 45–46, 56–57, 59, 65, 70, 73, 80–81, 91, 97, 104–5, 111, 117, 132, 140, 148, 165, 178, 185, 192
2:8	56, 78, 111–12, 130, 148, 165, 180
3	203
3:1	102, 126, 133, 141, 196
3:4	124, 133, 140, 142, 195
3:5	38, 47–48, 65, 67, 70, 85–87, 91, 93–94, 97–98, 142, 195, 197
4	206
4:6	129–30, 133, 141
8	206
8:5	120
8:6	112, 130, 133, 141, 198
16	158–59, 162, 166, 174, 203
16:1–9	178, 184
16:1	174, 178, 185
16:3	174
16:7–8	176
16:8–11	27–28, 158, 160
16:8	176
16:9–11	197
16:9–10	170, 178, 184
16:9	162
16:10	33, 145, 162, 170
18	203
18:43	172, 178, 185, 199
19:4	110
19:5–6	123, 130
21:4	93
22	24, 35, 38–39, 47–48, 59–60, 67, 86, 121, 125–27, 203
22:1–22	65, 70

22:1–18	35	31	203
22:1	24, 28, 35, 38, 60, 196	31:5	126, 133, 141, 197
		33:6	119
22:2	124, 133, 140, 195	35	203
22:6–21	196	35:12	125, 133, 141, 196
22:6–8	38, 41, 60	37	158
22:6–7	48	40	203
22:6	169, 178, 184	40:6–8	36, 41
22:7–8	48, 67, 126, 133, 141	40:6–7	193
		40:8	186
22:7	48	41:9	170
22:9–10	121, 133, 140, 194	45	202, 206
22:9	121	45:1	104–5, 109, 117, 132, 140, 148, 163, 177, 186, 192
22:10	121		
22:14–20	86		
22:14	174, 178, 185	45:2–5	112
22:15	61	45:2	109
22:16	47–48, 67, 125–26, 133, 141	45:6–11	53
		45:6–7	31, 41, 63, 65, 67, 70, 90–92, 97, 105, 129, 135, 198
22:18	47–48, 67, 125–26, 133, 141		
		45:7–8	181
22:19–21	35	45:7	92, 105, 149
22:20	61	50	203
22:21	126, 133, 141	50:16–18	151, 154
22:22–31	35	59	128, 203
22:22	35, 38, 41, 60–61, 127, 133, 172–73, 178, 180, 185, 198	59:11	128, 133, 141, 199
		68	203
22:23	180	68:26	127, 133, 141, 200
22:24	60	69	169, 178, 184, 203
22:25	127, 133, 198	69:1–28	145
23	206	69:4	125, 133, 141
23:5	152, 154	69:5	169
24	54, 172, 190, 202	69:21–22	196
24:7–10	159, 171	69:21	86, 125, 133, 141, 169
24:7	53		
24:8	116	71	203
24:10	54, 62, 65, 70, 112, 197	71:18	102, 126, 133, 141, 196
27	170, 203	72:1	115
27:1–3	170, 178, 184, 197	73	204
28	203	73:14	87, 91, 93, 97
28:1	171, 178, 184	78	159, 166, 204
28:7	38	78:1–2	178, 185, 200
29:3	116	78:1	175
30	203	78:2	23, 123, 133, 140, 160, 175, 195
30:9	171, 175, 178, 184–85, 197		
		78:3–8	175

Psalms (continued)

81	204
81:11–12	161, 177–78, 184–85, 195
82	204
82:2	176
82:6–7	91, 97, 178, 185
82:6	88, 175, 200
82:7	88, 175
88	204
88:4–5	171, 178, 184, 197
91	202
91:11–12	159
91:13	108, 132, 140, 193
102	202
102:25–27	32, 41
104:4	31
105	204
105:15	173, 178, 185
109	204
109:1	167, 177, 184
110	23, 26, 33, 39, 51–53, 78, 115, 131, 165, 202, 206
110:1–3	46, 200
110:1	5, 7, 26, 28, 32–33, 39, 41, 45, 53, 62–63, 65, 67, 70, 73–74, 78–80, 89–92, 97, 102, 111–15, 128–30, 133, 141, 145–48, 154, 165, 178, 185, 198
110:2	115, 133, 141
110:3–4	52–54, 65, 70, 75, 104
110:3	52, 104–5, 117, 132, 140, 148, 192
110:4	33, 41, 52, 115, 133, 141, 150, 154, 165, 178, 185, 198, 200
118:22–23	23

Proverbs

8	57–58, 82, 117–19, 167, 204
8:15–16	88, 91, 97, 199
8:21–25	58–59
8:21	58
8:22–36	57–58, 65, 70, 79, 82, 89
8:22–31	118–19, 132, 140, 153
8:22–25	117, 192
8:22	58, 116–18, 167, 177, 184
8:24	118
8:25	167, 177, 184
8:27–31	192
8:27–30	117
8:27	118
8:28	118
8:36	58
12:4	xiii

Song of Songs

1	204
1:8–10	173, 178, 185, 200
1:15	173, 178, 185, 200
2	204
2:1–2	173, 178, 185
2:1	173
2:2	173
2:5	174
2:10–15	173, 178, 185
4	204
4:8	123, 133, 140
4:9–12	173
4:12–13	151, 154
4:12	151
5:2	150
6	204
6:8–9	173
6:9	151, 154

Isaiah

1	204
1:2	151, 154, 176
1:3–4	45
1:11–15	45
1:16–20	46
1:18	122, 133, 137, 140, 195
2	204
2:8–9	151, 154
7:14	23, 46–47
8	202, 204
8:14	113, 133, 141, 199
8:17–18	35, 40–41, 198
8:17	35
8:18	172–73, 178, 181, 185
9:6	47
11:1	46
14	204
14:10–11	171
14:13–16	151, 154
28	202
28:16	113, 133, 141, 198
29	204
29:13	40–41, 151, 154
29:14	123
32	204
32:9–10	124, 133, 140, 195
35:2–4	122
40	204
40:6	151, 154
40:9	123
41	204
41:4	118, 132, 140
42	55, 112, 202
42:1–4	55, 65, 70, 77, 91, 97
42:1	55, 102, 112–13, 133, 141, 199
42:2–3	109, 132, 140, 193
42:4	55, 112, 133, 141, 199
42:5–13	55
42:6–9	55
42:6–7	55, 65, 70, 112–13, 133, 141, 198
42:6	112
43	204
43:1–3	151, 154
43:1–2	199–200
43:20	124, 133, 140
44	107, 202, 204
44:5	124, 133, 140
44:24	107, 118, 132, 140, 192
44:25–26	107, 132, 140
44:25	123
45	202, 204, 206
45:1	73–74, 77, 80, 91, 97, 102, 110, 128–29, 133, 135, 141, 147
45:3	123
45:7	118, 132, 140, 192
45:21–24	5
48	204
48:16	168, 177, 184, 193
49	56, 164, 202, 204, 206
49:1–6	169
49:1–2	177, 184
49:2–3	174, 178, 185
49:3	164, 169, 177, 184
49:5–6	74, 80–81, 86–87
49:5	91, 97, 177, 184
49:6	56, 65, 70, 77, 81, 88, 91, 97, 102, 113, 130, 133, 141, 165–66, 168–69, 177, 184, 198
49:8	56, 65, 70, 198
49:9	173, 178, 185, 199
49:18	124, 130, 133, 140–41
49:21	124, 133, 140
50	204
50:4–9	128
50:4	124, 133, 140, 195
50:5–7	196
50:5–6	87, 97, 151, 154
50:6–8	47–48, 65, 67, 70
50:6	93, 116, 126, 133, 141, 169, 178, 184

Isaiah (continued)

50:11	128, 133, 141
51:5	46
52–53	108
52	202, 204
52:5	40–41
52:6–7	133, 140
52:6	123
52:7	123
52:13—53:12	40
52:13—53:5	93
52:13	93
52:14	109, 132, 140, 193
53	93, 206
53:1–14	37
53:1–2	102, 128–29, 133, 141
53:7–8	23
53:7	169
53:8	93
53:12	122
55	202
55:3	33
55:4–5	113
55:4	113, 133, 141, 199
55:5	113, 133, 141
57	204
57:1–4	55
57:1–2	93
57:1	87
57:6	151, 154
57:16	118, 132, 140, 192
58	205
58:2	47, 67
58:6–7	45
58:6	151, 154
58:7	124, 133, 140
60	206
60:8	131, 133, 141, 200
61	205
61:1	85, 91, 97–98, 102, 124, 133, 140, 149, 154, 167, 176–78, 184–85, 193, 195
61:10	123, 130, 133, 140
63	172, 205–6
63:2–3	197
63:2	152, 154, 172
63:3	172, 178, 185
65	205
65:1–3	48, 61–62, 65, 70
65:1	89, 91, 94, 97, 167, 172, 177–78, 184–85, 199
65:2–3	199
65:2	47–48, 67
66	205
66:1	45
66:2	151, 154
66:12	173, 178, 185, 199

Jeremiah

1	202, 205
1:5	160
1:9	124, 133, 140, 195
2	205
2:13	151, 154
3	205
3:9–10	151, 154
3:15	151, 154
7	205
7:16	151, 154
11	205
11:19–23	169, 178, 184
11:19	126, 133, 141, 169, 196–97
12	205
12:7	168, 177, 184, 193
15	205
15:10	162, 177, 184, 195
23	205
23:16–17	151, 154
23:21–22	151, 154
23:23–24	173, 178, 185, 200
23:23	173
23:28	151, 154
23:30	151, 154
23:32	151, 154
31	205
31:26	86, 97, 195

ANCIENT DOCUMENT INDEX

Lamentations

3:30	93
4:20	130

Ezekiel

18	205
18:20	151, 154
34	205
34:3–6	151, 154
34:4–6	151
34:10–16	151, 154
34:10	151
34:16	151

Hosea

1	202
1:7	148, 154, 193
6	205
6:1	151, 154
8	205
8:4	151, 154
9	205
9:4	151, 154
9:12	169, 177, 184
12	205
12:4	125, 133, 140
12:10	166, 168, 177, 184, 194
13	205
13:14	171, 178, 184, 197

Joel

2	205
2:12–13	151, 154
2:13	151
2:29	149

Micah

5:2	47
7	205
7:1–2	162, 175, 177–78, 184–85

Nahum

1:15	124

Habakkuk

3:2	86
3:3	148

Zechariah

1	205
1:3	173, 178, 185, 200
9:9	47

Malachi

2	205
2:1–2	151, 154
3	202
3:1	107–8, 132, 140

Old Testament Apocrypha

Sirach (Ecclesiasticus)

16:1–2	151

New Testament

Matthew

1:22–23	23
5:17	95
7:7–8	172
7:9–11	151
11:19	85
12:29	171
13:14–15	24
13:34–35	23
13:35	23, 160
15:8–9	24
16:15	22
21:42	23
25:35	174
26:56	125
27:39–43	48
27:46	162
28:19	103

Mark

7:6	40
12:35–37	5, 26, 28
15:34	24, 35, 60
16:19	79

Luke

4:4	162
4:18–19	24
4:18	85, 149
5:16–26	122
5:27–39	122
5:34	123
6:12	123
8:22	116
8:30	116
9:51–56	109
10	108
10:19	108
15:7	151
22:27	164
23:46	170
23:53	170
24:13–35	1, 22
24:27	1, 189

John

1:1–4	23
1:1–3	119, 163
1:1	58, 118
1:3	118–19
1:18	117
9:1–12	82
13:18–30	170
15:26	63
19:24	24
20:28	5, 188

Acts

1:11	114
2	160
2:14–36	27
2:25–31	158
2:25–28	27
2:25	27, 160
2:27	170
2:31	27
2:33–35	5
2:34–35	33
4:25–26	33
8:32–33	23
13:33	33

Romans

1:3–5	14
1:5	110
8:29	190
8:34	14
10:13	5, 188
13:14	176
15:3	24
15:8–12	23

1 Corinthians

1:24	117
10:4	49, 82
12:12–31	174
15	115
15:3–7	14
15:3–5	1
15:3	16
15:24–28	79, 114
15:24–25	113–14
15:24	114
15:25	114–15
15:27–28	114

2 Corinthians

4:6	130

Galatians

2:20	176

Ephesians

1:18–22	112
1:18	111

1:19–22	111–12	10:5–7	36
4:8	171	10:5	36
4:9	170		
6:12	165		

1 Peter

3:18–22	14

Philippians

2:5–10	42
2:6–8	164
2:8	169
2:9–11	5

Jude

5	49, 82

Colossians

1:15–20	42
1:15	117

Revelation

2:20–22	151
12	145
12:5	145

1 Timothy

3:16	42

Early Christian Sources

1 Clement

16.1–2	37
16.2	37
16.3–14	37
16.15–16	38–39, 60
16.17	38
26.1–3	38
36.2–6	34
36.4–5	39
44	37

Hebrews

1	xi, 34, 39
1:1	29
1:2	29
1:5–14	29, 33, 67
1:5	x, 30–31, 58, 105
1:6–7	31
1:6	31
1:8–13	31–32
1:8–9	31–32, 105
1:8	30
1:9	31
1:10–12	32
1:13	32
2	34
2:11–13	34
2:12–13	40, 172
2:12	35, 38, 60, 127
4:14	165
5:5–6	33, 36
5:5	105
7:1–21	33
7:17	33, 36
7:21	33, 36
10	36

2 Clement

3.5	40
4.1	40
13.2	40–41
13.3	40

Clement of Alexandria

Christ the Educator

1.2.5	180
1.2.6	180
1.5.14	181
1.5.15	180
1.7.53	180

Christ the Educator (continued)

1.7.56–61	180
1.7.56	180–81
1.8.67–70	180
1.8.69	180
1.8.72	180
1.8.73	180
1.9.75	180
1.9.76–82	180
1.9.84–86	180
1.9.87	180
1.10.90–94	180
1.11.96	180
1.12.98	181
1.13.102	180
2.1.7–8	180
2.1.8	180
2.3.24	180
2.3.27	180
2.3.28	180
2.3.30	180
2.4.41–42	180
2.4.44	180
2.7.54	180
2.7.58–59	180
2.8.62	180
2.8.65	181
2.8.75	180
2.9.79	180
2.10.87	180
2.10.89	180
2.10.91	180
2.10.95	180
2.10.99	180
2.10.109–10	180
2.10.113	180
2.12.126	180
2.12.129	180
3.1.3	180
3.2.9–10	180
3.3.20	180
3.4.27	180
3.8.44	180
3.11.67	180
3.11.72	180
3.11.75–76	180
3.12.86–87	180
3.12.89–93	180
3.12.100	181

Exhortation to the Greeks

8–9	180
10	181
11	180

Miscellanies

2.20	180
2.23	180
4.22	180
4.26	180
5.4	180
5.14	180

Cyprian

The Advantage of Patience

22	152

To Demetrian

6	152
17	151
20	151

The Dress of Virgins

1	151
6	151

Epistles

6.4	151
8.1	152
17.1	151
39.5	151
51	151
51.22–27	151
53.4	151
54	151
54.3–5	151
54.5	152
54.15	151

ANCIENT DOCUMENT INDEX

54.21	152
61.1	151
62	152
62.4	150
62.7	152
62.11	152
62.18	151
63.1	151
64.1	151
66.4	151
67.2	151
67.3–4	151
69.1	151
73.8	151
73.11	151
75.2	151
75.9	151

To Fortunatus: Exhortation to Martyrdom

4	151
10	151–52
12	152

Jealousy and Envy

8	152
15	151

The Lapsed

10	151
27	151
36	151

The Lord's Prayer

5	152
31	150
33	151–52
35	151–52

Mortality

11	152
23	152

To Quirinius: Testimonies against the Jews

1.pref	153
2.1	153
3.pref	153

The Unity of the Catholic Church

4	151
7	151
8	151
10	151
11	151
24	151

Works and Almsgiving

2	152
5	152
9	152

Epistle of Barnabas

5.14	93
12.10–11	129

Eusebius

Ecclesiastical History

3.38	37
6.2–3	182
6.8	156
6.25	37

Hippolytus

Against Noetus

1	145

Christ and Antichrist

61	145

Irenaeus

Against Heresies

1.7.3	95–96
1.10.1	95–96, 98
1.10.3	15
1.22.1	96
2.28.7	79
3.4.2	96, 98
3.6.1	78–79, 83, 88–90, 92, 105
3.6.2	83
3.9.3	85
3.10.6	79
3.11.6	77
3.12.9	77
3.16.7	86
3.18.3	85
3.19	98
3.19.1	88
3.21–22	98
3.21.7	75
4.pref.4	76
4.12.4	83
4.14.1	75
4.20.1	75–76
4.20.3	82
4.20.5	84
4.20.9	83–84
4.21.3	78
4.29.2	83
4.31.1	85
4.31.2	85–87, 94
4.33.1	95
4.33.7	95
4.34.4	87
4.35.2	95
5.1.3	76
5.12.2	75
5.15.4	76, 82–83
5.20.1	96
5.24.1	88
5.27	98

Demonstration of the Apostolic Preaching

2	83
6	96–97
9	83
12	83
24	83
32–33	98
34	86–87, 126
41	98
42–100	92
43	75
44–45	83
45	84, 98
46	83–84
47–49	92
48–49	78
48	75, 79
49–50	73–74, 88
49	75, 77, 80
50–51	77, 79–80
50	77, 80, 113
51–52	77
51	80–81
52	97
53–54	98
53	85
55	76
62	75
68	75, 87, 93, 126
69–70	93
70	93
72	93
73	87, 93
79–80	86
79	86
82	86
83–85	97
85	75, 79
88	97
92	89, 94

Justin Martyr

1 Apology

21.1	69
30–35	44, 46
31.7	69
35	47, 49, 67
35.3	47
36–45	66, 74
36	44
36.1–2	44, 74
36.1	47, 57
36.2	47, 50
36.3	45
37.1–9	45
38	46, 48–49, 60, 66–67
38.1–8	47–48
38.1	50, 126
38.3	93
38.4	93
39–45	50
39.1	50
40	46
42.4	69
44.1	50
44.2–4	46
45.2–4	46
45.4	106
46.5	69
47.1	50
49	94
49.1–4	48
50–51	93
51.1	93
53.2	66
53.6	50
61.13	50
62.3	49, 82

Dialogue with Trypho

11.3	56
11.4	55
13.1–9	57
14.4–8	57
16.4	55
19.4	52
24	94
24.1	61–62
24.3	61–62
26.1	62
26.2	55
26.3–4	56
31.1–7	57
32.3	52
32.6	52
33.1–2	52
33.1	52
33.2	52–53
36	54
36.2	53
36.5–6	55
36.6	54, 62
43.3–8	57
49.2	57
52.4	57
53.1–6	57
56–60	67, 92
56.12–14	67
56.14	62–63, 92, 105
56.15	68
57.2	57
58.4	57
59–60	49
61.3	58
62.1–2	58
62.1	53, 57
62.3	53
62.4	53
63.1	69
63.3–4	53
63.3	106
65.7	55
66.1–3	57
68.5	57
83.1–4	52
83.4	52, 106
85.2	69
86.3	57
87.2	57
88.8	56, 59, 105
91.1	56
97–106	57, 59, 67
97	67

Dialogue with Trypho (continued)

97.1	93
97.3–4	59
97.4	61
98.1	59–60
98.2–5	126
99.2	60
99.3	60
100.1	60
101.2	61
102.2	61
103.6	56
103.9	61
105.1	61
106.1	60–61
118.1	52
120.3	56
121.1	56
121.2	57
121.4	56, 113
122.3	55
122.5	56
122.6	56
123.8	55
126.1	58, 69
127.5	53, 147
129.1–2	57
129.1	53
129.3	2, 53–54, 59

Methodius

Symposium

7.1–4	173

Novatian

The Trinity

9.6–8	148
9.8	148
12.1	148
12.7	148
13.1	148
15.6	148
17.3	148
17.4	147
18.2	149
18.10	149
18.19	149
19.1–14	149
26.3–7	146–47
28.10–12	149
29.2	149
29.13	149
29.14	149

Origen

Against Celsus

2.9	163
2.37	169
2.62	170
2.78	172
3.15	179
4.8	165
5.12	173
5.32	165
5.37	163

Commentary on John

1.110	163
1.133–35	169
1.135	169
1.191–96	162
1.204	165
1.220	171
1.228	169
1.230	164, 169
1.231–32	164
1.231	169
1.280–88	159
1.282	163
2.79	167–68
2.116–32	160
2.116	161
6.175	170
6.196	167
6.202	173
6.289	172
6.295–96	165
10.222	169
13.5	172
19.28	173
19.102	170
19.140	170

ANCIENT DOCUMENT INDEX 231

20.398	167	3.1	173
28.223	173	3.4	173
32.157–58	170	3.8	174
32.162–68	170	3.14–15	173
32.183–97	183		
32.285	170		
32.296	170		

Dialogue with Heraclides

7	170

Commentary on Matthew

10.11	167
10.14	168
11.11	167
12.2	163
12.20	176
12.43	168
13.9	176
13.18	168
15.23	165
15.27	171
15.28	175
16.21	175
16.29	175
17.14	167

First Principles

pref.4	183
pref.5	183
4.2.4	171

Homilies on Ezekiel

1.5	162, 171
6.3	165
9.3	173
13.4	173

Homilies on Genesis

1.7	173
9.3	165
13.4	163
14.1	166

Commentary on Romans

2.11.2	157
2.11.3–5	157
5.1.36	171
5.5.6	157
5.10.10	171
5.10.12	171
6.9.3–4	157
6.9.11–12	157
6.10.2	157
7.13.8	169, 172
7.16.4	157
8.6.2–3	157
8.6.6	157
8.6.9	157
8.6.11	172
8.7.5	159

Homilies on Isaiah

6.7	173
7.1	173

Homilies on Jeremiah

1.6	160–61
1.7	161
9.4	167
10.1	169
10.2–5	169
10.7	168
14.5	161
14.6	162, 171
17.4	161
18.6	173
19.12	169

Commentary on the Song of Songs

1.1	173
2.5–7	173

Homilies on Leviticus

12.1	165
12.2	173

Homilies on Luke

14.8	169
29.5	162
31.4	159

Homilies on Numbers

17.5	165

Homilies on the Psalms

15H1	175
15H1.2	158–59, 170
15H1.3	165, 174
15H1.6	174
15H2	175
15H2.1	159
15H2.2	162
15H2.3	162
15H2.5	176
15H2.8	159
15H2.10	162
36H1.1	158–59
67H1.2	173
74H1.1	159
77H1.1	160
77H1.2–3	159
77H1.2	159–60
77H1.4	175
77H8.3	174
80H2.6	161
81H1.1	173
81H1.3	176, 190

Homilies on the Song of Songs

1.1	173
1.9–10	173
2.4	173
2.6	173
2.8	174
2.12–13	173

Prayer

6.5	167
15.4	173

Tertullian

Against Hermogenes

18.1	118
18.3	104–5, 109
20.1	118
32.2	118
45.1	118–19

Against the Jews

7.2–3	110–11
9–14	136
9.23	107–8, 119
10.4	125
10.13	125–26
12.1–2	112
12.1	111
13.27	128
14.12	111

Against Marcion

1.1	137
1.20	137
2.4	104–5, 107, 109
2.27	119–20
3	127, 130
3.5	116, 126
3.6–7	116
3.9	120
3.14	112
3.16	119
3.17	109
3.19	126
3.20	111–13
3.22	127
3.23	128
3.24	131
4	122, 126, 136
4.10	122, 137
4.11	123, 130, 150

4.13	123–24, 142	12.1–2	106
4.14	104–5, 109, 124	13.1–4	129
4.19	124	14.7	120
4.20	116, 119	14.10	130
4.22	105	16.3	120
4.23	109	16.4	119–20
4.24	108	16.7	121
4.25	113, 123	19.2	117–18
4.31	124	19.4	107
4.39	119, 125	19.5–6	118
4.40	126	19.6	118
4.41	112	22.5	124
4.42	126	23.9	124
5.2	112	27	121
5.5–6	113	28.11	129
5.8	107	30	162
5.9	115	30.4–5	114
5.11	113, 130		
5.17	111–12, 130		

The Flesh of Christ

6.7	120
20.3	116, 126
20.4–5	121
20.6	121

Against Praxeas

2.1–2	138
4.2	113–14
6.1–2	117
6.1	117
7	105
7.1–2	105
7.1	104, 109, 117, 148
7.9	117–18
11	101–4, 113, 115, 134–36
11.2	104–5, 109
11.3	105
11.4	101, 134–35, 190
11.5–8	135
11.5	113
11.6	124, 126
11.7–8	128–29
11.7	115–16
11.8	147
11.9–10	102
11.9	135
12	106

Prescription against Heretics

13	138–39, 141
13.6	137
26.9	137

The Resurrection of the Flesh

6.4	107

The Soul

55	131

The Veiling of Virgins

1.3–4	139
1.3	139

www.ingramcontent.com/pod-product-compliance
Lightning Source LLC
Chambersburg PA
CBHW031732230426
43669CB00007B/332